HOW TO
SURVIVE
AND THRIVE

HOW TO
SURVIVE
AND THRIVE

IN THE MERCHANT SERVICES INDUSTRY

MARC J. BEAUCHAMP

ISBN: 978-0-57862649-9

Printed in the U.S.A.

"Our mission is to provide cutting-edge tools, education, and consulting services to provide our customers a true competitive advantage."

ACKNOWLEDGEMENTS

It's hard to believe this is the 3rd version of *How to Survive and Thrive in the Merchant Services Industry*. With so much changing at such a rapid pace, it was time for a comprehensive update.

I'd like to thank everyone who had a part in the development and production of this book, especially the guest contributors, interview participants, and my editor, Kate Gillespie.

I understand that time is a precious commodity, and you were willing to spend some of yours helping me with this project.

And finally, to my family for putting up with the late nights and weekend marathons; without your support nothing is possible.

ABOUT THE AUTHOR

Marc Beauchamp is a dynamic and engaging entrepreneur who has developed several successful companies. He has over 30 years' experience in sales, training, and marketing in various roles.

He has worked in the payments industry since 1995 and has hired and trained several thousand merchant services professionals over the span of his career. His most recent position he served as President of a Super ISO with over 2,000 sales partners and 2B in annual processing. Marc now manages a portfolio of investments in the payment processing, consumer finance and fintech space.

Marc has created a unique program called the *The Framework* which combined with live training and interactive modules helps ISOs and agents take responsibility for their results and expand their production across Body, Being, Balance and Business. He is uniquely aware of the challenges facing sales representatives, sales managers, issuers, acquirers, banks and ISOs.

Marc lives in The Woodlands, Texas with his wife of 25 years and three daughters.

*"Give a man a fish and he will eat for a day.
Teach a man to fish and he will eat for a lifetime"*

—CHINESE PROVERB

CONTENTS

CHAPTER 1
WHY I WROTE THIS BOOK

In 2003, when I wrote the first edition of *Survive and Thrive in the Merchant Services Industry* I had just over 8 years of experience in the industry and after working with multiple ISOs and financial institutions, I came to the realization that there never had been an industry guidebook written for field salespeople. I wrote this book because I saw a need and wanted to create a resource that covered everything from basic industry information to traditional sales techniques and new sales strategies.

Fast forward to today in 2020, and although the industry, regulations and technology have evolved dramatically, the basics of helping small business owners change or implement payment processing is pretty much the same. Sure, everything now happens on those little devices many of us are addicted to, but the same principles apply when educating, building a relationship and supporting our merchant clients.

I now have over 25 years of experience in this business and we're still facing some of the same challenges around product training, sales training and professional development that we did in 1995. It's gotten better for sure, but there is room for improvement, my hope is that I can fill in some of the gaps in this latest edition. In the chapter "The 10 Distinctions" I share the keys that separate the elite producers from the average.

I remember the first company I went to work for: they trained me for one hour in a coffee shop, gave me some brochures, and said, "Go Get'm, Tiger." I was one of the lucky ones; I actually made it. I've seen hundreds of salespeople leave this industry because the time and effort was not invested in order to educate them properly.

There was no roadmap or material that provided a general overview of the merchant services industry or explained how everything really worked, let alone something that would help me develop and execute an effective sales plan.

Even today there continues to be a significant gap in the skill level of merchant services salespeople when they are compared with their counterparts in other industries. Other industries, such as telecommunications, computer services, insurance, financial investment products, loan origination, and real estate, offer in-depth training and industry information for their salespeople.

The agent out in the field is often left to his own devices. This creates an uneducated salesperson who projects a negative image for the ISO, acquirer, member bank, card brands, and the industry as a whole.

My purpose in writing this book is to fill in the gaps and help you become a knowledgeable, creative, professional salesperson. In this book, I hope to educate, motivate, and empower you to better represent your ISO, the industry, and yourself in a more informed and ethical manner.

You'll find a history of the industry; how the bankcard system works; explanations about rates and fees; and overviews of existing and future products. You will also find valuable information and interviews about industry trends and product development, as well as a step-by-step approach to prospecting, lead development, and the sales process.

There is a difference between knowing *about* something and truly *knowing* something. If I tell you how to ride a bike, you will know *about* riding a bike. But you won't really *know* how to ride a bike until you get on it and pedal. I know how to sell merchant services; there are a lot of people who know *about* the business. I've taken my lumps for sure; hopefully, my experience will help you avoid some of the "bumps in the road."

Like any book, this will continue to be a work in progress. I welcome any comments on how I can make this a better tool for new and experienced salespeople. I've move many of the previous chapters and resources online, so I can keep them up to date as the business evolves and grows.

Please e-mail comments, suggestions, or ideas to me at:
marcb@surviveandthrive.biz

Online resources are at:
www.surviveandthrive.biz/resources

SECTION 1

INDUSTRY BASICS

CHAPTER 2
THE MERCHANT SERVICES INDUSTRY

The merchant services industry is a dynamic, ever-changing business. New regulations, technological advancements, and competitive pressures keep the excitement level high, to say the least.

What is our industry called? I've heard many names for the business, including the Bankcard Industry, Merchant Processing Industry, Transaction Processing Industry, Payments Processing Industry, the Financial Services Industry, the Electronic Transaction Industry, and the Credit Card Industry.

Whatever name you want to call it, we are in the same business as every other company on the planet: serving our customer, the merchant.

Without the merchant we have no industry. Our purpose in this endeavor is to add value to the merchant so he can add value to his customer. We do this by offering a variety of financial services and value added products.

The following is a breakdown of the most common products offered today, keep in the mind this list is always changing. I have divided them into three groups: Core Product, Tier I Products, and Tier II Products.

CORE PRODUCT

- Credit Card Processing
    - Card Present (Face to Face)
        - Brick & Mortar Businesses
        - Mobile/Wireless
    - Card Not Present (CNP)
        - Business to Business (B2B)
        - Mail Order/Phone Order (MOTO)
        - Ecommerce
    - Omni Channel
    - Businesses that process both Card Present and Card Not Present transactions

TIER L PRODUCTS

- Debit Processing
    - Online/Offline
    - ATM
    - EBT
- Gift/Loyalty Products
- Check Processing:
    - ACH
    - Electronic Check Conversion
    - Guarantee/Verification
    - Online
    - Remote Deposit Capture (RDC)

TIER II PRODUCTS

- Stored Value or Pre-Paid Products
- Alternative Lending (MCA, LOC)
- POS Financing (consumer lending)
- Point of Sale Systems
- Commercial Credit Cards
- Custom Applications
  - Age Verification
  - Background Screening
  - Online Ordering/Pickup
  - Time and Attendance/Payroll Cards
  - Smart Card Applications
    - Government ID
    - Mass Transit/Parking Systems
    - Healthcare
      - Benefits Verification
      - Electronic Claims Processing
    - Information Security
    - Biometric

Credit card processing is the foundation of our product offering; in the majority of cases, we will build upon this core product. This is the one service that retail, and Internet merchants alike, require if they want to succeed in business.

Tier I products such as debit, Electronic Benefits Transfer (EBT), and check processing are secondary products that appeal to a large percentage of retail merchants.

Tier II products are more specialized in nature and provide specific benefits to certain types of merchants. Many times, you can lead with a Tier II product in order to acquire merchants' credit card processing business.

I'll discuss these products in the following chapters.

CHAPTER 3
HOW THE SYSTEM IS DESIGNED

For an in-depth history of the payments industry please visit: *www. surviveandthrive.biz/resources*

Visa and Mastercard are card brands and payment networks that offer a comprehensive set of payment products and services, they are composed of member institutions. Thus, Visa and Mastercard are commonly referred to as bankcards. To become a member of Visa and Mastercard an organization must be a financial institution, aka a bank. The member bank may then be licensed to issue cards and/or acquire merchant transactions.

Member banks are required to provide cash advances on Visa and Mastercard cards at their teller windows. Member banks are issued a Bank Identification Number (BIN) and pay membership dues and assessments to the card associations.

Other cards such as American Express, Diners Club, Discover, and JCB are also common in the electronic payment industry.

They are structured differently from Visa and Mastercard primarily in that they do not have "members" (member banks). They are self-contained companies that control issuing, acquiring, payment, fraud, rule setting, and disputes.

Market share is also dramatically less for these "non-bankcards."

Visa and Mastercard do not:

- Issue credit cards
- Establish criteria for evaluating applicants
- Set credit limits offered to cardholders
- Determine procedures for billing customers

Visa and Mastercard are managers of their respective brands. As such, they:

- Create advertising and promotion programs to support their brands
- Develop new products
- Conduct clearing and settlement processing of transactions (interchange)
- Set and enforce rules and regulations governing the use and acceptance of their bankcards, such as operational procedures, interchange procedures, and graphic design approval of their cards.

MEMBER BANKS/ISSUERS

Member banks are financial institutions that have entered into membership with Visa and/or Mastercard. The member bank must designate its intended use of the cards, either to issue these cards to consumers and/or to acquire new merchants.

Members can perform both of these activities or utilize other companies to perform services.

The issuer is responsible for the cardholder account program, which encompasses nearly all aspects of cardholder account activities ranging from acquiring new customers to billing current ones.

The issuer's responsibilities include:

- Acquisition and marketing of new accounts
- Processing applications, establishing credit limits and policies
- Overseeing design, manufacturing, and embossing of cards
- Handling of issuing and reissuing of cards
- Overseeing PIN issuance
- Maintaining authorization file
- Providing customer service
- Processing payments and handling settlement
- Establishing collections operations

Managing a credit card program is expensive. Smaller banks can issue cards without becoming an issuing member by acting as an agent, which are called agent banks.

The issuer usually keeps most of the income from the cardholder account. The agent receives a small compensation for providing the application. This allows small banks to retain customers who want a credit card program.

ACQUIRER

The acquirer is usually, but not always, a member of Visa and Mastercard and contracts with merchants to accept merchant sales drafts, and provides authorization terminals, direction, support, and the processing of merchant credit card transactions.

The key responsibilities of the acquirer are:

- Sales
- Fraud investigation
- Pricing

- Merchant acceptance
- Support services
- Risk management

The acquirer charges a fee or "discount rate" for handling the transactions. The acquirer is registered with Visa and Mastercard and agrees to follow the association rules and regulations.

Here are the top 8 acquirers, according to The Nilson Report published in March 2018:

1. Worldpay
2. First Data
3. Chase
4. Bank Of America
5. Global Payments, Inc.
6. Wells Fargo
7. Elavon
8. TSYS

PROCESSOR

The processor is a company contracted by a member bank to authorize, capture, settle, and clear transactions.

With the increasing costs of technology associated with electronic payments, many members do not have the resources to create their own transaction network. Most processors are also large acquirers and some even issuers.

Examples of processors are:

- Global Payment Systems (merged with Heartland Payments)
- First Data Resources (FDR) now owned by Fiserv, Inc.
- TSYS (formerly Vital) now part of Global Payments
- WorldPay now owned by FIS

ISO/MSP

An independent sales organization or member service provider is a non-association organization that performs merchant solicitation, sales, or services on behalf of a member bank.

Many acquirers are labeled as ISOs, and those without a member bank partner, are not association members. These larger acquirer/ISOs are commonly referred to as "super ISOs," while the smaller companies that perform mostly sales and support roles are considered their "sub-ISOs."

MERCHANT

A merchant, or any business that sells goods or services and accepts Visa or Mastercard as payment, is an acquirer or ISO's customer.

BANKCARD FEES

The components of bankcard fees are:

- Interchange/assessments
- Authorization fees
- Processing fees
- Processor optional fees
- Chargeback and retrieval fees
- T & E authorization and processing fees
- PCI compliance fees
- Ancillary communication and network fees
- Hardware and software fees

INTERCHANGE (SEE ALSO CHAPTER ON INTERCHANGE)

Visa and Mastercard are at the center of the transaction process, maintaining the flow of funds between issuers and acquirers. During interchange, fees are deducted by the issuer from the transaction amount and the issuer pays the net amount to the acquirer. These are called interchange fees. Interchange is often used to refer to the amount the acquirers pay the issuers for each transaction and is determined on a transaction-by-transaction basis depending on many factors, including risk, merchant type, and method of payment.

Clearing refers to the exchange of financial information. Settlement refers to the exchange of the actual funds for the transaction and the associated fees.

Clearing and Settlement occur simultaneously. The acquirer credits the merchant's deposit account for the dollar amount of the sale (less the merchant discount fee). The acquirer sends the transaction to a processor, who transports it through a data network, to Mastercard or VisaNet (for Visa transactions). (Note: some acquirers are also processors.)

Visa and Mastercard transmit the transaction to the issuer, credit the acquirer, and debit the issuer for the amount of the transaction. The acquirer/processor then funds the merchant for the sale; again, less the discount fee.

In essence, the issuer pays the acquirer for the transaction via the Visa and Mastercard interchange system. Interchange makes it possible for the issuing banks and acquiring banks to exchange information, transactions, and money on a standardized basis.

Visa and Mastercard each own and operate their own international processing system. These systems connect thousands of banks around the world. Member institutions use these networks to transmit information about bankcard transactions.

VISA AND MASTERCARD

To summarize:

Both Visa and Mastercard offer products on both the cardholder-issuing and merchant-acquiring side of the business to facilitate a complete system of electronic currency.

Cards are issued to consumers with credit spending limits, revolving interest rates, and fees.

Merchants are enrolled to accept and deposit credit card sales through member acquiring banks.

The Associations' role is primarily branding and marketing; governing and enforcing the issuers to the acquirers' rules and regulations; and managing and settling interchange.

A member bank may be both a card-issuing and merchant-acquiring institution.

The Card Associations have rules and regulations governing how industry risk is handled.

Merchant interchange fees are paid from the acquiring bank to the issuer.

Interchange fees vary depending on the type of card product and how it is accepted.

CHAPTER 4
THE ANATOMY OF A CREDIT CARD

ANSI Standard X4.13-1983 is the system used by most national credit-card systems.

Illustration by Rosaleah Rautert

What the numbers mean.

The first digit in your credit card number signifies the system:

3 – Travel/Entertainment cards (such as American Express and Diners Club)

4 – Visa

5 – MasterCard

6 – Discover Card

The *structure* of the card number varies by system. For example, American Express card numbers start with 37; Carte Blanche and Diners Club, with 38.

American Express – Digits three and four are type and currency, digits five through 11 are the account number, digits 12 through 14 are the card number within the account, and digit 15 is a check digit.

Visa – Digits two through six are the bank number, digits seven through 12 or seven through 15 are the account number, and digit 13 or 16 is a check digit.

MasterCard – Digits two and three, two through four, two through five, or two through six are the bank number (depending on whether digit two is a 1, 2, 3, or other). The digits after the bank number up through digit 15 are the account number, and digit 16 is a check digit.

CHIP EMV TECHNOLOGY (SEE CHAPTER ON EMV)

This chip is an alternative method of holding the cardholder's information, in addition to the magnetic stripe (which is on the back of the card). It is a more secure and modern form of information storage, providing better protection against fraud.

This is known as EMV technology, which stands for "Europay, Mastercard, Visa." This is the global standard for this chip technology, which comes in two forms:

- Chip-and-Signature
- Chip-and-PIN

Chip-and-Signature cards require your signature to complete a transaction, while Chip-and-PIN cards use a PIN that you create, much like a debit card. Credit cards can be either one of these types, or both. It is most common to find only Chip-and-Signature cards in the U.S. as of now, but that situation is changing, and more cards will be enabled with both in the future.

Instead of swiping the credit card through a groove, you insert a chip-enabled card into a slot on the reader, usually on the bottom, and leave the card there until you are prompted to remove it. This is referred to as "card dipping."

Credit cards issued in the United States are required by law to be chip-enabled by the beginning of October, 2015, and at that date merchants who do not comply with the new standards by providing the correct technology for the chip cards will be held liable for fraudulent credit card activity.

Now that we know what the numbers stand for, let us examine the stripe on the back.

THE STRIPE

The stripe on the back of a credit card is a *magnetic stripe*, often called a *magstripe*. The magstripe is made up of tiny iron-based magnetic particles encased in a plastic-like film. Each particle is really a tiny *bar magnet* about 20-millionths of an inch long.

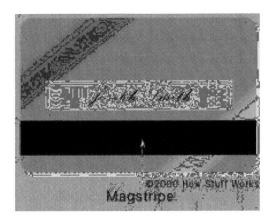

Illustration by Rosaleah Rautert

Your card has a magstripe on the back and a place for the signature.

A magstripe reader, as found in electronic data capture (EDC) terminals, registers, and numerous other electronic devices, can understand the information contained in a magstripe. If a terminal won't accept your card, the stripe may be dirty or scratched.

An erased magstripe (the most common causes for erased magstripes are exposure to magnets, like the small ones used to hold notes and pictures on the refrigerator, and exposure to a store's electronic article surveillance (EAS) tag demagnetizer) will also make your card unreadable when you swipe it through an EDC terminal.

> **CVV Security Code:** This code is a fraud prevention tool, used when making card-not-present transactions, such as online purchases that don't require you to actually have the physical credit card. You just need the information printed on it.

These are the opposite of those transactions where you actually use the plastic card, such as when checking out at a grocery store, where you would use the magstripe or chip.

CVV codes are a 3-digit number for Visa, Mastercard, and Discover cards, and a 4-digit number for American Express.

INFORMATION ON THE STRIPE

There are three tracks on the magstripe. Each track is about one-tenth of an inch wide. The ISO/IEC standard 7811, which is used by banks, specifies:

- Track one is 210 bits per inch (bpi), and holds 79 6-bit plus parity bit read-only characters.
- Track two is 75 bpi, and holds 40 4-bit plus parity bit characters.
- Track three is 210 bpi, and holds 107 4-bit plus parity bit characters.

Your credit card typically uses only tracks one and two. Track three is a read/write track (which includes an encrypted PIN, country code, currency units and amount authorized), but its usage is not standardized among banks.

For more info on standards, go to *www.ansi.org*.

CHAPTER 5
THE TRANSACTION FLOW

Here are the steps involved in a typical retail credit card transaction:

TRANSACTION FLOW

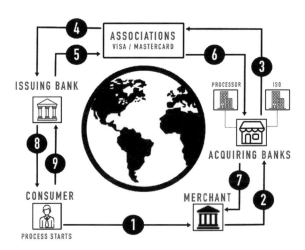

Step 1:	The consumer purchases goods or services from the merchant.
Step 2:	The merchant transmits the transaction to the acquirer, by sliding the card through the terminal or magnetic stripe reader. The most common device is a credit card processing terminal. If the device cannot read the card, the merchant will manually enter the card information and get a manual imprint of the credit card.
	The terminal then transmits the sales authorization request via a standard phone line connection to the acquiring bank.
Step 3:	The acquiring bank routes the transaction to a processor and then to the associations – Visa System (Visa Net) or MasterCard System (INET).
Step 4:	The association system then routes the transaction to the issuing bank and requests an approval.
Step 5:	The issuing bank sends back the response. If the cardholder is approved the issuing bank assigns and transmits the authorization code back to the association.
Step 6:	The association then sends the authorization code back to the acquiring bank.
Step 7:	The acquiring bank routes the approval code or response to the merchant terminal. The merchant terminal prints a receipt for the cardholder to sign, which obligates the cardholder to pay the amount approved.
Step 8:	Issuer bills the consumer.
Step 9:	Consumer pays the bill.

SETTLEMENT

Settlement is the actual transfer of funds to the appropriate parties. Generally, at the end of the day, a merchant will review all the sales, credits, voids, and totals in its terminal. Once all transactions are verified the merchant will settle, or close, its batch and transmit the information to the acquirer for deposit to its bank account. The acquiring bank routes the transaction through the appropriate settlement system against the appropriate card-issuing bank.

The card-issuing bank routes the transfer back through the settlement system for the amount of the sales draft, less the appropriate discount fee, to the acquiring bank's account.

The acquiring bank then deposits the amount to the merchant's bank account. The merchant usually receives its money within 48–72 hours.

There are several variations of this procedure on the front end depending on the program the merchant is utilizing.

For example, a restaurant may want to be able to track servers to more easily settle tips at the end of the shift. A hotel or car rental agency may want to get a pre-approval before the customer checks in or uses the service. A bar may want to open a tab for its customers.

Each processor has pre-built programs that can be requested based upon the merchant's type of business.

ONLINE PROCESSING

Here are the steps involved in a typical Internet transaction. This is assuming the merchant has a shopping cart and payment gateway installed on its Website.

Step 1:	The cardholder selects goods or services from the merchant's Website. As each item is selected it is placed in the customer's shopping cart.
Step 2:	The customer verifies the items to be purchased, then selects the shipping method and any other delivery options. The checkout button is clicked and the order is totaled for the customer. If all is acceptable the customer clicks the appropriate selection; i.e., Process Order, Buy Now, Order Now, or Checkout.
Step 3:	The customer is then transmitted to a secure payment gateway. This allows the customer to enter the credit card information in a safe mode.
Step 4:	Once the information is entered, the gateway encrypts the data and transmits the transaction to the acquirer.
Step 5:	The acquiring bank routes the transaction to the Visa System (Visa Net) or MasterCard System (INET), which then routes the transaction to the issuing bank and requests an approval. Issuing banks use AVS (Address Verification System) and/or CVV (Card Verification Value) to prevent fraudulent use of the consumer's credit card information.
Step 6:	The issuing bank sends back the response. If the cardholder is approved, the issuing bank assigns and transmits the authorization code back to the acquirer bank.
Step 7:	The acquirer bank processes the transaction and sends the authorization code back to the merchant's secure gateway.
Step 8:	The gateway displays an approval number for the customer, which usually advises the customer to print out a receipt at that time.

Step 9:	The gateway software will also e-mail a receipt to the customer at this time and an order notification to the merchant for processing and shipment.
Step 10:	The merchant ships the merchandise to the customer.
Step 11:	The payment gateway will automatically process the batch for the day, usually at a specified time.
Step 12:	The acquirer/processor routes the transaction through the appropriate settlement system against the appropriate card-issuing bank.
Step 13:	The card-issuing bank routes the transfer back through the appropriate settlement system for the amount of the sales draft, less the appropriate discount fee, to the acquiring bank's account.
Step 14:	The acquirer then deposits the funds into the merchant's bank account. The merchant usually receives its money within 48–72 hours.
Step 15:	The cardholder's bank bills the cardholder for the amount of the purchase.
Step 16:	Consumer pays the bill.

Remember that a payment gateway serves the same function as a credit card terminal. There are multiple payment gateways on the market. Many have sophisticated fraud prevention tools and can assist the merchant in controlling chargebacks.

Payment gateways also provide what is commonly called a virtual terminal along with a shopping cart. The virtual terminal allows the merchant to process manual credit card transactions from locations where there is an Internet connection.

For instance, a merchant may have a Website taking orders 24 hours a day and he may also travel to trade shows twice a month. If he has Internet access at the trade show or at his hotel, he can process manual orders from a virtual terminal, which is Web-based.

Many virtual terminals today also allow online electronic check processing via their virtual terminal.

Internet transactions use several encryption technologies including Secure Socket Layer (SSL) protocol.

CHAPTER 6
INTERCHANGE

*"Talking about Interchange to a merchant
is like talking about sex to your teenager –
If you don't do it, somebody else will."*

—Source: ETA Presenter

Suffice it to say, in order for an MLS or ISO to be successful it must understand Interchange concepts and be able to communicate that information to a prospect or merchant.

Interchange is dynamic and is typically updated with bi-annual releases in April and October. With the evolving nature of the payment space, however, Interchange changes and the introduction of new Interchange rates have been occurring outside of the traditional release dates.

Visa describes interchange as *"Visa uses interchange reimbursement fees as transfer fees between acquiring banks and issuing banks for each Visa card transaction. Visa uses these fees to balance and grow the payment system for the benefit of all participants.*

Merchants do not pay interchange reimbursement fees—merchants negotiate and pay a "merchant discount" to their financial institution that is typically calculated as a percentage per transaction. Merchants can receive a variety of processing services from financial institutions that may be included in their merchant discount rate." (SOURCE VISA)

Here are some Interchange fast facts:

- Interchange cost is the same for all processors, regardless of processing volume or size. All small bank pays the same interchange cost as say a First Data.
- Interchange is paid by the acquiring bank to the issuing bank on sale transactions.
- Interchange is refunded to the acquiring bank for refunds and chargebacks.
- Interchange compensates issuing banks for free interest loans for transactors and credit/fraud losses.
- Interchange represents a large portion of an issuer's gross income
- Interchange is the single largest cost component in a merchant's total bankcard charges.
- Interchange is in addition to assessments and other fees, which are paid to Visa, MasterCard, Discover and American Express as opposed to the Issuing Bank.

Gone are the days when we can think of one Interchange rate for retail and one for keyed or Internet. Interchange has evolved into a complex grid where, depending on the card type, MCC merchant's actions, and card attributes, the Interchange rate can vary quite dramatically.

The online posting for Visa's and MasterCard's Interchange may be found at their respective websites: www.usa.visa.com and www.mastercard.us

One of the highest cost categories of interchange are reward cards. Reward programs have dominated the new card segment, and consumers now look for the added value when selecting a credit card. Issuers need the higher Interchange payments in order to fund their marketing and new customer incentives. As reward cards have continued to dominate the new card market, and as issuers have gravitated towards higher-Interchange cards, the range between the lowest cost transaction and most expensive transaction has widened.

The Wal-Mart settlement brought about the separate Interchange schedule for signature debit, the rates were set lower than credit Interchange. The reasons why signature debit Interchange rates were set lower were to account for:

- Lower credit risk
- Lower fraud risk
- Lower cost of funds

Credit losses are lower because the issuer is not extending credit beyond the funds that the issuer has on hand in the depositor's account. Certainly, there are overdrafts and fraudulent purchases, but banks have a solid history of dealing with overdrafts. Fraudulent transactions are more quickly reported on a debit card than with a credit card because cardholders are more in tune with their deposit balance than with their credit line. Also, because funds are deducted from the cardholder's checking account, there is no carrying or interest cost to the issuer either.

Although issuing banks have a greater expense associated with the rewards and signature products, they too benefit from the increased balances and corresponding interest income and – in addition to the premium interchange – cardholder loyalty increases and attrition decreases.

Historically, acquirers benefited from the increased transactions. To be sure, there is far more work caused by the complexity of the Interchange schedule manifesting in increased customer service and more complex pricing, training expense and merchant dissatisfaction. Nonetheless, the increased volume more than compensates us for the additional work. Further, many premium or rewards cards are down-graded (or charged a higher discount rate) making up for the higher Interchange.

Many merchant classes, however, are not made whole. A petroleum retailer will not experience an increase in sales simply because a cardholder upgraded their card. Grocery stores, doctor's offices, auto body and automotive repair shops, gyms, lawyers, dry cleaners, newspaper subscriptions, and dentists will not see sales increase because a cardholder upgraded their card to a new reward card. These merchants will, however, face an increasing cost for processing, simply because the cardholder used a high cost product.

All acquirers must cover the following variable costs, just to break even.

- Interchange
- Assessments (V/MC/DIS/AMEX)
- Base II Fees
- Numerous other fees like, FANF, Integrity, Kilobyte, NABU, AVS, Cross Border, Location, Downgrades, Data Usage, Auth fees, etc.
- Bank Sponsorship Fee
- Sales Commission / Residual

Moreover, acquirers would also like to ensure they are being compensated for overhead and merchant loss with something left over for profit.

Interchange is typically priced with both a percentage component and a flat fee. A common Interchange rate is 1.65% + $0.15. As you can see from the illustration below, when converted to a percentage of the transaction, a smaller average ticket equates to a higher calculated Interchange percentage. For example,

Average ticket = $1,000.00, Interchange rate of 1.65% + $0.15
1.65 x 1,000 =$16.5 + $0.15 = $16.65
$16.65 is 1.66% of $1,000

Average ticket = $100, Interchange rate of 1.65% + $0.15
1.65 x $100 = 1.65 + $0.15 = $1.80
$1.80 is 1.80% of $100

Average ticket of $10, Interchange rate of 1.65% + $0.15
1.65 x $10 = $0.165 + $0.15 = $0.270
$0.270 is 2.70% of $10

Consequently, it is extremely important to ensure merchants are priced with both a percentage rate and a per transaction (or authorization) fee, especially for smaller average ticket merchants.

There are many different pricing schemes, but the two most prevalent are pass-through pricing and tiered pricing.

Pass-through pricing is becoming ever more prevalent. What was once a pricing plan reserved only for the largest accounts is now being used regardless of merchant size.

True pass-through pricing works by passing through only the amount of the increase above Interchange. Assessments may or may not be included in the mark-up above Interchange. The beauty of pass-through pricing is its transparency. By marking up the downgrades, the merchant has to deal with the complexities of the numerous Interchange structures and penalty fees associated with downgrades.

Ideally, merchants will see all the Interchange tiers on their pass-through statements so only the more sophisticated businesses will be suited for this pricing. In addition to the fixed mark-up over Interchange, pass through pricing has an authorization or transaction fee to cover processor cost and the fixed component of Interchange.

The mark-up above interchange is fixed regardless of the Interchange category. This assists the merchant in knowing that the acquirer's margin is reasonable and known regardless of card type or Interchange category.

The acquirer is assured a fixed margin. Unfortunately, there is little financial incentive for the acquirer to assist the merchant in optimally routing the transaction, but they do know that whatever Interchange category a transaction falls into they will make a set margin – This applies to newly introduced categories as well.

Some acquirers have taken pass-through pricing and morphed it into a version that further marks up down-grades and has variable authorization costs depending on the Interchange category. I expect to see more of this type of pricing as the margins are compressed in tandem with the shift away from tiered pricing towards pass-through pricing.

Another common pricing strategy is Tiered pricing. The terms "Qualified," "Mid-Qualified" and "Non-Qualified" are industry invented terms used to define the three tiers that all Interchange Categories are traditionally lumped into. The tiered pricing scheme is meant to simplify the multitude of Interchange levels into a few tiers. Nowhere in the Visa and MasterCard regulations; however, will you find the terms Qualified, Mid-Qualified, and Non-Qualified.

With the Wal-Mart settlement, the number of Interchange tiers were nearly doubled (for signature debit.) May acquirers, now price credit and signature debit separately causing acquirers to now have separate signature debit tiers. Effectively when signature debit is priced uniquely there are six rates (qualified, mid-qualified, and non-qualified for credit and signature debit.)

It is critical to understand that not all acquirers down grade transactions consistently. One acquirer may "Qualify" a transaction that is either Mid-Qualified or Non-Qualified at another.

EMERGING MARKET OPPORTUNITIES

Visa and Mastercard have incentivized certain markets with lower interchange rates, these are called emerging markets. The strategy is to offer these markets lower interchange pricing to promote more card usage. These are great opportunities for you to approach these emerging markets and offer card services. Examples are current emerging markets are; charity, government, schools, utilities and insurance companies. Check their respective websites for the current emerging markets incentives.

My suggestion to you is to understand the top 5 Interchange categories for card present and card not present merchants within your market. Your acquirer should be able to provide this for you.

I further suggest you know the Interchange costs to each of those categories and where they fall within your tiers. Understand the qualifications of those specific categories and you will understand the Interchange for 85% of your customers. And if you understand Interchange for 85% of your merchants, you will be ahead of 99% of your competitors.

Many ISOs have statement analysis services that will break down each prospective merchant's current pricing plan and prepare a proposal to present to the merchant. There are also several software tools now that can assist in preparing pricing analysis for your merchants.

CHAPTER 7
TYPICAL MERCHANT FEES

Let us review the most common fees that may be charged to merchants (in alphabetical order):

ADDRESS VERIFICATION FEE

The fee charged to the merchant to perform address verification.

ANNUAL FEE

This is a yearly fee charged by ISOs and acquirers to maintain a merchant's account. This is also called a renewal fee, subscription fee, or annual membership fee.

APPLICATION FEE

This is the fee associated with processing an initial application from a new merchant. This covers the overhead costs of credit bureaus, phone verifications, and data input.

CANCELLATION FEE

This is the fee charged by the ISO or acquirer if a merchant cancels his contract before the specified contract period expires.

CHARGEBACK FEE

This is the fee charged by a bank when a chargeback is issued to a merchant. This varies from $15.00–$25.00 per transaction, plus the actual amount of the chargeback sale.

CHECK GUARANTEE FEES

Check guarantee fees are basically structured similar to credit card processing fees. There is usually a percentage rate, transaction fee, statement fee, monthly minimum, and application fee.

CHECK VERIFICATION FEES

Check verification does not guarantee checks. Check verification verifies whether the check writer has a history of writing bad checks. There is usually not a percentage fee associated with check verification.

Standard fees usually include a flat fee transaction fee, monthly minimum, and/or statement fee.

COMPLIANCE FEE

This is a fee, which is currently in vogue, to help ISOs and processors underwrite the cost of PCI compliance.

DEBIT FEES

Debit fees vary based on the debit network that issues the debit card. Debit fees are comprised of network fees and transaction fees. Check with your ISO or acquirer for your exact debit fees.

The network will either charge a flat fee or a small percentage of the transaction. The acquirer may also have a debit card statement fee ranging from $3.00–$10.00 per month.

DISCOUNT FEE (PER TRANSACTION)

The discount rate is the fee charged by the acquirer to the merchant to process each transaction. This rate is dependent upon several factors, but usually the rate is either a retail (card present) merchant or a MOTO/Internet (card-not-present) merchant. (Refer to Interchange Chapter)

Retail rates are lower because they present less risk than card not present transactions. Conversely, card-not-present rates are higher due to the increased risk exposure to the bank.

For instance, if the retail discount fee is 1.85% for a swiped transaction, then the merchant will be charged $1.85 for a $100.00 sale.

Rates with no transaction fee are called bundled rates. The cost of the transaction is built into the discount rate; bundled rates are usually used for merchants with a very small average ticket, like a dry cleaner, quick-serve, or restaurant.

Also, if a retail merchant swipes a card and the magnetic strip cannot be read, an additional fee will apply because the card number will have to be manually entered. This is called a mid-qualified transaction or surcharge (these are high profit transactions.) These terms vary depending upon your bank. Always check with the acquirer or ISO if there are rate fee questions.

If a merchant processes retail and Internet transactions, the bank may require that the merchant maintain two accounts, one for each type of transaction.

EQUIPMENT WARRANTY PLAN

This is a monthly or annual fee that will replace or repair a merchant's terminal if it malfunctions or breaks.

INTERNET PAYMENT GATEWAY FEES

A monthly fee associated with maintaining a merchant's secure payment gateway.

Payment gateways also vary. Usually there is a setup fee, a monthly gateway fee, and/or a transaction fee.

The monthly gateway is usually $10.00–$25.00, and the transaction fee ranges from $0.05–$0.15 per sale.

INVESTIGATION FEE

This fee is charged by some banks to investigate or research merchant transactions.

IRS REPORTING/REGULATORY FEE

An IRS reporting fee, also known as an "IRS regulatory fee" is a fee imposed to recover the administrative costs for reporting a merchant's annual credit card processing volume to the IRS.

MONTHLY STATEMENT FEE

This is the monthly fee charged to the merchant in order to produce a monthly accounting of all transactions. This will break down the merchant's total sales by day, average ticket amount, and total charges.

MONTHLY MINIMUM FEE

This is a set minimum the bank wants to earn from each account. Monthly minimum fees range from $10.00–$25.00. That means if the merchant doesn't process any transactions, the bank will still receive the monthly minimum fee income in order to service the account.

For example, let's consider a merchant with a monthly minimum of $25.00. If they processed $1,000.00 in charges and the discount rate is 1.85%, the monthly discount fee will be $18.50 – the merchant did not reach the $25.00 minimum, so it will be charged the difference of $6.50.

If the merchant ran $10,000 in sales at a 1.85% discount rate, however, the monthly discount fee would be $185.00, so the merchant would not be charged a $25.00 monthly minimum fee. The monthly minimum only comes into play for low sales volume merchants.

PCI COMPLIANCE FEE

This is a fee charged by the ISO for PCI Compliance. Merchant's typically must complete compliance on an annual basis.

PCI NON COMPLIANCE FEE

This is a fee charged for merchant that have not completed their PCI compliance for the year. These fees can range from $0-$129.00 per month.

RETRIEVAL FEE

Fee charged to process a retrieval request.

TRANSACTION FEE

This is a fee charged to the merchant to authorize a transaction. This fee for retail is usually $0.20–$0.25 per sale; for MOTO, it ranges between $0.28–$0.35 per sale. In a bundled discount fee, the transaction fees are included in the discount rate.

VOICE AUTHORIZATION FEE

This is the fee charged if the merchant calls Visa/MasterCard for a manual voice authorization.

WIRELESS FEES

Wireless terminals require a wireless network to process transactions. Monthly wireless access fees range from $15.00–$30.00 and additional per-transaction fees can range from $0.05–$0.35 per transaction, depending on the carrier. Often, a wireless setup fee is required that can range from $50.00–$99.00.

CHAPTER 8

CHARGEBACKS 101: UNDERSTANDING CHARGEBACKS & THEIR ROOT CAUSES

CONTRIBUTING WRITER SURESH DAKSHINA

Chargebacks are one of the biggest challenges facing merchants today. Not only do they equate to millions in lost sales every year, but because of associated fees—the costs to manufacture, market and ship the product, and the potential damage to valuable merchant accounts—they typically mean a financial loss of 2.5 times the sale price.

Sadly, the problem is getting worse, too. From 2016 to 2017, the rate of chargebacks jumped 179 percent from four years prior, and merchants lost a whopping 1.9 percent of their revenue.

Merchants who want to stop the ever-growing chargeback trend and protect their revenues, merchant accounts and reputation, must take steps to understand the problem. Knowing the causes of chargebacks, as well as how the overall chargeback process works, is vital to both fighting customer chargebacks and preventing them in the first place. What is a Chargeback?

A chargeback occurs when a consumer contacts their bank or credit card issuer, disputes a charge on their account, and requests a refund. It typically occurs when they spot a charge on their bank or card statement that they either 1) don't recognize or 2) are unhappy with in some form or fashion.

Consumers may file chargeback disputes for various reasons, including dissatisfaction with the product or service they purchased, a higher-than-expected cost, late or delayed shipment, or unknown charges due to true fraudulent activity or identity theft.

HOW DOES THE CHARGEBACK PROCESS WORK?

The chargeback process has many steps and includes the consumer, the issuing bank, the retailer and the retailer's acquiring bank. If the retailer has engaged a chargeback representment firm, they will also be involved in the process.

Here's how it works:

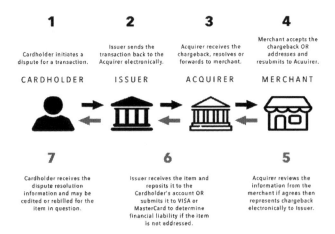

1	2	3	4
Cardholder initiates a dispute for a transaction.	Issuer sends the transaction back to the Acquirer electronically.	Acquirer receives the chargeback, resolves or forwards to merchant.	Merchant accepts the chargeback OR addresses and resubmits to Acuuirer.
CARDHOLDER	ISSUER	ACQUIRER	MERCHANT

7	6	5
Cardholder receives the dispute resolution information and may be cedited or rebilled for the item in question.	Issuer receives the item and reposits it to the Cardholder's account OR submits it to VISA or MasterCard to determine financial liability if the item is not addressed.	Acquirer reviews the information from the merchant if agrees then represents chargeback electronically to Issuer.

TYPES OF CHARGEBACKS

1-10% of all chargebacks
are caused by criminal fraud

60-80% of all chargebacks
are caused by friendly fraud

20-40% of all chargebacks
are caused by merchant error

There are three main categories of chargebacks: merchant error, true fraud and friendly fraud.

Merchant error involves charges made accidentally or erroneously by the retailer. These may occur when a merchant makes duplicate charges, authorizes the wrong transaction amount or, in some cases, fails to issue a refund as promised.

True fraud chargebacks stem from identify theft, hacking or credit card theft. In short, someone other than the cardholder made the charge, and the customer had no knowledge that their card was being used.

Friendly fraud chargebacks occur when a customer disputes a charge they – or a family member – knowingly made. They may dispute the charge if they were unhappy with the transaction, product or purchase, or if the charge was more than they expected.

Instances of family fraud also fall into the friendly fraud category. These occur when a cardholder's spouse, mother, father or other loved one uses their card without their permission. When the transaction shows up on a statement as unrecognizable, the cardholder disputes the charge, not knowing it was their family member that made the purchase.

CHARGEBACK CLASSIFICATION BY REASON CODE

A reason code is a numeric code that describes the motivation behind a chargeback dispute. Each major credit card network – Visa, MasterCard, Discover and American Express – has its own unique set of reason codes. As a merchant, reason codes can shed light on why your customers are filing chargebacks and help you both fight and prevent future disputes.

VISA

As of April 15, 2018, the card network, as part of the Visa Claims Resolution (VCR) Initiative, consolidated 22 legacy reason codes into four dispute categories. Previously there were 23 reason codes. To review a list of old and new codes go to: www.surviveandthrive.biz/resources

CHARGEBACK THRESHOLDS

Every card network sets a maximum chargeback threshold for its merchants, which caps the merchant's monthly chargeback ratio. This ratio is determined by dividing the total number of charge-backs per month by the merchant's total number of transactions for that time period. For example, a retailer that has 10 chargebacks in May on a total of 100 transactions would have a 10 percent chargeback ratio for the month. (10 divided by 100).

These thresholds help ensure merchants are operating a fair and honest business, and that consumers are served to their expectations. Merchants who exceed their card issuers' thresholds may see their merchant accounts shut down as a result. They will be unable to open a new merchant account without a new business or company ID.

Here's what the thresholds for each card network look like:

VISA

Visa's chargeback threshold is 75 chargebacks per month and a 0.75 percent chargeback ratio. If a merchant hits these numbers for any given month, Visa will place them on a pre-monitoring program. If they surpass 100 chargebacks and a 1 percent chargeback ratio, the network moves them to a Merchant Monitoring program.

MASTERCARD

MasterCard's chargeback threshold is similar in structure to Visa's, though it leaves a little more room for error, capping chargebacks at 100 per month and a chargeback ratio of 1 percent. If a merchant exceeds these, they are placed on what's called a Chargeback Monitored Merchant program. If they exceed 100 chargebacks and a 1.5 percent ratio in a month, they're considered an Excessive Chargeback Merchant.

AMERICAN EXPRESS

American Express doesn't have hard-and-fast thresholds but instead considers the merchant's overall risk level, chargeback count and chargeback ratio. Generally, merchants should avoid exceeding 100 chargebacks and 1 percent chargeback ratio in a month.

DISCOVER

Like American Express, Discover is also more relaxed when it comes to its chargeback thresholds. Again, merchants should attempt to keep their chargebacks under 100 for the month and avoid exceeding a 1 percent chargeback ratio.

CHARGEBACKS VS. RETRIEVAL REQUESTS

Merchants often confuse chargebacks and retrieval requests, as notifications for both come straight from the merchant's bank. Sometimes called "soft chargebacks," retrieval requests occur when a consumer wants more information on a purchase they've made from a merchant.

Here's how it works: the customer calls their card issuer to request more information on a recent purchase. The issuer contacts the acquiring bank, who then contacts the merchant. The merchant must then produce the receipt, invoice, tracking number, shipment info or other details requested by the consumer, which is then sent back to the issuing bank.

While retrieval requests don't result in immediate financial losses, they can lead to potential chargebacks if the merchant doesn't produce adequate documentation. If merchants respond to retrieval requests thoroughly and on time, they may be able to prevent some chargebacks from occurring.

PRE-ARBITRATION AND ARBITRATION

In some cases, a card issuer may decide to take a chargeback dispute into arbitration. This may be because the reason code changes, new information has come into play, or the merchant's documentation or evidence was incomplete or inaccurate. The issuing bank and the acquiring bank can also request arbitration, should they be unhappy with the result of the initial dispute.

When arbitration occurs, the merchant will once again have a chance to produce evidence and fight the dispute. The card network will have the ultimate say in the outcome of the case. For Visa card-related disputes, there is an added step just before entering arbitration, dubbed "pre-arbitration."

Arbitration typically comes with a few overhead costs. For MasterCard disputes, for example, there a filing fees ($150), administrative fees ($250), withdrawal fees ($150) and technical fees ($100). These costs and fees vary by card network. Merchants are best served by preventing arbitration by responding to retrieval requests and chargebacks promptly and thoroughly at the outset.

3.	REPRESENTMENT	
Process ends if bank **is satisfied** with representment.	Process advances to the next cycle if issuing bank **isn't satisfied** with the representment.	

4.	PRE-ARBITRAITION	
Process ends if Merchant **accepts liability**	Process advances to the next cycle if Merchant decides to **request arbitration**	

5.	ARBITRAITION (final phase)

MOST COMMON CAUSES OF CHARGEBACKS

As you can see by the list of reason codes, there are hundreds of reasons a customer may dispute a charge. Still, the majority of chargebacks stem from one of five common root causes. These include:

FRIENDLY FRAUD

Friendly fraud is a category that includes a number of different scenarios. Many times, the customer is trying to cheat the system, purchasing the product or service and then filing a chargeback to obtain that purchase for free. In other cases, customers may dispute a charge because they never received the product or service, their purchase was defective, the merchant continued to charge them after cancelation, or they never received a refund after being promised one. A shocking 60 to 90 percent of chargebacks are due to friendly fraud.

AFFILIATE FRAUD

Affiliate marketing can often lead to chargebacks, particularly when merchants don't vet their affiliates carefully. Many unsavory affiliates will generate large numbers of bad transactions in order to increase their income. By the time the merchant notices the significant volume of chargebacks on these transactions, the affiliate has cashed out and left. Affiliate-related chargebacks account for 10 to 60 percent of all charge disputes, depending on the industry.

BAD CUSTOMER SERVICE

Poor customer service is another common cause of chargebacks. Long waits with call center representatives, delayed response times, understaffing and otherwise lacking operational policies can push a customer to file a dispute out of dissatisfaction. Bad customer service accounts for 10 to 30 percent of all chargebacks.

FULFILLMENT ISSUES

Fulfillment and shipping issues often lead to chargebacks. Shipments sent late, to the wrong address, without tracking numbers or without proper quality control checks, may cause a customer to file a chargeback and dispute a transaction. These issues account for anywhere from 1 to 15 percent of chargebacks.

CANCELED SUBSCRIPTION

For subscription-based merchants, canceled subscriptions are one of the most common reasons behind chargebacks. Customers file these disputes if they were charged after already canceling their subscription. They may also file them as a way to cancel their subscription or after they receive the product, so as to keep both the product and service charge.

CHARGEBACK REPRESENTMENT & PREVENTION

Merchants have the right to dispute a chargeback should they feel it is unmerited. If the merchant knows they've fulfilled their obligation to the client, delivered their goods and services, and has proof, they may be able to fight the chargeback and recover their lost funds. This is called chargeback representment.

Here's what the chargeback representment process looks like:

It's very important that merchants fight chargebacks whenever possible. As chargebacks cost merchants in lost sales, cost of goods, marketing expenses, transaction fees and more, they often result in significant financial losses. They can also threaten the very merchant accounts necessary to do business.

Ultimately, the best way to fight chargebacks is through prevention. Merchants can often keep chargebacks from ever occurring with honest, ethical and efficient back-end operations.

This means:

- Being up-front, honest and ethical in marketing and advertising efforts
- Clearly explaining all terms and policies
- Having iron-clad quality control and fulfillment processes
- Tuning in to customer feedback and responding appropriately
- Employing a 24-7 customer response team

Because the chargeback industry is constantly evolving, with changing regulations, rules and timelines, enlisting a chargeback representment firm is the best way to successfully fight and prevent chargebacks.

CHAPTER 9
DEBIT AND CHECK CARD PROCESSING

- Usage of signature and PIN-based debit cards has been steadily rising, with $2.88 trillion dollars in spending and 82.6 billion transactions reported in 2017.

- In Q2 2018, 521 million VISA debit cards were in circulation in the U.S. and 1.65 billion VISA debit cards in circulation worldwide; 66% of those cards are active.

- In Q4 2018, 216 million Mastercard debit cards were in circulation in the United States and 933 million Mastercard debit cards in circulation worldwide.

- As of 2017, Visa and Mastercard debit cards account for 76% of debit card purchases.

- Over 77% of all adult bank account holders in the U.S. have at least one ATM/debit card.

- Over the years, debit has held its status as the preferred payment type with over 44% of ATM/debit cardholders using their card(s) to make purchases at the point of sale.

- 98% of debit transactions are made with EMV-enabled cards.

- Since EMV liability was enacted in October 2015, EMVCo reports that globally, 69.6% of transactions where both the card and the device are chip-enabled, are EMV transactions.

Source: The Federal Reserve Payments Study: 2018 Annual Supplement; 2017 TSYS U.S. Consumer Payment Study; Pulse 2018 Debit Issuer Study

Debit is the fastest growing form of payment. A debit card accesses the cardholder's bank account to secure and hold the authorization amount against available funds.

There are two types of debit transactions:

- Online (PIN-based) – ATM-like
- Offline (signature-based) – check card

A regular debit or ATM card (without the Visa or Mastercard logo) may only be used through the debit networks.

This means that the debit card will work at any ATM machine but, in order to be accepted at a merchant business, the merchant must have the debit service activated and a PIN pad attached to the credit card terminal.

A check card (Visa or Mastercard logo) can access all debit/ATM networks and has the ability to run through the credit card networks like a credit card transaction.

Rates for online debit are usually just a small transaction fee and possibly a reduced discount fee (get current pricing from you processing provider). Pricing for check cards is similar to a credit card transaction, which has a percentage and transaction fee.

Here are the top ATM networks, according to the Federal Reserve Update published in 2018:

- STAR
- Plus Alliance

- NYCE
- CO-OP Financial Services
- PULSE
- Jeanie Network
- AFFN (Armed Forces Financial Network)
- Accel Network
- SHAZAM

CHAPTER 10
EMV (EUROPAY, MASTERCARD, VISA)

BACKGROUND

EMV is a payment method based upon a technical standard for payment cards and the payment terminals, mobile payment devices, and ATMs that can accept them.

EMV cards – also known as smart cards or chip cards – are cards that store the cardholder's account data on an integrated circuit embedded within a chip, in addition to the traditional magnetic stripe. Payment cards that comply with the EMV standard are often called *Chip & PIN* or *Chip & Signature* cards, depending on the authentication methods employed by the card issuer. Chip cards that must be physically inserted, or "dipped" into a reader, as opposed to "swiping" the card through the mag-stripe reader. EMV also applies to contactless cards that are read or "tapped" against a terminal scanner to read the computer chip data via NFC technology.

EMV originally stood for **E**uropay, **M**astercard, and **V**isa, the three companies that created the standard, which was created to facilitate the acceptance of secure payment transactions through the development and testing of EMV specifications and processes.

The EMV standard was initially written in 1993 and was widely adopted in Europe as smart card technology the following year. JCB and American Express joined the consortium in February 2009, and UnionPay and Discover both joined in 2013.

EMVCo's work is overseen by EMVCo's six member organizations – American Express, Discover, JCB, Mastercard, UnionPay, and Visa – and is supported by many banks, merchants, processors, vendors and other industry stakeholders who participate as EMVCo Associates.

EMV LIABILITY SHIFT 2015

In the wake of numerous large-scale data breaches and increasing rates of counterfeit card fraud in the US, EMVCo established new technology to further protect consumers and reduce the costs of fraud nationwide. The EMV fraud liability shift was implemented October 1, 2015, by 9 major US payment card networks (Accel, American Express, UnionPay, Discover, Mastercard, NYCE, SHAZAM, STAR and Visa) to combat card-present counterfeit fraud.

At the time, card-present counterfeit card fraud costs in the US equaled $7.86 billion in 2015, according to The Nilson Report. Card issuers lost $4.91 billion and merchants lost $2.95 billion to counterfeit card fraud.

Once enacted, the EMV liability shift moved the financial liability of chargebacks for fraudulent in-store credit card transactions from the credit card issuers to the party -- either the card issuing financial institution or the merchant -- that had not yet adopted chip technology.

Prior to this shift, credit card issuers were primarily responsible for covering fraud affecting consumer accounts, reimbursing cardholders for lost funds as a result of counterfeit (or other) fraud. With the EMV liability shift, financial institutions will still cover cardholders' accounts as before, but in some cases the institutions may be able to seek reimbursement from the merchant or merchant acquirer if the retailer was not prepared to accept EMV payment technology. And if both parties have integrated the hardware and solutions to process EMV transactions, then the environment remains precisely as it is now; the issuing bank will reimburse the customer as they have done in the past. It's also important to remember that the liability shift is not a mandate, it's simply a financial incentive to make the switch to EMV acceptance.

EMV CONVERSION STATISTICS

- Since October 2015, EMV integration according to EMVCo has grown at a slow but steady pace:
- 47% of card-present transactions in the US are EMV; 69.6% globally.
- 54.6% of issued Cards are EMV chip-enabled cards; 54.6% world-wide.
- 785 million EMV cards have been issued in the US – 58.5% of all cards issued.
- The cost of issuing a new EMV card is $2-4, per First Data.
- *In 2015, there was an estimated 15 million* total number of POS terminals that needed to be upgraded to accept chip cards, per Javelin Research & Strategy; as of 2018, 1.81-2.3 million POS terminals have been enabled to accept chip card payments.
- *In 2015, Javelin Research & Strategy* estimated that it would cost $6.75 billion to replace the 15 million existing magstripe POS terminals with chip card-compliant machines; as of 2018, close to 52% of merchant locations process chip card payments according to VISA and Strawhecker Group estimates.
- Counterfeit fraud rates have already decreased in the U.S. as a result of EMV adoption, according to Mastercard and Visa. In March 2017, chip-enabled merchants saw a 58% percent drop in counterfeit fraud compared to a year earlier.

LIMITATIONS OF EMV INTEGRATION

Slow adoption of EMV: The adoption of EMV integration and certification has been slow, but steady since October 2015, partly due to the elongated time needed for software certification from the OEMs, processors, gateways and card issuers. To accept EMV card transactions, payment terminals and applications must be tested and certified as EMV-compliant by the processors, gateways and card networks that process their transactions. If a merchant has EMV equipment in place but must wait for certification before using the chip reader, under the terms of the EMV liability shift, the merchant could be responsible for fraud chargeback costs until the certification process is complete.

EMV Integration can be costly or unnecessary: The cost to migrate to EMV acceptance can be overwhelming to many small merchants. Purchasing and installing new equipment can be a lengthy and possibly costly process if they must shoulder the expense of a chargeback while waiting for EMV certification.

Merchants who don't experience a high rate of card-present fraud, such as small, local shops and restaurants, may not need to worry about integrating the EMV terminals. If their risk for fraud is low, then so is the risk of being liable for chargebacks

Merchants, both large and small, should partner with their ISO/MSP to learn about chargebacks and about the level of fraud protection that they'll need to help determine if purchasing chip-enabled terminals is the right strategy for their business. Once they have that information, they can better decide whether the added protection and the investment is worthwhile.

The liability shift does not apply to card-not-present fraud: At the present time, card-not-present transactions via eCommerce sites aren't included in the EMV liability shift mandate. However, merchants should be aware that the focus of fraudulent activity will shift to online shopping, since there is no PIN verification for online transactions being developed in the foreseeable future.

Another large industry still exposed to fraudulent activity is Petroleum. Gas stations with pay-at-the-pump acceptance have until 2020 to integrate EMV acceptance.

CHAPTER 11
ELECTRONIC BENEFITS TRANSFER (EBT)

EBT programs allow participants to receive and access their government-paid SNAP (Supplemental Nutrition Assistance Program) benefits electronically using a magstripe card and to redeem their benefits for cash assistance or food stamp programs.

The 2014 Farm Bill states that most retailers authorized to accept Supplemental Nutrition Assistance Program (SNAP) benefits must pay for their own EBT equipment and services. Only exempt retailers such as farmers markets, direct marketing farmers, military commissaries, non-profit food buying cooperative and community meal services & programs are eligible for State-supplied POS equipment that handles only EBT transactions.

Source: USDA: SNAP EBT Third-Party Processor List and Guidance to Retailers Updated as of November 27, 2018.

WHAT ARE THE BENEFITS OF EBT?

- EBT offers a more cost-efficient and secure benefit delivery system. Each month, SNAP benefits are directly deposited into the household's EBT card account.

- Recipients no longer have to go to banks or check cashing agents to receive their cash or food stamp benefits.

- Recipients no longer need to carry large amounts of cash or food stamps. They can withdraw their benefits as needed.

- Recipients are no longer stigmatized by using food coupons since EBT makes shoppers with food stamp benefits look like any other shoppers.

- If the EBT Access Card is lost or stolen, it cannot be used without the PIN. The card is easily canceled and replaced.

- EBT eliminates the labor-intensive process of storage, delivery, and accounting for the paper coupons at the federal and state levels.

- Retailers are able to provide better customer service in the checkout lane because EBT transactions are faster and more efficient than paper coupons.

- Retailers no longer have to count, bundle, and deposit paper food coupons at their bank because the EBT settlement process is automatic and provides a payment to the retailer's account within two business days.

- All of the food stamp dollars are spent on food because change is never given.

- EBT creates an electronic record of transactions, making it easier to identify and document instances of fraudulent activity.

- EBT cards, by law, have no interchange fees and, therefore, should be much lower in cost to implement.

- EBT does not require Payment Card Industry (PCI) or EuroPay Mastercard VISA (EMV) compliance for terminals, so merchants can continue to support mag-stripe terminals to read EBT data.

EBT is not a big money maker for our industry but is required if selling into niche markets like grocery or convenience retailers.

CHAPTER 12
ACH & CHECK PROCESSING

CONTRIBUTING WRITE PATTI MURPHY

Checks have been around for centuries. They became popular in the 17th century because they eliminated the need for merchants to carry large amounts of currency for purchases of goods and services. A writer of a check instructs their bank to withdraw (pull) funds from their checking account for delivery to the payee.

Consumer adoption of checks grew, particularly in the United States, with the economic expansion that followed World War II. Between the 1950s and the 1990s, the annual total number of checks written by U.S. consumers and businesses grew more than six-fold to 50 billion. Check writing began tapering off in the mid-1990s, as they were supplemented (but not replaced) by electronic alternatives. In 2016, Americans wrote just over 19 billion checks totaling nearly $27 trillion.

According to data and analysis from the Federal Reserve, consumers write a majority of checks (10.6 billion in 2016), but their use of checks has been declining as they have made greater use of credit and debit cards and electronic bill-payment services. In 2016, consumers with checking accounts (93% of adults, according to government data) wrote an average seven checks a month.

U.S. businesses wrote on average 24 checks a month in 2016, making checks the preferred payment method among businesses, behind automated clearing house (ACH) payments. Checks represent 50% of business-to-business payments, according to several estimates. Business preferences for checks are rooted in historical practices and in legacy systems that streamline integration of check payments with corporate financial controls and accounting systems.

ACH AS ELECTRONIC ALTERNATIVE TO CHECKS

As check usage grew, check clearing became an automated process, but the need to move large bundles of paper checks within and between banks was labor and time-intensive. The ACH emerged in the 1970s as an electronic alternative to the check system. It took more than 40 years, however, for ACH payments to unseat checks as the number one source of noncash payments in America. In 2018, 23 billion transactions were processed through the ACH system, representing $51.2 trillion in payments.

ACH payments originate through banks and/or credit unions based on customer instructions. Like checks, ACH payments clear in batches. A key difference is that ACH transactions can be initiated by either credit (push) or debit (pull) payments, with debits being the transaction type that most closely resembles checks.

Another important difference: ACH payments get initiated, exchanged and processed as part of electronic batch files, with processing occurring at intervals throughout the day.

ACH payments are less expensive for businesses to make than are check payments. The Association for Financial Professionals (AFP) estimates the median cost of sending and receiving an ACH payment is 55-cents (internal and external costs, combined). The median cost of sending a check is $3.00; the median cost to payees of handling a check once received is $1.57, AFP reports.

The first big use case for the ACH credits was Direct Deposit of payroll, in which payments initiated by businesses and government entities are pushed to consumer accounts at banks, credit unions and even prepaid debit card accounts. Today, over 80% of U.S. workers get paid by Direct Deposit, according to NACHA. NACHA is a private-sector association that develops operating rules and regulations for the ACH.

ACH credits have many other uses aside from Direct Deposit, including consumer bill payments, where funds get pushed from a payer's bank account to the bank account of the biller. Residual payments to ISOs and merchant level salespeople from upstream card acquiring partners also are commonly sent as ACH credits.

In an ACH debit transaction funds get pulled from the payer's bank account, on accountholder instructions, and are credited to a payee's bank account. Recurring loan payments are a common use case for ACH debits, as are other recurring transactions, such as payments for subscription-based services.

B2B transactions have been slow to move to the ACH, in terms of sheer numbers of transactions, but the value of those payments tells a different story. NACHA reports that in 2018, 3.6 billion trans-actions (or 15.6% of all ACH transactions) were B2B payments. At $34.9 trillion, B2B transactions represented 68% of total dollars sent via the ACH in 2018.

One reason for the slower than expected migration of B2B pay-ments to the ACH is that ACH file formats can't accommodate the detailed remittance details that accompany many B2B payments and are required to update backend accounting systems. Another reason has been ACH processing schedules, which often result in lags of several days between origination of an ACH payment instruction and when funds actually get credited to the recipient's bank account.

NACHA, working with the Fed and others in the payments space, has been addressing the need for more ACH processing cycles, and also has introduced same-day settlement options for ACH credits and debits. In 2018, just under 178 million transactions valued at $159.9 billion cleared as same-day ACH payments, according to NACHA.

One of the fastest growing uses of ACH has been for e-commerce payments. These so-call WEB transactions, which can clear as ACH debits, grew by more than 14% between 2017 and 2018, when they totaled 5.9 billion transactions valued at $2.9 trillion, according to NACHA. WEB transactions can also flow through the ACH as credits, and WEB credits are growing too, driven by person-to-person (P2P) payment schemes, like PayPal's Venmo and the bank-controlled Zelle network.

CHECKS GO ELECTRONIC AND GET FAST, REAL FAST

In keeping with its mission as an electronic replacement for the check system, ACH formats have been developed for the conversion of paper checks to electronic payments. One of the earliest iterations of this was the RCK format, which continues to be used to re-present checks returned to business depositors for insufficient funds in the payer's checking account.

Other ACH check conversion transactions include:

- ARC, used to convert mailed-in consumer bill payments to ACH debits;
- POP, which converts checks written at points of purchase to ACH debits; and
- BOC, for back office conversion of checks that written at points of sale.

In each of these cases, the original check serves as a source document from which the check writer's account, routing and check serial number, plus the dollar amount are captured and used to originate

ACH debits. In 2016, the last year NACHA broke-out data on check conversions, 1.3 billion ARC, 125 million BOC, 265 million POP and nearly 2.8 million RCK transactions were processed through the ACH.

If the history of payments has taught us anything, it's that old payment methods never die. Instead they continue to exist alongside newer methods of payments. And sometimes they improve through the application of new technologies. Such has been the case with checks.

Thanks to the evolution of high-speed imaging and network technologies, and passage of the Check Clearing for the 21st Century Act (better known as Check 21), the labor- and time-intensive process of clearing checks has given way to electronic clearing of checks. Twenty years ago, it wasn't uncommon for a check to be handled as many as a dozen times during a multi-day clearing cycle before funds got debited from the check writer's bank account and were made available to the payee. Check image exchange eliminates most of those touch points.

Remote deposit capture (RDC) further reduces paper check handling by enabling consumers and businesses to deposit images of checks (captured on desktop or free-standing check scanners, or using smartphone apps) instead of taking paper checks to local bank branches for in-person deposits.

The end result: better than 99% of checks clear through the Federal Reserve and banking system today as image files, the Fed reports. And a small but growing share of those checks are entering the banking system as image files. Mitek, the financial technology firm that holds patents supporting mobile RDC, estimates, for example, that about 20% of consumer deposits are mobile RDC transactions.

Banks have made significant inroads marketing RDC to large corporations and are ramping up plans to expand usage among small and mid-sized businesses (SMBs), said John Leekley, Founder & CEO of RemoteDepositCapture.com, an independent Web site focused on the RDC market. "Our research suggests as many as

44% of small businesses could be using RDC by year-end 2019. Furthermore, nearly one in four financial institutions we've surveyed has plans to offer, expand and/or enhance mobile RDC offerings to SMBs," he related.

"The combination of RDC and image exchange means it is now possible for checks to clear on the same day they are presented for deposit," Leekley added. In other words, a check payment can now clear as fast, if not faster, than it takes to initiate and clear an ACH payment.

CHECK SERVICES AVAILABLE TO BUSINESSES

No business wants to inconvenience customers, and not offering the payment method a customer prefers to use can be a major inconvenience. But check acceptance can be risky, with check fraud being a major pain point.

Several services have been designed to help businesses control check fraud losses. These fall into two broad categories – check verification and check guarantee. Service providers may offer these individually, in combination with one another, and/or in combination with RDC thereby eliminating potential fraud and paper check deposits as well.

With Check Verification the merchant enters information from the check into a terminal for transmission to the service provider; phone-based authorization is another option. That information is used to ascertain whether a check-writing customer is in a negative data base (one that keeps tabs on individuals with histories of writing bad checks), and that the account the check has been written against has not been closed. They also take into consideration other factors (e.g.: time of day, type of purchase). Based on all this information the service provides a recommendation that the merchant accept or not accept the check. All of this takes about the same amount of time needed to complete a credit card authorization.

The business paying for verification services assumes the costs and hassles associated with collecting any checks returned for non-sufficient funds (NSF), although check services companies often also offer collection services.

Check Guarantee takes verification a step further, with the service provider reimbursing merchants for the full value of any checks returned for NSF.

Here are a few examples of businesses that are candidates for check authorization and/or guarantee services.

- Automobile Dealers
- Auto After-Market Shops
- Auto Repair Shops
- Building Suppliers
- Check Cashers
- Convenience Stores
- Dry Cleaners
- Electronics Retailers
- Equipment Rentals
- Grocers
- Home Furnishings
- Home Renovators
- Jewelers
- Medical Offices
- Veterinarians

A relatively recent innovation in check services are electronic checks, or eChecks. As the name implies, eChecks are an electronic version of the paper check. They leverage the RDC infrastructure to support electronic creation, presentment and processing of checks. Customers provide their checking account information to a merchant who in turn sends an electronically-created check through their payment processing company for clearing through the banking system. Anyone with a checking account can pay using an eCheck. eChecks are particularly well suited to eCommerce merchants, telephone sales companies, and other businesses that don't rely on face-to-face sales.

WHEN AND WHERE ACH PAYMENTS MAKE SENSE

ACH remains an important payment option for businesses of all sizes. It can be faster and less expensive to process an ACH payment than credit and debit card payments or wire transfers. And as an electronic option, ACH payments are safer than accepting cash.

Unlike card acceptance, there are no PCI compliance requirements associated with ACH payments. However, NACHA rules require businesses originating ACH transactions to take "commercially reasonable" steps to ensure the validity of customer identity and routing numbers, and to stay on top of fraudulent activity.

The appeal to a business's customers is simplicity as they no longer need to write and mail checks; they just instruct their banks or credit unions to initiate recurring bill payments and let the system do the work.

The following is a list of likely prospects for ACH processing services. This list is by no means complete, but a starting point.

- Churches
- Collection Agencies
- Day Care Centers
- Delivery Services
- eCommerce Businesses
- Furniture & Equipment Rentals
- Government Agencies
- Health Clubs
- Home Security Companies

- Home Services Businesses
- Hospitals
- Insurance Companies
- Internet Service Providers
- Janitorial Companies
- Leasing Companies
- Mail Order/Telephone Order Firms
- Medical Offices
- Multi-Level Marketing (MLM) Firms
- Non-Profits
- Nursing Homes
- Pest Control
- Property Management Companies
- Rental Companies
- Schools
- Subscription-Based Services Businesses
- Telemarketing Companies
- Uniform Rentals
- Utilities
- Web Hosting Companies
- Yoga Studios

CHAPTER 13
GIFT CARDS

CONTRIBUTING WRITER CHRISTIAN MURRAY

GIFT CARD HISTORY

The concept of the gift card was originally introduced by retailers like McDonalds and JC Penney in the early 1970s and 1980s using paper and thin plastic cards.

Gift card programs began getting more exposure and recognition in 1995 with their introduction by a few larger retailers, such as Blockbuster and Kmart. These retailers adapted gift card systems to replace paper gift certificates and to help streamline tracking and reconciliation.

The systems continued to gain momentum and popularity after other large retailers began aggressively promoting the cards through the media and TV. Within a few short years, the gift card concept had proven its worth and overall necessity to retailers of all types. One of the reasons the gift card technology continued to grow and become mainstream with retailers of all types was ultimately because of the media and consumer awareness that other retailers helped build. It was also a product that solved issues that all businesses had with using manual paper certificate systems.

The gift card market has come a long way over the years, and today card sales represent an enormous market with volume exceeding $160 billion by 2018.

Today there are many providers that offer these solutions but only a select few that specialize in supporting the ISO sales channels exclusively.

Source: Giftcards.com, 2018.

GIFT CARD FACTS

Information relating to the growth and usage of gift cards can be obtained online from hundreds of sources. Below are key statistics you may find useful.

- Gift card sales totaled $160 billion in 2018, up from $149 billion in 2017, according to data from Statista.
- According to First Data, in 2017, US shoppers purchased an average of 6.5 gift cards and 6.1 eGift cards, up from 5.9 and 4.0, in 2016.
- According to the Blackhawk Network, 80% of holiday shoppers surveyed plan on purchasing at least one gift card during the holiday season; 81% estimated that almost half of their gifts are likely to be gift cards. First Data notes that in 2018, shoppers planned to spend 55% of their annual holiday budget on gift cards, with 33% percent of purchasers spending more on a gift card they would on a traditional gift.
- The National Retail Federation's Gift Card Spending Survey found that those planning to buy gift cards will spend $153.08, an average of $44.83 per card. Total spending is expected to reach $25.9 billion.

- According to an NRF 2018 Holiday Report, early in-store shopping plans increased by 9 percent, with 47% of consumers shopping in stores before December. Most consumers use gift cards as a last-minute gift.
- The biggest change in the past 10 years is the growing acceptance of purchasing and giving digital or eGift cards. Blackhawk Network reported in 2018 that 55% of consumers have given digital gift cards that can be added to a mobile app or digital wallet, especially Millennials. 67% are interested in receiving a digital gift card.
- Although over 60% of consumers request gift cards as a present, an estimated 9% of gift card recipients never cash in cards. Gift card recipients also bring new customers into stores that they might not have otherwise visited.
- The 2018 Prepaid Consumer Insights Study published by First Data reported that the average consumer spends $59 more than the original value of their gift card, an increase from $21 in 2017. Industries with the highest results are restaurants and grocery.
- While 74% of shoppers buy purchase gift cards from third-party providers (Gift Card Mall or grocery stores), 49% prefer to buy directly from the store where the gift card will be redeemed.
- One in six adults had "re-gifted" a gift card they received.

GIFT CARD PURCHASERS SAY

- 42% of consumers say that they use the gift cards the receive immediately.
- 59% spend more that the gift card's value.
- 42% of consumers purchase gift cards for themselves in order to earn more loyalty points for gas, credit cards or airline mileage.

Over the years gift cards have become a staple value-added product that many ISOs and MLSs offer to their merchants. These solutions continue to serve as a very important retention tool within the payment industry. Despite the growth in eGift cards, physical cards are still preferred. According to the NGC Annual Report, 75% of all cards redeemed are physical versus the 25% of eGift cards. The programs continue to assist merchants with improved tracking, reduced fraud, streamlined operations, and increased cash flow.

TYPE OF GIFT CARD SYSTEMS

There are two types of gift card systems that are offered today. These systems are divided into "closed loop" and "open loop" programs.

Closed Loop Programs are able to be used within the locations that have an application or download inside of a terminal or POS system. Some software options for processing cards may include windows-based and virtual terminals. These cards can be used within a "closed loop" environment and are not able to be used outside of the merchant's locations.

- Closed loop programs offer a wide variety of options for merchants of all sizes. The cards can only be used within the location(s) designated by the merchant. Closed loop programs are very easy to manage and give merchants the tools needed to track and reconcile sales and redemptions.

- Closed loop programs are a preferred option as they are affordable and easy to launch.

- Merchants can customize the cards with their logos or artwork.

- *Open Loop Programs* are cards that have a Visa, MasterCard, American Express, or Discover logo. These programs allow merchants to become an issuer and add pre-paid value to the card. Cardholders are not limited to using the card within a specific merchant location; they can use it anywhere that accepts the card brand.

These programs are more complex and are targeted to merchants that typically are not concerned with keeping the money within their location(s).

TYPES OF GIFT CARD PROGRAMS

Merchants can utilize plastic card programs in many ways other than standard gift cards.

Depending on the provider and the programs available, merchants can select the package and features that best fit their individual business. Adapting alternative ways of selling cards to merchants is always helpful and can differentiate a sales agent from the competition.

Below are examples of several unique forms as prepaid program can take:

Standard Electronic Gift Card The standard electronic gift card replaces the traditional paper-based gift certificate. Cards are activated with a pre-paid balance and may be used multiple times until the original balance is depleted.

RETAIL MERCHANT CREDIT

Cards are issued in place of a cash refund or traditional credit certificate, to provide an in-store credit, or to provide an incentive for customers to visit the store.

- Allows merchants to keep money in the location without giving cash back on returned items. Separate tracking for merchants so they can report on returned items.

   Merchant types: retail, storefront, or other tangible product that is purchased from a merchant location.

CORPORATE VOUCHER CARD

Replaces paper voucher systems typically used by retailers for business-to-business transactions or "House Accounts."

- Can be used by any type of merchant that wants to offer a house account charge or extend credit to customers.
- Merchant types: bars, restaurants, service-related, golf courses, "over-55" properties, corporations, fleet accounts, and more.

SINGLE-AUTHORIZATION CARD

Normally used to provide a vehicle for a single purchase of a qualified product or amount against the card. Only one transaction will be authorized against the card regardless of the value of the purchase.

- Merchants utilize this type of program for donations or charity.

- Can also be used for marketing; for example, a merchant could activate a group of cards for $5.00 and pass them out at an event to attract new customers.

EMPLOYEE INCENTIVE CARD:

Incentive cards are mainly used to reward employees who meet specific criteria. Value may be added at any time for additional incentives. This program is very helpful to businesses that wish to track employee incentives.

SO DOES THE MERCHANT BENEFIT?

There are many benefits to merchants that implement these systems. Below is a list of benefits that merchants can take advantage of when launching a gift card program. Results may vary depending on a variety of factors and their local demographics.

INCREASED SALES AND CASH FLOW

- The sale of a gift card itself immediately generates revenue for the merchant.
- Revenue generated can be as much as 60% depending on marketing and ongoing promotions.
- Allows upfront cash to be utilized by merchants to expand and grow business.

BREAKAGE AND UNREDEEMED BALANCES

- 10–20% breakage on average.
- In most states, breakage can be retained by the merchant.

BETTER TRACKING AND REPORTING CAPABILITIES

- Less time reconciling sales vs. redemptions.
- The ability to capture cardholder information.

- Provides sales and card activity by location(s).
- Manage user privilege levels at locations.

REDUCES FRAUD & DUPLICATE USAGE

- Random non-sequential numbering helps prevent fraud and theft.
- Systems have additional security features to help control users and clerks.
- Eliminates the potential of duplicate cards from being issued.

BUILDS BRAND AWARENESS

- The card itself acts as an advertisement in someone's purse or wallet, where it may be seen on a regular basis by the recipient.
- Attracts shoppers to choose merchants that offer card programs over others that do not.
- Great marketing tool in a local community.

NO CASH BACK TO CUSTOMERS

- System helps manage returns and exchanges without giving cash back to be spent outside of the location (s).
- On average, merchants can enjoy a 3-month float on funds collected.
- Reduces cash refunds because card users are choosing the gift they desire instead of receiving a gift they might return.

EASE OF USE AND FASTER TRANSACTIONS

- Helps speed up transactions at the point of sale.
- Processing gift cards is similar to a credit card transaction.
- Less steps at the point of sale increases sales and efficiencies

ELIMINATES MANUAL BOOKKEEPING

- Most online reporting systems can provide merchants with reconciliation reports and other data.

- Saves merchants lots of time with tracking and reporting total outstanding liability on cards.

- Point and click technology that can be used to track marketing or promotional efforts that a merchant has launched.

LOW COST OF ENTRY

- Considering how the systems streamline operations and tracking, many merchants are able to save time and money using these solutions.

- Most providers offer affordable options like transaction-based and flat-rate monthly solutions.

- No interchange fees, membership dues, or assessments associated with gift cards.

ATTRACT NEW CUSTOMERS

- Card programs promote businesses and help turn one-time buyers into lifetime customers.

- Cards that have been received as gifts typically draw in customers to the location that would have never otherwise visited or purchased from the merchant.

HIGHER TICKET PRICES OR PURCHASES FOR MERCHANTS

- Average ticket prices on gift card transactions are 20% to 50% higher... research shows that people spend, on average, 61% more than the value of their card.

- Promotes higher-than-normal ticket sizes for merchants.

PROMOTES IMPULSE PURCHASES

- Cards are often bought as an impulse purchase that otherwise would not have occurred.

- Customers will tend to buy cards that are promoted at the point of sale.

- Offering cards solves last-minute gift ideas for customers that don't have the time to shop.

- Can be the "perfect gift" for loved ones who have no idea what to purchase.

ADDED CONTROL OVER ACTIVATED CARDS

- Most systems offer the merchant real-time controls to block or cancel cards within their system.

- Merchants are able to block lost or stolen cards that have an active balance.

- They can issue new ones without having lost certificates picked up and used in addition to the replaced one. With paper certificates, the merchant would traditionally issue another certificate in the same amount to accommodate their customers.

HELPS MANAGE DONATIONS AND CHARITABLE CONTRIBUTIONS

- Tracking cards separately from gift cards can help merchants with ongoing donations and charitable offerings.

- By issuing these cards, merchants can utilize the marketing efforts of local schools and charities in their communities.

ISOS AND MLS BENEFITS:

For many within the payments processing business, gift cards greatly increase retention and profits. Merchants are less likely to cancel a bankcard account or leave a processor if they have outstanding gift cards in customer's hands. For some, gift cards are the glue that holds together long-term merchant relationships.

For many agents and MLS sales professionals, the gift card programs offer a doorway into accounts that normally would not be interested in their processor's services.

- Helps increase sales and merchant retention for ISO.
- Promotes additional terminal upgrades and leases with merchants.
- Differentiates sales agents from the other agents who are solely selling on price.
- Offers merchants additional products other than standard credit card processing.
- Builds confidence and helps agents secure closer business relationships with merchants.
- Helps with setting appointments with and cold calling on merchants that otherwise would not book an appointment.
- Builds more intimate long-term relationships that can lead to additional sales and profits.
- Increases opportunities for selling agents to receive local referrals to other merchants that may want a gift card solution.

Review our free gift card sales tactics go to: *www.surviveandthrive. biz/resources*

As you can see, just selling gift card programs is not enough. The key is uncovering unique ways in which your merchants can benefit from this technology. Depending on the target merchant types that are being focused on, a selling agent or ISO needs to understand more about the type of business and in what ways the card can help improve efficiencies and generate cash flow.

Finding unique ways of marketing different types of card programs can greatly strengthen and diversify your portfolio.

Sources: Gift Card FACTS Report, BIGresearch, American Greetings, Profit Point, American Bankers Association, ZDNet Research, Corporate Research International, Stored Value Systems, National Retail Federation. All material and studies listed are owned by their respective sources.

CHAPTER 14
LOYALTY CARDS

GUEST WRITER CHRISTIAN MURRAY

According to a recent article by Colloquy Magazine, *"A loyalty program is one that seeks to identify, maintain, and increase the yield from customers through long-term, interactive, value-added relationships."*

In this competitive business climate, many merchants are looking for more, innovative, ways to increase customer loyalty. This is one of the hottest segments of the merchant services industry. There are thousands of loyalty programs in the marketplace. The loyalty industry is estimated at $5 billion and rising.

That is why loyalty and rewards programs have taken center stage for many payment professionals. Merchants can truly benefit from day one that a loyalty and rewards program is launched. Loyalty- and rewards-based solutions are the 'stickiness' that is critical to helping merchants retain loyal business and increase visits and profits.

Companies everywhere are implementing and advertising customer loyalty programs. Loyalty programs are now available at your local carwash, auto repair, video store, retailer, and restaurant.

Companies realize that their most precious asset is their existing customer base. Merchants are acutely aware that it costs much more to acquire a new customer than to market to an existing customer.

WHAT IS A LOYALTY OR REWARDS CARD?

Loyalty or rewards programs are launched using a card made of PVC plastic that has a magnetic stripe on the back. The card can be used to accumulate points, dollars, or rewards in a merchant's store or business. The card tracks visits, products purchased, or total dollars spent. The merchant can predetermine the levels of rewards or points available in the program.

Consumers would then visit the location(s) and present the card at the time of sale. The card is then swiped and the system calculates the reward or dollar-based credit to the card. After a predetermined level is reached or a particular product is purchased, the customer can be rewarded with a credit or with the cash value on the card.

Programs vary from merchant to merchant depending on the provider, equipment, and applications available.

TYPES OF LOYALTY/REWARD CARD PROGRAMS

Several types of programs are available and can be easily implemented into most the majority of business types. Some reward-based systems may also be combined with a gift card program. The "Combo Card" offers a pre-paid balance and accumulates ongoing points or dollar-based rewards. This allows merchants to provide rewards based on the number of times a consumer visits or how much a consumer spends. Here are some examples:

- **Frequency Reward Program:** The Frequency Reward Program offers a flexible way for customers to purchase a set number of items or receive a free or discounted item or service.

- **Dollar Reward Program:** The Dollar Reward Program offers customers a way to earn rewards based on their spending. The points can be converted to a dollar value, added back onto the card automatically, and used toward future store credit.

- **Rebate/Discount:** Allows merchants to reward consumers based on a percentage of the sale amount. Most systems will handle the conversion and calculations and add the percentage to the card after the purchase.

- **Frequency Program:** Frequency programs offer a customer a reward based on a set number of items purchased or visits. The merchant can choose the number of purchases required and the item/service that the reward balance can be redeemed for.

Building a successful program that will generate positive returns on investment for merchants requires some basic analysis of the surrounding demographics and local competitive landscape.

Not all merchants will use the systems the same, and many will require customized solutions to help match their marketing goals. For some, it's simply time and money that is required to manage a successful campaign. For others, creating enough value and marketing the programs effectively is what is needed.

TYPES OF MARKETING STRATEGIES USING CARDS

Loyalty is a useful predictor of how customers will respond to marketing offers. Moreover, customer loyalty is increasingly viewed as an important indicator of retailer performance. There are a variety of marketing strategies that a merchant may deploy. Finding the right fit depends on the type of business, type of service, or specific local demographics.

- **Relationship Card Marketing:** Usually focuses on developing a long-term relationship with customers. This program often helps merchants target what type of items or services each customer desires the most. This marketing tactic often results in much more word-of-mouth activity, long-term purchasing behavior, and a willingness to participate in surveys and other targeted marketing.

  - Example: Merchants may include a questionnaire that asks what the consumer's interests are and then utilize that data to send specialized product specials or offerings.

- **Transactional Card Marketing:** This strategy is most widely used in a retail environment and continues to be an effective way to reach larger amounts of customers with minimal effort. This approach creates passive, reactive, and short-term customer relationships and does not focus on long-term customer loyalty and customer retention, as relationship card marketing does. This is often used in formulating marketing campaigns that result in greater success in a shorter period of time.

  - Rewards can be instant or can be easily reached by customers. Program is designed to offer faster results and build a loyal customer base with minimal effort other than internal promotion and marketing.

- **Shop Local/Coalition Card Marketing:** Programs that can be used at multiple locations and benefit the customer by offering more value. Consumers can visit the participating locations within the closed-loop circle and earn rewards based on standard or custom program types. These solutions are becoming very popular with small-to medium-sized businesses. Building more value and combining marketing efforts can greatly increase the success of the programs.

  - Example: Use the card to go to dinner for Italian tonight and then use it the next day in a shoe store followed by a sub shop for lunch. Offering consumers a multitude of discounts or rewards on a single card creates substantial benefits to the cardholders in that community.

- **Frequency card marketing:** Can increase the number of visits, purchases, or items that customers buy in a location and rewards consumers based on their activity and purchasing behavior.

  - Example: A merchant may reward consumers on a card based on how many times they frequent a location or on how many advertised items they buy.

- **Enforced card marketing:** Would require a consumer to automatically register or participate in the program in order to become a valid member or to receive long-term services or perks from the merchant.

  - Example: requires a login online or in-store sign-up in order to begin utilizing services or benefits on a card.

- **One-to-one card marketing:** Provides direct customization for each user or customer. Not typical of card programs, but can benefit merchants by customizing the solution to offer in-person discounts or other promotions that may be chosen by the consumer.

  - Example: Offer specific reward levels based on options that can be offered to each consumer. Criteria can be length, account status, or dollar volume in purchases. Cards can be used to track and reward.

- **Punch Card Marketing:** One of the original marketing methods that has been in existence for many years. Most effective type of marketing to attract repeat business.

  - The majority of these solutions are managed on a paper card and holes are punched for each visit or purchase made.

- Cards can replace this manual punch-hole system very easily. Card is swiped and processed vs. punching holes. Utilizing the cards would provide much better tracking and functionality for the merchant.

HOW DO MERCHANTS BENEFIT BY UTILIZING A LOYALTY AND REWARDS PROGRAM?

There are several major benefits that come with operating a loyalty or reward system. Some of the many benefits are the following:

- Enhanced image/brand reinforcement.
- Promotes increased spending and repeat business.
- Ability to capture customer information and track purchase history.
- Tracking and reporting allows merchant to easily manage program.
- Creates a more personal relationship with customers.
- Distinguishes the merchant's business from the local competition.
- Card members are more likely to refer others to visit.
- Promotions or special events can also be launched using cards.
- Solutions are affordable yet offer robust functionality to manage programs.
- Better ROI than traditional marketing methods.
- Reduces labor cost and provides a streamlined process at the POS.

Additional benefits can be realized by business owners if they truly get behind the program and promote it aggressively. You, as a merchant-focused salesperson, need to ensure they are taught how to use the program properly or it will not generate the desired results.

Keep in mind not all programs require the card to be printed with "loyalty card" or "rewards card"; each merchant should name its program based on how it plans to come to market.

Examples may include: *Preferred Guest Card, Savings Card, Discount Card, VIP Guest Card, Your "Club Card,"* or any other branded name that fits best.

THERE IS A TRUE NEED WITHIN THE MARKET

Successful loyalty or rewards systems are the 'stickiness' that merchants need in today's competitive market. Finding the right "value added" solution for each merchant is not cookie-cutter and does require probing and needs analysis on the part of the selling agent.

The true power of card marketing is a valuable tool in the payment professional's product suite.

Loyalty applications are another excellent way to get your foot in the door of a potential customer. Merchants are much more willing to talk to someone about an opportunity to increase their traffic, profit, and customer retention than they are about saving money on credit card processing.

Want more information on the loyalty industry?

Visit *www.colloquy.com/default.asp*.

CHAPTER 15
MOBILE PROCESSING

HISTORY

Less than 15 years ago, transaction processing for the typical brick & mortar retail merchant (both large and small- to mid-sized) consisted of installing a traditional countertop point-of-sale (POS) terminal, connecting to a landline, and Voila! the "plug-and-play" solution was ready to go. If the business had an online presence, the merchant simply needed to connect the online terminal to the appropriate software to enable e-commerce transactions.

At the time, most ISO (Independent Sales Organizations) and MSP (Merchant Service Provider) agents focused on the tried and true methods to support their merchant's payment strategy. But as mobile processing (mobile and wireless) has seen steady growth in the payments industry, the experienced salesperson should be fully aware that offering mobile can help the merchant find an affordable and efficient solution, and still have the profit margins that help grow their own business.

WHAT IS MOBILE PROCESSING?

Where e-commerce uses the Web on a computer screen to run transactions, mobile processing uses a wireless payment device to transact via the internet. Wireless credit card processing terminals are available in retail or POS form; they allow for MSR (magstripe reader), EMV (chip cards) and NFC (near field communication) processing, giving the merchant the options to swipe, dip or tap the card for real-time transactions. With mobile commerce (m-commerce), Bluetooth and WIFI connectivity helps eliminate the need for a phone jack or electrical outlet, and transactions basically take only a few seconds to complete.

M-commerce operates in the same capacity, but instead of using a wireless terminal, the merchant simply installs the payment processing app from Google Play or the App Store on their smart phone or tablet to enable payments. A card-reading device, mostly referred to in the industry as a dongle, is either plugged into the headphone jack of the phone or tablet or is used in a wireless capacity. The devices allow for swiped (MSR), dipped (EMV) and contactless (NFC) processing.

The mobile processing space is rapidly growing, and the numbers published showing both merchant and consumer adoption are compelling to anyone still undecided about integrating a mobile strategy.

- Usage of mobile point-of-sale (mPOS) devices are expected to grow rapidly, with over 27 million devices in use by 2020 (Mobile Payments Today, Feb. 2019).

- Statista predicts that m-commerce sales will make up over 44% of total US e-commerce sales in 2019, up from 39.6% in 2018.

- eMarketer predicts that US retail m-commerce sales will reach $268.8 billion in 2019 – up nearly 30% year over year. They predict that by 2020, the figure will increase to $338.02 billion, accounting for nearly half of all retail e-commerce sales.

- By 2021, US issuers predict that over 50% of cards issued – 500 million – will be equipped with NFC technology for contactless payments.

- A 2019 report published by Allied Market Research predicts that the food delivery mobile application market (i.e. Grubhub, DoorDash) is predicted to grow at a rate of 27.9% – $16.6 billion in the next 5 years.

- According to a 2019 *BRP In-Store Mobility Report*, 66% of retailers offer mPOS capability in their stores; 40% of consumers admit they are more likely to shop in a store that offers both mPOS and POS functionality.

MARKET POTENTIAL

Millions of businesses operate in a non-traditional environment – outdoors, without walls, or on-the-move – where a traditional countertop POS solution isn't feasible. Many businesses in various mobile industries may find wireless credit card processing very appealing. A few examples are:

- Delivery & distribution companies
- Plumbers & electricians
- Towing & locksmiths
- Heating, ventilation, & air conditioning (HVAC)
- Messenger services
- Taxi & limousine companies
- Food delivery
- Tool trucks
- Window & door installation
- Carpenters & home maintenance
- Furniture delivery
- Lawn & pool services
- Bike rentals

- Stadiums & arenas
- Amusement parks
- Concert pavilions
- Trade shows
- Park & recreation centers
- Farmers' markets
- Flea markets
- Marinas
- Golf courses
- Colleges & universities
- Raceways

It's also important to remember that using a mobile processing solution isn't limited to non-traditional merchants. As brick and mortar stores are in fierce competition with e-commerce giants for sales, many retailers are incorporating mobile solutions into their sales strategy to help meet the needs of the mobile shopper.

ADVANTAGES OF MOBILE PROCESSING

Being mobile doesn't mean that accepting credit and debit cards can't be a part of a merchant's payment strategy. Using a mobile processing solution makes taking credit cards cheaper, safer, and more efficient. The advantages of using a mobile payment solution are many:

- Merchants who previously couldn't accept credit cards can now accept them.
- Merchants pay lower discount rates for card-present transactions, due to swiping, dipping or tapping the card.
- No power outlets are needed (good for trade shows, taxi drivers, sidewalk sales.)
- Merchants can easily expand checkout lanes and remote promotional sales within their store.

- No phone lines are required, and merchants save on installation costs.
- The risk of accepting a bad card, or incorrectly entering the credit card number into the system, is greatly reduced.

THE TECHNOLOGY

When selling a wireless solution to a mobile merchant, it is important to understand what network/communications technology is used and on which processing platform the device is certified. Each service provider works best in specific areas; ensure you check the merchant's connectivity options against the wireless plan your ISO is providing.

The important sales points to stress when talking about wireless are:

- Wireless processing works with the merchant's existing account provider. The merchant simply purchases and integrates the wireless device into the structure of their merchant account, including the pricing and fees charged for wireless processing.
- The wireless device works just like your cell phone. If your cell phone can get a signal, so can your payment device.
- It's not satellite-based. There must be a cell signal to process a transaction.
- If there's no signal, most devices allow "store and forward"; the transaction is stored on the device until it finds a signal, then forwards the transaction for processing.
- Wireless devices use powerful encryption technologies to protect sensitive transaction data. Transactions are safe and secure.
- Wireless devices may have additional plugin capabilities – printers, signature capture devices – features to help provide complete customer service.

The same holds true for using a mobile device – such as a smart phone or tablet – for accepting credit cards, with the following exceptions:

- The merchant opens a mobile credit card processing account with a merchant account provider or adds mobile processing to their existing account.

- The merchant receives a credit card reader or a dongle that plugs into the headphone jack of a smartphone or tablet, or a wireless card reader that's connected via Bluetooth or WIFI.

- The merchant downloads the provider's payments app from either Google Play or the App Store, enabling credit card processing on their smart phone or tablet.

SECURITY AND FRAUD CONSIDERATIONS

As more merchants integrate mobile devices into their payment strategy, security and fraud experts caution users to be aware of the risks involved, and to understand how to minimize them.

- One of the biggest risks with wireless and mobile systems is the risk of physical theft or loss. A recent 2019 report finds that only 56% of employees using mobile credit processing devices know how to remotely wipe sensitive data from them. It's important to train all employees on how to lock their devices and restrict access to sensitive data.

- Ensure that each device used to process credit cards has an approved security app installed to ensure that account holder data isn't at risk of being compromised.

- Make sure all employees use secured WIFI networks when transacting, and that the payment service includes point-to-point encryption (P2PE) from the point of swipe or dip, to the data center.

- Use only wireless devices that meet PCI standards and are EMV-compliant to ensure both you and your consumer are protected from card-fraud liability.

THE COMPETITION

In September 2018, the Nilson Report published that the number of mPOS devices sold totaled 28.8 million worldwide, up 70%6 from the previous year; accounting for 41.88% of all shipments, up from over 30% year-over-year.

All the major original equipment manufacturers (OEMs) now produce both wireless payment devices and dongles or readers for mPOS functionality. The top OEM manufacturers of Wireless and mPOS devices are listed below, with China capitalizing over 60% of the market:

- Ingenico
- Newland
- Centerm
- Verifone
- PAX Technology
- Ition Electronices
- BBPOS
- Dspread Technology
- Xinguodu Technology
- Castles Technology

Every ISO/MSP sells equipment and mobile processing based on their partnerships with banks or processors and certifications with the various processing platforms. Their competition is not only within the traditional merchant industry, it's also been with disruptors new to the game.

New players in the market have come along within the last 10 years to forever change the existing landscape of how small- to mid-sized businesses and mobile merchants accept credit cards. Not only have they changed the way the merchant accepts payments on-the-go, they've challenged the status-quo for how fees, pricing, and interchange rates are structured and charged to the merchant. Here are three of the top game-changers within the mPOS market:

Square: Launched in 2010, Square began targeting the SMB market by offering easy, flat-rate pricing for merchants. For little money, merchants could initially start transacting, using only their smart phone or tablet, and a free dongle card reader that plugged into the headphone jack. The product line has expanded to tablets, stands and registers for POS environments. The Square app can process transactions offline and comes with bonus features like sales reports and inventory tracking.

PayPal Here: For any business that wants to integrate PayPal payments into their business, PayPal Here is a logical choice for mobile card processing. PayPal offers very competitive flat-rate payment processing. It's a smart choice for businesses that already use PayPal to accept online payments.

QuickBooks GoPayment: GoPayment's mobile credit card reader and mPOS app give merchants payment processing, sales tracking, and business management tools through their phone or tablet, and all sales directly sync to QuickBooks data – both online and desktop versions. QuickBooks processing rates are very competitive, and if used in conjunction with QuickBooks to manage their business, merchants find that using GoPayment is ideal for easy back-office integration.

HOW TO SELL MOBILE PROCESSING

Before we consider tips for selling wireless or m-commerce, let's figure the return on your investment for focusing on the wireless segment, since it primarily involves the merchant purchasing an additional terminal. That was a big list of potential target market segments, so the best thing to do is to test a couple to see what works best for your interests and in your geographic area.

One wireless device manufacturer tested paper-based direct marketing campaigns to the plumbing and HVAC segments since these segments tend to generate multiple unit deals (one unit for each truck in the field) and tend to charge at least $5,000 per month per truck.

The company generated these results over an eight-month trial period:

- 1% response rate (10 direct inbound calls for every 1000 letters sent)
- Two closes per ten inbound calls
- Average deal size of 2 terminals

You can easily find your own lead source, write your own letter, and do a similar mailing. With the right presentation, you can sell 4-6 terminals for each $500 to $600 you spend on marketing. Think about the rate of return on the direct mail. Say you make $100 margin on each terminal you sell – that's $800 up front. Beyond that, you'll earn the residual from processing fees, wireless band-width resale fees, transaction fees, and other value-added services you sell. If you call your prospects to follow up on the mailing you sent them, your response rate will be even higher.

That's why the wireless and m-commerce niche can be so lucra-tive. Yes, it's harder to sell than standard landline accounts, but it can be worth much, much more to your portfolio since it's often a multiple unit sale.

The main difference in selling a wireless account is that often it may be viewed as a "nice to have" and not a "must have" for merchants used to the typical countertop system. If a merchant opens a new convenience store, for example, there is generally no-question as to whether he'll need to accept credit and debit cards at the point of sale. He will be bombarded by offers for "free" equipment and sometimes deceptively low rates. Aside from the fact that nothing is free, that's a tough battle to win.

A small plumber or HVAC contractor, by comparison, is probably not using any device to take payments in the field. You can now offer him a wide range of wireless payment or mPOS solutions to process credit cards or even checks at the customer's home. The main challenge you must overcome is to convince the contractor to change his business processes. Yes, he can continue to do things the old way. He can still call in the numbers to the home office, but how much time does that waste? How much more expensive is his processing by not getting card-present rates? Yes, he can still write down the card number on an invoice and process it back at the office. How often does he get the number wrong? Has data ever been stolen from his truck? How does he know the card is good?

You can overcome the inertia of old business processes, but you must change how you sell. You must become a consultative seller. You must become the expert on wireless and mPOS payments as you communicate the benefits of moving the transaction closer to the customer. You should view yourself as selling a solution to the merchant's problems, not just a reseller of terminal equipment. Building a relationship based on the needs of the merchant will help set you apart from providers that on the surface, may seem like a less expensive solution.

Moreover, and this is the most important thing, you must absolutely make service and education your number one priority if you want to be successful in the mobile processing space. If you simply drop off the terminals or devices and then wave goodbye as you head for the door, you will fail.

Since you are changing a merchant's business process, your customers are going to have questions on how to use the terminal or the device/app. Many ISOs and even the manufacturers have downloadable materials, videos, and live training classes to help merchants better understand the equipment.

The hour you spend with the merchant at the time of sale will prevent ten hours of hassle down the road and will encourage the merchant to maximize the use of the terminal or the mobile app, which is nothing but good news for your residual.

CHAPTER 16
E-COMMERCE

CONTRIBUTING WRITE STEVEN PIESNER

There were over 3.9 billion active Internet users in Q4 2018.

With easier access to computers and an increased use of smartphones to shop online and connect with friends and family via social media platforms, people around the world are able to use the internet more frequently and with more security and convenience.

In 2018, it was reported by Statista that retail e-commerce sales amounted to $504.6 billion US dollars and is projected to surpass $735 billion US dollars in 2023. Retail e-commerce, namely apparel and accessories, is projected to generate over 138.7 billion U.S. dollars in revenue by 2022. Understanding that a growing percentage, more than 10% of all retail sales are made online, merchants shouldn't underestimate the importance of having an online presence.

E-commerce is not only the buying of goods and services over the Internet, but it is the advertising of goods and services as well. E-commerce business is its own economy. The amount of e-commerce transactions has nearly surpassed the amount of retail (card swipe) transactions in the United States. With consumers carrying less cash and becoming more reliant on credit cards, debit cards, payment apps and mobile payments, the Card-Not-Present (CNP) transaction can longer be ignored.

Since 2013, the percentage of households that use debit cards has dropped from 74% to 58%. According to data from a ValuePenguin study, the downward trend of debit card usage can be attributed to the change in consumers' financial habits; an increased use of online and mobile banking, including payment apps like ApplePay and Venmo, as well as the increased use of prepaid debit cards.

THE TOP TEN LANGUAGES OF THE INTERNET ARE:

- English 1.055B or 25.4%
- Chinese 804.6M or 19.3%
- Spanish 337.8M or 8%
- Arabic 219.1M or 5.3%
- Portuguese 169.1M or 4.1%
- Indonesian/Malaysian 168.7M or 4.1%
- French 134.1M of 3.2%
- Japanese 118.6M or 2.9%
- Russian 109.5M or 2.6%
- German 92.1M or 2.2%
- Rest of the World 950.3M or 22.8%

Source: www.Internetworldstats.com

The top ten advertisers in the U.S. by media value in December 2017 were:

RANK	ADVERTISER
1	Comcast Corp.
2	Procter and Gamble
3	AT&T
4	Amazon
5	General Motors
6	Verizon Communications
7	Ford Motor Co.
8	Charter Communications
9	Alphabet (Google)
10	Samsung Electronics Co.

Source: Statista.com

It should be noted that in the 2009 edition of the book, 60% of top the 10 advertisers were in the Online Trading and Online Lending space; AT&T was the only Telecommunications company that made the list; Telecommunication currently makes up 50% of the top ten. With the growth of online retail giants like Amazon and Shopify we can expect to see the demographics continue to shift.

The basic components of an e-commerce site are:

- Website Pages
- Shopping Cart
- PCI-Compliant Payments processing Gateway
- Order Fulfillment System
- Social Media Links
- Website Hosting Solution

What are the benefits of e-commerce?

1   Convenience. E-commerce sites operate 24 hours a day, 7 days a week, which leads to lower internal costs.

2   Internet commerce allows firms to eliminate the middleman in buyer-supplier transactions. Firms interact with customers through e-mail rather than through direct mail and direct sales associates. Information is distributed online instead of through costly catalogs.

3   Cheaper processing costs. Electronic payments are less expensive than paying via live assisted calls.

4   Increased speed of the selling process. E-commerce companies receive revenue faster than traditional retail sellers.

5   Reduced errors. The automated process tends to produce fewer errors than the traditional selling process.

6   Unlimited shelf space. E-commerce companies can display/shelve an unlimited number/amount of goods.

7   Increased global presence. People from all over the world can access e-commerce companies.

One of the most important components of e-commerce is transaction security.

The acquirer is responsible for making sure that the merchant is PCI DSS (Payment Card Industry Data Security Standard) compliant, but ultimately it is up to the merchant to make sure that his site is compliant as fines are passed from the card associations to the acquirer and on to the merchant per processing agreements.

PCI Compliance should be of the utmost importance to the merchant due to potential fines for noncompliance.

CHAPTER 17
PAYMENT GATEWAYS

WHAT IS A PAYMENT GATEWAY?

In today's technologically-driven environment, it's vital for any merchant doing business to have an e-commerce solution as part of their payment strategy. According to Statista, US retail e-commerce sales are projected to accelerate within the next 5 years, going from $505 billion in 2018 to over $735 billion by 2023.

Whether the merchant has an in-store, online or mobile presence, it's important for them to understand how a payment gateway helps drive their business successfully. It's even more important for you to understand which payment gateway is the right choice for your customers, so they can transact payments flawlessly.

So, what is a payment gateway? A payment gateway helps merchants process credit, debit, check/ACH, gift card/loyalty, and other payment transactions electronically via an e-commerce application. The gateway truly acts as a portal, allowing customer account information to transmit between the merchant and their payment processor/acquiring bank for authorization and settlement.

Payment gateway providers come in a variety of shapes and sizes; gateway services are typically bundled with the merchant's existing account based on their business needs and the recommendations from you, their sales representative. Gateways may also be integrated into POS systems or software platforms to provide a seamless payment experience for your merchant.

HOW DOES A PAYMENT GATEWAY WORK?

Three seconds. That's how long it takes to complete a payment transaction. But it's important to know what happens the behind the scenes of that transaction to better understand how a payment gateway works. Let's take a look at how a credit card is processed through a payment gateway.

1   A customer makes a purchase of an item – in-store, online or on-the-go – and the account number is either keyed, swiped, dipped or tapped into the system.

2   Details of the purchase and the customer's sensitive account information are sent to a payment gateway for processing through various levels of encryption. Encryption ensures that the data is passed securely through the various connections.

3   The payment gateway then forwards the transaction information to the payment processor used by the merchant's bank, which is then transmitted to the credit card issuer.

4   The credit card issuer routes the transaction to the customer's card issuing bank for authorization. If approved, the issuing bank sends an authorization code back to the processor; if declined, the authorization code provides details for the decline.

5   The authorization code (authorization or decline) is then sent back through the payment gateway to the merchant's bank to process or cancel the transaction.

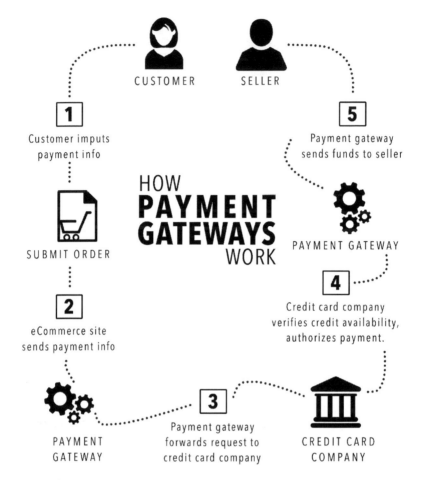

CUSTOMER

SELLER

1 Customer imputs payment info

5 Payment gateway sends funds to seller

HOW
**PAYMENT
GATEWAYS**
WORK

SUBMIT ORDER

PAYMENT GATEWAY

4 Credit card company verifies credit availability, authorizes payment.

2 eCommerce site sends payment info

3 Payment gateway forwards request to credit card company

PAYMENT GATEWAY

CREDIT CARD COMPANY

6   At the end of each business day, the merchant "batches" all the approved transactions and sends the files to their bank for settlement. Through the payment network, transactions are shared so that customer's banks and merchant's banks can complete the transfers to one another.

7   The merchant's bank will deposit the funds into their account in a specific period of time, typically 24-48 hours.

WHAT ARE THE BENEFITS OF A PAYMENT GATEWAY?

With the explosion of online retail giants like Amazon and eBay, e-commerce shows continued growth year after year, and customer satisfaction in the US is highly favorable towards online shopping. Statista reports that:

- As noted at the beginning of this chapter, 2018 online sales in the US equaled $504.6 billion with projections to surpass $735 billion by 2023.

- Even though online sales still represent a smaller portion of US retail sales – about 9.6% as of Q3 2018, the percentage consistently increases year after year.

- An estimated 78% of US internet shoppers made an online purchase in 2017; 32% made an internet purchase once a month and 29% shopped online once or twice a week.

The numbers are important because they drive home the concept that enabling an e-commerce solution is not only a necessity for online retailers, it's also vital for brick and mortar retailers who want to stay relevant in today's ever-changing retail landscape.

Value-priced: Using an integrated payment gateway is a cost-effective way to enable payment acceptance for both the online and in-store merchant. Working with a trusted merchant salesperson to set up a merchant account through their processor, the merchant has the potential to save on interchange and services fees, and perhaps take advantage of volume pricing discounts for multiple locations and devices.

Compliant: When selecting a payment gateway provider, it's important for merchants to partner with a company that has gone through the rigorous testing and certification necessary to ensure that their software meets all compliance standards as mandated by the Payment Card Industry (PCI). A trusted gateway will have software that is PCI-DSS or PA-DSS compliant to ensure that a customer's sensitive data is never compromised.

All-inclusive: Using an integrated payment gateway provider is beneficial to the small and mid-sized merchant who needs a complete business solution; one that provides a full suite of services for back-office support, in addition to transaction processing.

Integrated services mean that the gateway provider can tailor the agreement based on the needs of the merchant. Will they need back-office support for accounting software plug-ins for QuickBooks®, inventory management, recurring payment processing, account updater functionality, and CRM? Will they offer gift/loyalty cards, or EMV functionality? Understanding your merchant's current and future needs will help instill trust and build a healthy partnership.

THE LEADERS IN PAYMENT GATEWAYS

With so many powerful and popular payment gateways in the market today, how does your merchant know which one best meets the needs of their business? Every payment gateway has a variety of solutions and services, as well as pricing and fee structures, and most of the time the merchant will choose the gateway that is certified with their bank's processor.

Below is a list of some of the leading payment gateways in the US according to a 2019 comparison study completed by FinancesOnline.com; some are tried and true gateways, and some are disruptors to the status quo. Even though this list doesn't endorse one gateway over another, it's important for agents to understand the competition in order to meet the needs of their merchants.

- Amazon Payments
- Authorize.Net
- BlueSnap
- Braintree
- PayPal Payments Pro
- PayU

- SecurionPay
- Skrill
- Stripe
- WePay

THE FUTURE OF PAYMENT GATEWAYS

The payments industry has seen significant growth in the past few years with technological innovation, shifts in consumer expectations and shopping habits, and new regulation all contributing to its evolution. Even though there is no indication that the pace will change in the immediate future, it's important to understand current trends that dominate the industry news. Here are just a few trends that are seeing an increased adoption from both providers and consumers.

OMNICHANNEL

Omnichannel, also known as Omnicommerce, is a relatively new concept in the payments industry. Omnichannel is a multichannel approach to retail that provides customers with a seamless shopping experience, whether they shop online, in-store or on their mobile device. What really drives the omnichannel experience is integrated technology; the effectiveness to which all the processing software (the merchant's retail, e-commerce, and mobile applications) interconnects to drive consistency across all customer touchpoints.

Implementing an omnichannel solution helps merchants better understand and meet the purchasing needs of their customers; providing a consistent message across all customer touchpoints helps increase sales, builds customer loyalty and builds referrals.

BOPIS

To help enhance the omnichannel experience, retailers have come up with innovative ways to bring online and mobile shoppers back to the stores. With new opportunity comes a new acronym:

BOPIS, known as Buy Online Pickup In Store. And it's a key part of what's driving growth for small and large retailers competing in the fast-fulfillment Amazon era.

According to a survey by Doddle, more than 68% of shoppers recently made click-and-collect purchases, and cited reasons why:

- 48% were incented to save on shipping fees
- 39% needed the item the same day
- 28% believed that the process was more convenient

BOPIS sales during the 2018 holiday season increased 54% from the previous year, and it's expected to have a larger impact this year. BOPIS services are a great conversion tool for retailers. 50% of shoppers decided where to make online purchases based on BOPIS availability, and once they were in the store, 85% made additional in-store purchases. Working with your merchants to implement innovative solutions like BOPIS can be the driving change they need to further bring in-store and online together.

P2P INTEGRATION WITH MOBILE PAYMENTS

The world of digital payments – payment by a digital wallet on your phone – is evolving faster than ever before. The development of P2P (Peer to Peer) options, such as PayPal's Venmo and the bank-supported Zelle, allows consumers to quickly move funds from their phone's linked account to another digital account. Mobile payment revenue is expected to grow to more than $1 trillion by the end of 2019, and merchants are seeing the ability to pay via phone as a way to acquire new customers. According to Venmo, the number of merchants accepting Venmo as a payment method has exploded to over 2 million merchants. In addition, monthly active users increased 185% month-over-month from August to September 2018.

The service is especially popular with Millennials and the mobile-first Gen Z customers. A fall 2018 report from Rubix shows that

P2P is slowly overtaking ATM withdrawals as a preferred payment method for these two demographics, with 68% of Gen Z customers embracing digital wallets as a primary method of shopping with retailers.

PAY-OVER-TIME LOANS

Today's landscape of offering pay-over-time financing options to consumers is rapidly evolving. Consumer preference, especially younger generations like Millennials and Gen Z, is leaning towards a "buy now, pay later" philosophy, and it's a growing option even for online merchants. As younger generations become consumers in today's digital world, it's essential for merchants and service providers to be proactive in addressing their credit preferences.

According to a recent TransUnion study (Generation Revealed: Decoding Millennial Financial Health), data showed that while Millennials still use credit cards for purchases, they tend to utilize them less often, own fewer cards, and carry smaller balances. Instead Millennials rely more on debit cards for smaller purchases, and they prefer the ease of online loan origination, such as pay-over-time loans, to make larger purchases. Digitization and eCommerce have helped younger consumers comparison shop to find an item or service at the lowest price, as well as find the best rate when purchasing something over time.

In today's FinTech world, consumers are no longer dependent on bank loans, nor are they interested in carrying larger balances on their credit cards. They're looking to businesses to provide convenient pay-over-time loans –with low-interest rates and without the hassle or inconvenience of traditional loans.

There are many gateway providers in the marketplace, there is nothing wrong with attending software demos or training until you decide which you prefer to offer.

CHAPTER 18
PROCESSING EQUIPMENT

In order to process a retail transaction, the merchant must have terminal equipment.

Three of the largest equipment companies in our industry are:

1   Ingenico

2   PAX Technology

3   VeriFone (Acquired Hypercom in 2011)

These three manufactures represent the majority of U.S. terminal shipments.

Credit card processing equipment or point-of-sale (POS) devices give the merchant the ability to electronically transmit transactions to their acquiring bank.

Optional POS systems may include software packages installed on a PC or hosted in the cloud with a wireless unit, a kiosk, a mobile app or a custom-developed system (usually for very large merchants).

For small to mid-size businesses, a standard credit card terminal and printer will do the job.

Terminals have drastically evolved over the years. The majority of terminals now are multi-application capable. Multi-application capable means a terminal can process and support multiple services at the merchant's countertop. Many terminals are now connected to mobile apps, which allows the merchant to review real-time sales activity from their mobile device. Terminal manufacturers now have software APIs (Application Programming Interface) that connect terminal devices with software applications and platforms, this allows for an easy integration between hardware and software systems.

Current POS devices have the ability to process several types of applications:

- Credit Card Transactions
- Debit Transactions
- Gift/Loyalty Cards
- Prepaid Services (limited in number)
- Check Processing
- EBT
- Check Card Transactions
- Purchasing Cards
- Signature Capture
- EMV-enabled/Smart Cards
- NFC/Contactless
- Custom Applications, such as:
    - Medical Benefits Verification
    - Government License Renewals
    - Age Verification
    - Biometrics
    - And many more

Check with your ISO and acquirer to see what new products you will be able to offer in the future or conduct your own research. Here are the top three manufacturers' Websites:

www.ingenico.com
www.paxtechnology.com
www.verifone.com

Other notable terminal manufacture websites:

www.clover.com
www.dejavoosystems.com
www.exadigm.com
www.poynt.com

CHAPTER 19
POINT OF SALE PROCESSING

POINT OF SALE (POS)

If your primary clients are retailers or restaurateurs whose core business runs from a brick and mortar location, then you know how important a point of sale (POS) system is to them. The retail industry is one of the predominant users of standard POS terminals. POS software is the lifeline for retail, e-commerce, and restaurants selling goods and services to their customers. Not only can a robust POS system lower the transaction time for your customers, it can save and organize your sales data, store customer contact information, manage inventory, keep track of employee's hours, and so much more.

According to a recent report from Zion Market Research, the global POS terminal market was valued at over $45 billion US dollars in 2016 and is expected to increase to over $98 billion by 2022. Even with the fast-paced changes within the industry, the need for a POS system remains constant, especially for merchants who run an in-store business.

Choosing the right system is key for a small- to mid-sized business. A POS system should be cost-effective and easy to use and implement; it should have the integration necessary so that the terminals on the showroom floor work seamlessly with the back-office systems for successful business and inventory management.

Delivering the right payment solution to the merchant doesn't always mean trying to sell high-technology software and expensive hardware. It's vital to partner with the merchant to help strategically plan which POS system will be best for them to run their business; whether it be a simple in-store solution or integrated with an e-commerce and/or a mobile solution.

TRADITIONAL VS. TABLET POS

If your merchant is looking for a POS system, it really comes down to two different solutions – a traditional system, or a tablet, cloud-based solution. It's important for you to understand the difference between both to help your merchant determine which one makes the most sense for their business.

So, let's understand the difference between the two. Referred to as legacy systems over the years, traditional POS systems run on a closed internal network, and store data on a local server; think big box chains. Tablet, or cloud-based POS systems are web-based solutions that store and access data on remote servers, with information accessible online. With a tablet-based POS solution, merchants can access the software from anywhere they have internet connectivity.

When advising your merchants on choosing a POS solution, it'll be critical for you to understand the benefits and drawbacks of both traditional and tablet-based solutions in order to recommend a system that best suits the current and future needs of the merchant.

TRADITIONAL POS – STRENGTHS AND WEAKNESSES

To reiterate, traditional POS systems are installed as an in-house solution; the software runs on the merchant's own servers, and the terminals and ancillary devices are all maintained on-site.

Strengths

Although the upfront costs to implement a traditional POS system are far greater than a tablet-based one, there are certain advantages to investing in a long-term, on-premise solution.

- Security – Typically, traditional POS systems are purchased under the terms of a perpetual, non-exclusive license for the installation and use of the software. With the purchase agreement comes the ability to maintain and update the system as needed or mandated. An internal IT team is kept on-staff to ensure that the system is operating 24/7. By having an internal software system, businesses can ensure that their data is as secure and updated as needed.

- Customization – Since the merchant owns the hardware and software that runs the traditional POS system, they have the flexibility to customize and add solutions to the system to help manage and grow their business.

- Stability – Unlike a tablet, cloud-based system, a locally-owned, in-house solution doesn't depend on an internet connection, so connectivity to data is rarely an issue.

- Seamless integration – Since the merchant owns the system, they control how the hardware components – barcode scanners, card readers, cash drawers, signature capture, and other payment devices – seamlessly integrate with one another.

Weaknesses

One of the most glaring weaknesses of implementing a traditional POS system is cost. Although it's an ideal solution for established, multi-store organizations, the investment and commitment required for a traditional system may be too much to bear for most small to mid-sized businesses. With every strength noted above, there is a flip side of which to be aware.

- Maintenance – Merchants that own their POS systems are also responsible for maintaining the hardware and upgrading software to meet the needs of the business, as well as stay up-to-date with all regulatory mandates.

- Staffing – Most businesses that purchase a traditional in-house system have the IT experts on staff to ensure that regular maintenance and system upgrades are planned and scheduled according to industry updates. Even if contractors help with customization to new or existing software, the internal IT team is responsible for project management and implementation.

- Upfront costs – Implementing a traditional POS system requires upfront investment. Purchasing the system includes the costs for licensing fees, terminals and ancillary devices, installation and implementation fees, and systems training. Customer support usually comes at an additional monthly fee. Vendor support can also come at an additional cost.

TABLET POS – STRENGTHS AND WEAKNESSES

As much as traditional POS systems are the industry's past, tablet, cloud-based POS solutions are taking merchants into the future. Recent reports from Epson indicate that over 4 million tablets have been shipped to US businesses for specific use as POS systems. As more and more people are getting comfortable with using mobile devices in a cloud-based environment, adopting a tablet-based POS solution seems like a logical choice.

With so many tablet options in the market, it's still important to understand the varying degrees of functionality, as well as the benefits and drawbacks of the plethora of POS software systems entering the game.

Strengths

Tablet POS systems are great options for smaller merchants. The easy-to-use interface makes the implementation and on-boarding processes faster and easier, and the smaller price tag makes it more affordable for new merchants hanging up their OPEN sign. And since it operates in a cloud-based environment, merchants can operate from anywhere they have a wireless connection.

- Affordability – A tablet POS system typically costs less than a traditional system, both in implementation and on-going maintenance. A variety of add-ons needed to mirror an all-in-one POS system – check scanners, EMV chip readers, cash drawers and receipt printers – can affect pricing; the number of tablets needed can also drive the price up. But with multiple device discounts, merchants can typically expect to pay less per "terminal." Since most tablet POS systems are cloud-based, the cost for monthly subscription-based support is typically lower.

- Customer-friendly experience – Implementing a customer-friendly POS system is an easy way to interact with the customer during the sales process. Many tablet-based POS systems engage the customer with easy-to-follow prompts for order review, tip capabilities, and electronic signature capture. It also enables the customer to choose their preferred form of receiving a receipt.

- Easier integration – Similar to traditional POS systems, Tablet POS software includes capabilities for enhanced inventory reporting and analysis, and CRM tools for marketing and lead management. These integrated analytical tools are designed to decrease the time spent in the back office, and increase time interacting with customers on the sales floor.

- Increased mobility – One of the greatest advantages of a tablet POS terminal is the mobility it allows employees on the sales floor. Employees can interact with and better assist more customers, without having to be tied to a stationary, countertop solution.

- Reduced training time – Since people are familiar with the technology of Apple and Android devices, implementing a tablet POS system will be easier to use from the get-go. The familiarity with using the devices helps the merchant save on the time and costs associated with employee training programs.

- Easier software updates – A tablet POS system offers flexibility, lower pricing and a broader product selection of a preferred tablet device – Apple or Android. Apple devices are excellent, but POS software for Androids seems to be open to more customization. Merchants who choose Android over Apple devices like that the software updates are more fluid and faster, and customization is greater because the operating system allows for it.

Weaknesses

There are very few drawbacks to choosing a tablet, cloud-based POS system, but one very real drawback is connectivity. Since tablet POS systems work in a SaaS, web-based environment, when the internet goes down, or a merchant is in a "no-service zone," they're susceptible to being without service. No service could affect their ability to transact.

HOW TO CHOOSE THE RIGHT PROVIDER

When it comes to choosing a POS system for their business, a merchant has the overwhelming task of trying to find the perfect solution. As you partner with your merchants to help explore options, try asking qualifying questions to help narrow the field.

- What features will I need now, and is the system scalable for future add-ons?
- Do I want to save money upfront or keep my monthly costs down?
- What types of hardware and devices will I need to support my business effectively? Do they offer bundled or quantity discounts?
- Does the new system integrate with my existing business apps, like QuickBooks?
- Is the system easy to implement? What training is involved now and in the future?
- What level of customer service do I need, and what can I expect?
- Are there any custom features or applications required for your industry type? (To go pickup, takeout, online ordering, scheduling, table management, server reporting, tax reporting, etc.)

WHAT THE FUTURE HOLDS FOR POINT OF SALE

Know your customers: POS systems that expect to be relevant in the years ahead need to be developed on a platform that is flexible to support new functionality, such as mobile integration and enhanced CRM applications. Stores are trending towards being highly experiential and engaging in the customers senses (aesthetics, music); it's more about human interaction while allowing the customer to shop on their own terms.

Embrace mobile marketing: Merchants need to embrace the mobile experience as seen through the eyes of the consumer. In a recent study from Yes Marketing, more than 57% of shoppers are using mobile devices while shopping in-store. 65% are using their smart phones to redeem coupons, 57% to source mobile coupons, or 46% to locate on-sale items as featured on the merchant's website.

Build an omnichannel strategy: From the merchant perspective, 50% mentioned implementing a mobile shopping app into their payment acceptance strategy and 45% listed mPOS as another key element to embracing an omnichannel strategy (Shopgate). For 61% of merchants, BOPIS (Buy Online Pickup in Store) is another important element to completing the omnichannel strategy. Merchants need to adopt the right technologies and service partner if they want to deliver a seamless, user-friendly shopping experience that can increase both customer lifetime loyalty and revenue.

Accept Mobile Payments: Offering mobile payments, including NFC capabilities for contactless acceptance can also be key to gaining future customers. According to MobilePaymentsToday.com, last year, an estimated 31% of iPhone users made a purchase using Apple Pay, while 47% of users surveyed expect to use mobile payments and digital wallets by 2020. Embracing contactless payments is not only ideal for retailers but good for restaurants looking to comply with EMV standards for Chip & PIN issued cards.

There are literally dozens of POS systems on the market, start with your ISO to see what systems they recommend and support.

CHAPTER 20
LEASING

Leasing is the ability to finance merchant equipment over time. Leasing allows the salesperson to offer the merchant an alternative to paying cash. A large number of equipment sales in the bankcard industry are made utilizing lease financing.

When leasing equipment, the agent is paid a percentage of the payments the lessee (merchant) expects to make over the term of the lease. The lease company grades the lease, based on the merchant's credit, to determine the amount of funding or commission to the agent.

Gross funding amounts are based upon lease factors, which correspond to the term of the lease and customer credit rating. The lease company sets the factor assigned to each credit score.

Consider a $39.00 monthly lease payment for a term of 48 months with an "A" credit score with a lease factor of .0310. (Lease factors vary by credit and lease company)

To get the total funding amount, divide $39.00 by .0310 for a total funding amount of $1258.06 – this is your gross funding amount.

Remember you must deduct your equipment cost, doc fees if any, upfront payments not paid by the merchant, and any other overhead costs.

Usual lease terms are 12, 24, 36, and 48 months. Leasing is not renting – the merchant is committed to the contract for the term of the lease and it is non-cancelable. Most lease companies will let the merchant transfer the lease liability if the business is sold or will let the merchant pay the lease off early.

In addition to the monthly lease payment the merchant will pay tax and a loss destruction waiver. The loss destruction waiver is small fee charged per month and serves as an insurance policy on the equipment. It's like buying a car; if you finance a car, insurance must be purchased. The merchant can avoid this fee by providing its own coverage with the lease company named as the loss payee.

At the end of the lease term the merchant will either return the equipment to the leasing company or purchase the equipment for fair market value. Fair market value is determined by the leasing company.

The advantages of leasing are as follows:

- Requires very little upfront cash (usually 1 or 2 payments)
- Preserves existing capital, which can be used to start and maintain business
- Easily budgeted with a fixed lease payment
- 100% tax deductible
- Older equipment can be upgraded to take advantage of newer technology
- Excellent selling tool to close more business

Here are the normal steps to process a lease:

Step 1   Agent writes a contract between the merchant and lease company.

Step 2   Lease is faxed or sent to lease company for credit grading.

Step 3   Merchant is approved; equipment is downloaded and installed at merchant's location.

Step 4   Original lease and required paperwork is sent to lease company for funding.

Step 5   Merchant verbally verifies the terms of the lease with the lease company.

Step 6   Lease company pays ISO funding amount based on credit score.

Step 7   Agent is paid commission.

Most lease companies currently are leasing only hardware, which means a physical piece of equipment. A few will lease software and payment gateways.

CHAPTER 21
CONSUMER FRAUD

The major form of fraud hitting consumers and businesses is identity theft, which comes in several forms:

- Skimming
- Check Fraud
- Cyber Crime

According to complaints filed with the Federal Trade Commission (FTC) in 2018, identity theft is one of the top three crimes in America. In a recently-published FTC report, the *Consumer Sentinel Network Data Book 2018*, records show that over 1.4 million fraud reports were filed with the FTC, equaling about $1.4 billion in lost revenue. The loss equates to a median of $375 per individual, with some age groups (i.e. seniors) losing more than others.

Since 2017, credit card fraud has risen 24% from the previous year; the FTC received over 167,000 reports from consumers stating that their personal information was misused for fraudulent activity on both valid existing credit card accounts, and fraudulent new credit card accounts.

For more research go to:

www.identitytheft.gov
https://www.consumer.ftc.gov/topics/identity-theft

Let us look at the three most common forms of fraud.

Skimming

Even with enhanced security measures put in place to reduce fraud, a large percentage of potential online buyers remain highly concerned about the security of credit card transactions conducted over the Internet. The perception that credit card numbers could be compromised during the transmission between the browser and the website or hacked once stored in a merchant's database limits consumer confidence in buying online. Although these risks exist, the likelihood of a card number being compromised online is relatively low because of the widespread use of SSL encryption for secure communication, firewalls, and data encryption of stored information. On the other hand, few consumers consider the risk of their card numbers being compromised during face-to-face transactions by handing their cards to sales staff who often are complete strangers.

With the implementation of EMV technology, hackers and scammers probably still find it much easier to obtain credit card numbers in the physical world because of the security measures that are in place to protect card information online. The traditional way to collect card numbers is "dumpster diving," basically the act of gaining access to personal account information – credit card bills, receipts, bank statements, pre-approved loan applications – that might be thrown away by consumers. However, technology makes it easier for crooks to collect hundreds of credit card numbers is a much more efficient way – welcome to the world of credit card skimmers!

A skimmer is a small, self-contained device about the size of a pack of cigarettes. To avoid notice, credit card skimmers are sometimes disguised as pagers or Personal Digital Assistants (PDAs). Because of their size, they can be hidden in a pocket or behind a tie. The skimmer can read the information contained in a card's magnetic stripe and can store up to 1,000 card numbers in memory. The unit can then be connected to a PC to download the collected information. Unfortunately, credit card skimmers are easy to find and relatively inexpensive. The web provides plenty of underground "hacker supermarkets" advertising these devices, which can be purchased for as little as $600.

The modus operandi of skimmer-based credit card fraud is quite simple and has potential when a consumer provides a credit card with a mag-stripe for payment. Skimming can occur in situations where a collusive employee temporarily takes control of the card at a point-of-sale device located out of the consumer's sight. For example, a malicious restaurant waiter can quickly swipe the card through the skimmer, collecting card number and expiration date (some skimmers can also read "Track 1" data, which includes the cardholder's name) while walking toward the legitimate point-of-sale terminal. This process is much easier than breaking into a corporate database to access credit card numbers online. And with EMV integration, skimmers are becoming increasingly popular at ATMs and gas station pumps where there's been a lag in retrofitting or replacing expensive equipment to include the EMV chip-readers.

Because the cardholder is unaware that the card has been compromised, the number can be used for a month or two before unauthorized charges show on the cardholder's statements and action is taken. Obviously, the safest place for a criminal to use these compromised numbers is on the Internet, which provides anonymous worldwide access to thousands of commerce-enabled sites that don't have methods in place to verify the PIN assigned to EMV-enabled cards. Numbers are often posted in underground chat rooms and on hackers' websites for rapid exchange and distribution. To make matters worse, skimmed card numbers can be copied onto the magnetic stripes of counterfeit cards and used for face-to-face transactions.

WHAT MERCHANTS CAN DO

What are some ways online merchants can defend themselves from credit card skimmers? One protection scheme is already present on the majority of circulating cards, particularly in the United States. The 3-digit card validation code imprinted on the back of Visa, Mastercard, Discover, and Diners Club cards and the 4-digit code imprinted in the front of American Express cards provides significant protection. Although different acronyms (CVV2, CVC2) are used to describe these codes, the principle is the same. The code is not readable from the magnetic stripe and cannot, therefore, be skimmed. When the consumer is asked to provide these codes in card-not-present transactions, online or by phone, a correct answer provides at least some assurance that a legitimate cardholder is using the card. To protect the effectiveness of this security mechanism, card associations mandate that online businesses not store the validation code in their databases, even in an encrypted format.

Although card validation codes are not a complete solution to the skimming problem as the number could be annotated separately, they still provide a significant level of protection to both merchants and cardholders. For added protection, avoid storing card verification codes after the transaction has been completed and ensure that codes do not appear in Web server logs or other persistent files. Fortunately, most card processors support card verification mechanisms as part of the card authorization process and this protection is readily available to all online merchants.

For more research go to:

https://merchantriskcouncil.org/

Check fraud

Check fraud is still one of the largest forms of identity theft today. According to several government publications, check fraud takes on multiple forms, including:

- Forged signatures - legitimate blank checks with an imitation of the payor signature;
- Forged endorsements - often involving theft of a valid check, which is then endorsed and cashed or deposited by someone other than the payee;
- Counterfeit checks - the fastest-growing source of fraudulent checks, due to advances in color copying and desktop publishing capabilities;
- Altered checks - defined as valid check stock with certain information, such as the payee or written amount, changed to benefit the perpetrator;
- Check kiting – the process of depositing a check from one bank into a second bank without sufficient funds to cover it, then taking advantage of the conditional credits offered by the second bank to write a check for deposit back to the first bank to cover the original check.

For more in-depth information, research the following:

www.frbservices.org – to review the Federal Reserve Payments Study Fraud Report 2018.

www.fbi.gov

Cybercrime

Cybercrime takes many forms; one of the most devastating is online fraud.

A recent industry press release shows how real the threat of online fraud is.

> *WASHINGTON – (BUSINESS WIRE) – Three years after the switch to new chip-based credit and debit cards, a study released today by the National Retail Federation and Forrester says payment card fraud is still a top concern for large U.S. retailers as criminals move their activities online.*

"The implementation of EMV chip cards and chip card readers was supposed to dramatically reduce credit and debit card fraud," the State of Retail Payments report said. "So why is fraud still the top concern for merchants?"

The report found that fraud was the top payment-related challenge faced by retailers, cited by 55 percent of those surveyed. The reason is largely that Europay-MasterCard-Visa chip cards have moved payment card fraud away from stores and toward online transactions, the report said, citing a Forter study showing a 13 percent increase in online fraud last year. A Federal Reserve study said online fraud rose from $3.4 billion in 2015 – the first-year retailers were required to accept chip cards or face an increase in fraud liability – to $4.6 billion in 2016 and was an "increasing concern."

"In a post-EMV world, fraud is shifting from in-person to ecommerce channels, so retailers have been busy bolstering their defenses to mitigate the increasing costs and risks of ecommerce fraud," the NRF/Forrester report said.

To help fight fraud, the report found that retailers want better authentication of purchases no matter where they take place and that 33 percent have implemented 3-D Secure, a system marketed as Verified by Visa or Mastercard SecureCode that is intended to help authenticate online purchases.

For in-person purchases, 51 percent of merchants said biometrics would be the best way to verify transactions, and 53 percent expressed interest in implementing forms such as the fingerprint and facial recognition available on smartphones. But with that technology limited to phones rather than cards, 46 percent said personal identification numbers would be the best currently available way to approve card transactions.

For purchases made with cards, 95 percent of retailers said requiring PINs would improve security and 92 percent would implement it if it were available. While EMV cards in other countries are chip-and-PIN, virtually all EMV credit cards issued by U.S. banks have been chip-and-signature with PIN available only on debit cards. And the major credit card companies stopped requiring a signature last year.

"The chip in an EMV card makes it very difficult to counterfeit the card, but it does nothing to show whether the person trying to use the card is the legitimate cardholder," NRF Senior Vice President and General Counsel Stephanie Martz said. "If we want to stop card fraud, we need a better way of authenticating users and it should be one that's affordable, easy and safe. Someday the answer might be biometrics or technology that has yet to be invented but, in the meantime, we know PIN can stop criminal's dead in their tracks. With no signatures, no PIN and no biometrics, what we have right now is no authentication at all."

NRF has long argued that PIN is important because the chip in EMV cards only prevents the use of counterfeit cards while not stopping lost or stolen cards, and a PIN can also provide a backup for cases where the chip malfunctions or is tampered with.

In addition to the focus on cards, retailers have also been installing technology to fight data breaches and thereby keep criminals from stealing card data that can then be used to commit fraud. The report found 89 percent expect to have tokenization in place by the end of next year, and that 80 percent plan to do the same with point-to-point encryption.

The second-biggest concern was the cost of accepting payment cards, including the swipe fees banks charge to *process transactions, cited by 45 percent. While the survey found 49 percent of retailers have taken advantage of routing options required as part of a cap on debit card swipe fees passed by Congress in 2010, rising swipe fees for credit cards remain the subject of litigation between retailers and the card industry. Chargebacks of disputed purchases, which increased after implementation of EMV for some retailers, were the third-biggest concern, cited by 35 percent.*

"Eliminating fraud and improving authentication are clearly top priorities for retailers," Brendan Miller, principal analyst at Forrester, said. "As the answers to these challenges are found, the key will be finding ways to implement the solutions in a way that provides a frictionless experience for consumers."

Source: https://www.businesswire.com/news/ home/20181114005745/en/

Consider these basic steps to help you avoid risk and stay secure when you're online – whether you're using e-mail or shopping at your favorite merchant.

- *Protect your Visa card with Verified by Visa.* Added password protection helps ensure that only you can use your Visa card online.
- *Be discriminating when providing personal information online.* Never give out your personal or account information to anyone you do not trust. And make sure to verify a business's legitimacy by visiting its website, calling a phone number obtained from a trusted source, and/or checking with a reliable resource such as the Better Business Bureau's BBBonline Reliability Program.
- *Keep your passwords secret.* Some online stores may require you to register with them via a username and password before buying. Online passwords, including your Verified by

Visa password, should be kept secret from outside parties the same way you protect your ATM PIN.

- *Look for signs of security.* Identify security clues such as a lock image at the bottom of your browser, or an URL that begins with "https://." These signs indicate that only you and the merchant can view your payment information.

- *Keep current with anti-virus and anti-spyware software. Download only from trusted sites, and don't click pop-up windows or suspicious links in emails, even from people you know. These can all be tricks to install spyware and steal financial information.*

- *Never send payment information via e-mail.* Information that travels over the Internet (such as e-mail) is not fully protected from being read by outside parties. Most reputable merchant sites use encryption technologies that will protect your private data from being accessed by others as you conduct an online transaction.

- *Keep a record of your transaction.* Just as you save store receipts, you should keep records of your online purchases. Back up your transaction by saving and/or printing the order confirmation.

- *Review your monthly account statement thoroughly.* Immediately investigate suspicious activity to prevent any possible additional fraud before it occurs. Promptly notify your financial institution of any suspicious e-mail activities.

- *Be wary of "free trial" offers. Take time to read and understand all terms and conditions. Pay attention to any pre-checked boxes before you submit your payment card information for an order. Failing to un-check the boxes may bind you to terms and conditions you're not interested in.*

Here are some tips from *https://www.visasecuritysense.com/en_US/index.jsp* on buying online:

For more info on cybercrime, research the following:

https://www.justice.gov/criminal-ccips

CHAPTER 22
DATA SECURITY

CONTRIBUTING WRITER DR. HEATHER MARK, PH.D. CCEP.

The issue of data security is one that is "top of mind" for everyone in the payments industry. The very foundation of electronic payments is the exchange, and in some cases the storage, of personal information. While the ability to process payment card transactions certainly introduces a level of convenience and the ability to increase a merchant's customer base, it also introduces a level of risk. As technologies have evolved that make payments processing more convenient, criminals and their techniques to steal sensitive data have, unfortunately, also evolved. In accepting payment cards as a method of payment all merchants accept some level of risk. So, too, do service providers, independent sales organizations (ISOs), and others that may facilitate the payment process. Acquirers (banks and ISOs) assume a particular level of risk for their merchants as the card brands have specific penalties associated with noncompliance with card brand rules as well as with the compromise of data. In an attempt to mitigate the risk to cardholder data, the major payment card brands (Visa Inc., Mastercard Worldwide, Discover Financial, American Express, and JCB) have developed a minimum standard of security to which all companies that store, process or transmit cardholder data must comply.

As early as 1999, the major card brands began to introduce base-line security programs. These programs encouraged organizations handling cardholder data to implement a minimum standard of care around the storage and transmission of data. The programs were largely voluntary in nature, and adoption of the program among service providers and merchants was slow. That changed, however, with a large data breach in 2003. A fairly small payment processor suffered a breach that resulted in the compromise of more than 13 million Primary Account Numbers (PAN). This breach, and the attention it garnered, spurred the creation of what is now called the Payment Card Industry Data Security Standard, commonly referred to as the PCI DSS. The card brands also formed the Payment Card Industry Security Standards Council (PCI SSC) in 2006 to manage the standards and to qualify companies and individuals to conduct assessments against the PCI DSS.

The PCI DSS is a set of twelve high-level requirements and more than 300 sub-requirements that detail the way in which each objective should be met. The twelve main requirements are:

- Install and maintain a properly configured firewall
- Do not use vendor-supplied passwords
- Protect stored data
- Encrypt data in transmission across open public networks
- Use and regularly update anti-virus software
- Develop and maintain secure systems and applications
- Restrict access to cardholder data on a need-to-know basis
- Assign a unique user ID to each person with access to the system
- Restrict physical access to cardholder data

- Track and monitor all access to network resources and cardholder data
- Regularly test security systems and processes
- Maintain an information security policy

These standards are consistent with good security practices and seem straightforward. However, they can be rather daunting, particularly for smaller merchants and the acquirers that are liable for their compliance. They are exceedingly more challenging when one begins to examine the sub-requirements that accompany the standard. The goal of the standard, though, is the protection of cardholder data. That being the case, before one can understand how to protect cardholder data, one must understand the definition of cardholder data.

CARDHOLDER DATA AND SENSITIVE AUTHENTICATION DATA

The PCI DSS classifies two different types of data: cardholder data and sensitive authentication data. Organizations are permitted to store cardholder data, with certain stipulations, but sensitive authentication data must never be stored after the initial authorization response has been received. Understanding the definitions of these two classifications of data and how they must be handled can help merchants reduce their compliance burden and can help ISOs provide guidance to their merchants.

Cardholder data is defined, primarily, as the Primary Account Number (PAN). The PAN is the 15-19 digit number embossed on the front of the card. The PAN, by itself, is considered to be cardholder data and thus requires protection under the PCI DSS. A company that stores the PAN must protect the information by rendering that data unreadable as well as by adhering to the other requirements of the PCI DSS. If the cardholder's name, expiration date, or service code are stored in conjunction with the PAN, then those elements are now also considered cardholder data and must be protected as well.

Sensitive authentication data is defined as the magnetic stripe, track data, CVV (or equivalent), and CVV2 (or equivalent); in addition, PINs, PIN Blocks, and PIN Verification Values are all considered sensitive authentication data. These data elements can never be stored post-authorization.

COMPLIANCE VS. VALIDATION

As stated previously, all companies that store, process, or transmit cardholder data must comply with the PCI DSS. Due to their primary function, boarding merchants on behalf of acquirers, many ISOs believe that they are not required to comply with the standard. In the truest sense of the ISO, this may be correct. If the organization is simply acquiring merchants and is not providing any ancillary services that require the storage, processing or transmitting of data, validation of compliance may not be required. However, many ISOs provide a variety of complimentary functionalities, such as gateway services or fraud analysis and reporting, in which the cardholder data is a prominent element. In these cases, the ISO is defined as a service provider and will be required to comply with the standard and to validate compliance.

The discussion of validation and compliance is of vital importance in the industry, for both ISOs and merchants. Compliance is a state of being in which an organization or individual adheres to a given set of standards. Validation, on the other hand, is substantiating to a third party that the individual or organization of concern is in compliance with the standard. In 2018, Visa mandated that all merchants, regardless of size, must validate compliance.

As an ISO that provides ancillary functions, the methods of validation may depend upon the "level" of the ISO. If the organization is determined to be a gateway or other type of service provider, then the ISO must validate compliance. Depending upon the number of transactions processed on an annual basis, that validation may take the form of an onsite security assessment by a Qualified Security

Assessor. A Qualified Security Assessor, commonly referred to as a QSA, is a data security professional that has been approved by the PCI SSC to conduct assessments against the PCI DSS. Additional methods of validation for service providers include quarterly network scans and completion of a Self-Assessment Questionnaire (SAQ).

HOW MUST MERCHANTS VALIDATE COMPLIANCE WITH THE PCI DSS?

The determination of how a merchant, or a service provider for that matter, must validate compliance is dependent upon two major factors; 1) the number of transactions per card brand that are pro-cessed on an annual basis; and 2) the channels through which the merchant accepts electronic payments. Looking first at the number of transactions processed, merchants are categorized according to the following levels:

Level	Transaction Numbers
1	6M or more transactions of any one card brand on an annual basis.
2	1M-6M transactions of any one card brand on an annual basis.
3	20,000 – 1M ecommerce transactions of any one card brand on an annual basis.
4	Less than 20,000 ecommerce transactions annually and all others processing fewer than 1M transactions annually.

All Level 1 merchants must validate compliance annually with an onsite assessment. The assessment may be conducted by either a QSA or an Internal Assessor may be used, provided an officer of the company signs the Report on Compliance (ROC), which is then submitted to the acquiring bank. In addition, Level 1 merchants must conduct quarterly network scans conducted by an Approved Scan Vendor (ASV).

All Level 2-4 merchants must validate compliance by conducting a SAQ and submitting an Attestation of Compliance (AOC) to its acquiring bank. The SAQ to be used, and the obligation to conduct quarterly scans, is dependent on the channel through which the merchant accepts payments. Accordingly, the chart below details which SAQs should be used in certain scenarios.

SAQ	Merchant description
A	ecommerce and mail order/telephone order (MOTO) merchants that have fully outsourced all cardholder data functions. The cardholder data functions must be carried out by a PCI DSS compliant service provider and the merchant must have no electronic storage of any cardholder data and must not store, process, or transmit cardholder data. This SAQ cannot be applied to card present merchants.
A-EP	Merchants that use a "redirected" payment page that is hosted by a PCI compliant service provider. Like SAQ A, merchants using this questionnaire must not store, process, or transmit cardholder data. These merchants, by hosting the "redirect" may impact the security of the transaction, and therefore are subject to a more comprehensive questionnaire.
B	Merchants that are using either imprint machine or dial-out terminals only and do not store electronic data. This is not applicable to ecommerce merchants. Such merchants are also not generally required to conduct quarterly scans.
B-IP	Merchants that are using a stand-alone payment terminal with an IP connection to a payment processor. The merchant must not have any electronic storage of cardholder data and the terminal must be PTS approved.
C-VT	Merchants that accept payments only through a virtual terminal. The merchant must not have any electronic storage of cardholder data. Additionally, the virtual terminal must be provided by a PCI DSS validated service provider.

C	Merchants that have payment applications systems that are connected to the internet. There must be no storage of cardholder data.
P2PE	Merchants that are using hardware terminals that are included in and managed through a validated P2PE solution. There must not be storage of cardholder data.
D	All other merchants must complete the SAQ D.

In addition to managing their own compliance, it is important for merchants to select PCI DSS compliant service providers, as well. A service provider is defined as any entity that stores, processes, or transmits cardholder data on behalf of another entity, whether that is a merchant, another processor or an acquiring bank. Service providers should not only validate compliance but should also register as a service provider with the card brands. Merchants should be sure to monitor the PCI DSS compliance status of their service provider in order to maintain their own compliance.

Like merchants, service providers must also validate compliance. Level 1 service providers, those that process more than 300,000 transactions annually of any one card brand, must have an onsite assessment conducted by a QSA. Service providers must also undergo penetration tests and conduct quarterly vulnerability scans.

HOW DO MERCHANTS REDUCE THEIR PCI DSS SCOPE?

Compliance with the PCI DSS can seem daunting, but there are ways to mitigate the resources required to achieve and maintain compliance throughout the year. Merchants are often advised to find a means to "reduce their scope." To understand that, there are some important terms that must be defined. First, what is scope? The PCI DSS is concerned with the protection of "cardholder data," which is defined as the Primary Account Number (PAN) and a handful of other data elements if they are stored in conjunction with the PAN. Any systems that store, process, or transmit cardholder data, and any systems that are connected to those systems comprise the Cardholder Data Environment (CDE). When a merchant is undergoing a PCI DSS assessment, whether via a QSA or the completion of the SAQ, the environment being assessed is the CDE. This is often referred to as either the scope or the CDE. Reducing the size of the CDE, or reducing the scope, allows the merchant to achieve and maintain compliance in a more cost-effective way. Additionally, by reducing the scope, and thereby the volume of valuable data in the environment, the merchant can mitigate liability associated with a compromise of its systems. As payment technology continues to evolve, the industry has seen several methods through which scope can be reduced.

Hosted payment pages

Hosted payment pages offer merchants a channel through which to offer their customers an online shopping experience, without introducing cardholder data into the merchant environment. In this scenario, the payment page is hosted by a registered, compliant service provider. The payment information is entered by the cardholder and posted directly to the service provider. In this way, the merchant is still able to accept payments online, but does not increase the size of its CDE.

Hosted payment pages can be served in a number of ways. A common implementation is the use of a redirect. In using a redirect, the merchant hosts some script on its page that sends the users' information directly to the payment provider. This allows the merchant to maintain significant control over the look and feel of the page and provides the most seamless customer experience. The drawback to this implementation is that the merchant's web servers, those systems that host the "redirect," are considered to be "in scope" for the purposes of the PCI DSS.

An alternative implementation allows the payment page to be presented via an i-Frame (essentially an HTML document that is embedded within another HTML document). This allows the merchant to control the page, but the payment form is presented and hosted by a registered, compliant service provider. This, too, may keep some merchant systems in scope, but allows for the data to be posted directly to the provider.

A less common approach to the hosted payment page is to have it exist wholly outside the merchant's environment. In such a configuration, the consumer would click on the "pay now" button and a separate page, hosted by the service provider, would open to allow the user to make a payment. This is the "purest" implementation of the hosted payment page because it completely circumvents the merchant's environment.

Tokenization

In this solution, the payment information is replaced with a randomly generated value that is used to represent the payment mechanism. The merchant can still use that token to process subsequent payments, and may be useful for patients on payment plans, reporting purposes, patient payment analysis, and chargeback or dispute purposes. The benefit here is the reduced payment data footprint within the organization.

Point to point encryption

Over the course of the last several years, the industry has learned that data in transit can be just as vulnerable to theft or compromise as data at rest. As such, the PCI DSS has comprehensive requirements around the protection of data in transit. One way to simplify these requirements is to implement a point to point encryption (P2PE) payment solution. A *P2PE* solution is one in which the cardholder data is encrypted from the point of interaction (swipe, dip, entry) all the way through the processor. The cardholder data does not traverse the merchant's systems because the only data passing through their environment is encrypted and the merchant has no means to decrypt that data. P2PE is most often implemented in conjunction with tokenization, as this allows for the protection of data in transit and at rest.

The PCI SSC and the card brands recognize the value of P2PE and tokenization solutions, and so have introduced a P2PE validation program. The use of validated P2PE solutions can result in significant scope reductions. It is important that, if a merchant is using a validated P2PE solution, the product implementation manual (PIM) is strictly followed. Failure to follow the PIM may negate any scope reduction benefits to the solution.

It is important to note that a merchant can never fully be out of scope, regardless of the payment technologies being used. By virtue of accepting payment cards, a merchant must always comply with the PCI DSS and must validate that compliance to their acquirer.

PAYMENT APPLICATIONS AND THEIR IMPACT ON COMPLIANCE

For the past several years, the PCI SSC has managed a standard for payment application security called the Payment Application Data Security Standard (PA DSS). The PCI SSC is now shifting that standard to a more comprehensive program, called the Secure Software Framework, which consists of a Secure Software Standard (SSS) and a Secure Software Lifecycle Standard (SSLC). While the PA DSS addressed payment applications that were sold, distributed or licensed to third parties, it did not apply to software systems that were deployed as a service. The new SSS will apply to SaaS payment applications.

The SSLC also applies to software vendors, but provides a framework for the management of their development processes. A software vendor that validates against this standard can self-assess portions of their SSS assessment, resulting in lower assessments costs for the vendors. The two standards are separate, but both work to address issues of security within the payment applications. It is important to note that the PCI SSC will be sunsetting the PA DSS validation in 2022, when the last of the PA DSS v 3.2 validations expire.

The underlying notion here is that compliance and security must address all elements of the payment ecosystem. This includes applications, hardware, people, and processes. The standards put in place by the councils and enforced by the Card Brands help to address each of these elements.

CONSEQUENCES OF NONCOMPLIANCE

Noncompliance with the PCI DSS can result in fines being levied from the card brands to the acquiring banks. The acquiring banks will then typically pass these fines to the merchants or service providers, as appropriate. Fines can range from $2,000 to $25,000 per month. While noncompliance penalties are severe, they pale in comparison to the financial liability associated with a compromise of cardholder data.

Egregious cases involving full magnetic stripe data can result in fines of up to $500,000 from Visa, and similar fines from the other major card brands. In addition to the fines, merchants and service providers may also be responsible for reimbursing the card issuers for fraudulent transactions as well as the costs associated with account monitoring and card re-issuance. In some cases, the cost of re-issuance can be as high as $25 per card.

It should be noted that these noncompliance consequences are only those that are associated with noncompliance with the PCI DSS. The payments industry is subject to a number of laws that also dictate data protection measures and breach notification. These measures encompass a variety of different data elements that are not addressed by the PCI DSS. Merchants and ISOs alike are well-served to analyze the types of data that are stored and how they are protected. Violations of the various state laws and statutes can quickly add to the financial burden associated with a data compromise.

BEYOND THE PRIMARY ACCOUNT NUMBER

One of the predominant methods of stemming the tide of identity theft and financial fraud is by protecting the data elements that can be used to perpetrate those crimes. The payment card industry addressed this issue with the creation and enforcement of the PCI DSS. It is important to note, though, that the standard addresses only one class of information that can be used to perpetrate financial crimes; that is cardholder data.

A variety of other laws create a category of data that can be described as "protected." This protected data must be afforded certain protections related to its storage and transmission. Data breach notification laws, which require entities that have exposed, or potentially have exposed, non-public personal information to notify affected individuals. In addition to the notification requirements, some of these laws also create an affirmative duty to protect the sensitive data that is collected and stored by the organization.

Some states, Massachusetts for example, have actually created new information security standards. Given the vast number of these laws, and the rate at which new ones are being passed, it is vital that organizations understand their obligations under the regulations. For example, California's data breach notification law applies to any organization doing business in the state, while the Massachusetts data breach notification and their attendant data security requirements apply to any organization that stores information on a single Massachusetts resident. These laws represent an important shift in creating an obligation on the part of companies to provide sufficient security protections to data that can be used to steal identities or perpetrate other financial crimes. More recently, though, the focus has shifted to the privacy of data, as opposed to focusing narrowly on the security of the data.

The California Consumer Privacy Act, or CCPA provides an excellent example of that shift. Guided by the international movement to protect data that can be used to identify and categorize individuals, states have begun to mandate privacy protections that give consumers greater control over the use of their personal information. Data privacy is a relatively new regulatory front for the United States. While the U.S. has focused on the security of data, many other countries have focused on privacy. Therefore, these laws do represent a shift in perspective and may require merchants and ISOs to reflect and revise their data practices.

COMPLIANCE VS. SECURITY

With such a strong focus on compliance and the various standards in the payments industry, it is easy to confuse the concepts of "compliance" and "security." Addressing security through compliance, however, can be a dangerous and expensive route. Compliance, as stated earlier, is a state of being in which an organization or individual adheres to a given set of standards. Security is much more of a moving target. Security is the implementation of protective measures (process, policies, and technologies) to address identified risks to data, as well as methods for identifying and addressing new vulnerabilities. Conceivably, an organization can be in a state of compliance without fully addressing security and it is even possible to be secure without being compliant. In fact, the PCI SSC has published a white paper entitled "Ten Common Myths of PCI Compliance," in which one of the myths listed states, "PCI will make us secure." It is vitally important to understand that security is a much broader discussion than compliance with the PCI DSS or the various regulatory requirements.

The mindset in which PCI compliance and security are synonymous offers another roadblock, as well. That roadblock is the one that suggests that cardholder data is the only data that must be protected. Those who feel that PCI DSS compliance makes the organization secure lose sight of the fact that the systems that support the payment card transaction often store much more than cardholder data. This other data often falls under the purview of various state laws. PCI DSS is only concerned with the protection of cardholder data, which is narrowly defined. The various state laws have a much broader definition of data, "non-public personal information," with which they are concerned, so organizations should be aware of all classifications of data within their environment and develop policies for classifying, protecting, and disposing of the data.

SUGGESTIONS FOR ADDRESSING COMPLIANCE AND SECURITY

An oft-heard refrain with respect to reducing the compliance burden is "remove, protect, comply." The first step is to remove data that the organization either does not need or should not be storing. This can be accomplished through a variety of means, including the use of hosted payment pages, tokenization or P2PE solutions. Whatever means are selected, the reduction of the cardholder footprint results in a smaller CDE, lower assessment costs, lower cost associated with managing and maintaining compliance, and, perhaps most important, mitigating the impact of a potential compromise.

Secondly, implement appropriate controls around the data that is stored. This includes policy, process and technology. Make sure that those items are documented and tested throughout the year. These controls should evolve along with the business. As the business model changes, the controls should be evaluated and changed as appropriate.

Third-party management is also an integral part of maintaining both security and compliance. Requirement 12.8 of the PCI DSS requires merchants to *"Maintain and implement policies and procedures to manage service providers with whom cardholder data is shared, or that could affect the security of cardholder data..."* This requirement is consistent with regulatory enforcement actions and is increasingly a part of federal regulatory examinations. The management of vendors to ensure that their processes for the protection of data are commensurate with that of the data owner is critical, for both compliance and security.

While a comprehensive discussion of the steps to compliance would be quite lengthy, a vital element that is often overlooked is the culture. Cultivating a compliance- or security-focused culture empowers employees to watch out for and to report potential threats to data that the traditional control framework may not detect. Ensure that employees are aware of their responsibilities for the protection of data and that they know how to appropriately report suspected security incidents.

CONCLUSIONS

Payment technology is evolving faster than ever. While that provides customers and businesses with a multitude of new opportunities, it can also provide some challenges with respect to compliance and security. Understanding how new technologies can impact an organization's security posture is crucial to maintaining compliance with both industry standard and with regulatory requirements. It is also important to stay current with any changes to the industry standards. The latest information on the PCI DSS and its related standards can be found at *www.pcisecuritystandards.org*. By understanding the minimum security requirements of the industry, as well as the regulatory obligations with respect to the protection of non-public personal data, organizations can minimize their risk of data compromise and its consequences. Additionally, having such an understanding as an ISO means that an organization can provide its merchants with insights and guidance as to how they can minimize their compliance and security burdens.

SECTION 2

ADVANCED TOPICS

CHAPTER 23
HIGH-RISK PROCESSING

CONTRIBUTING WRITER ALLAN LACOSTE

"You don't concentrate on risks.
You concentrate on results.

—Chuck Yeager

Every business, in person or online, needs payment processing services. Acceptance of credit cards is critical to developing or scaling a business' revenue stream. And for e-commerce sites, cash payments aren't an option at all. Unfortunately, some merchants find themselves in a high-risk category, making fees higher or, in some cases, making it difficult to get a merchant services account at all.

For businesses that need high-risk merchant services, working with an established processor can provide the best opportunity to secure payment processing at the best possible terms. At the same time, the processor needs to ensure that the integrity of the payment eco-system is upheld by protecting the end consumers who expect their purchases to be honored.

A company can fall into the high-risk group based on initial capital-ization, revenue concerns, previous fraud issues, lack of adequate risk management protocols, or even because of the business owner's poor personal credit. In general, banks evaluate these merchants by one of the three categories: credit risk, reputational risk and transactional risk. Let's break down what each means.

CREDIT RISK

A credit risk is the risk of default on a debt that may arise from a borrower failing to make required payments. Although acquiring banks don't advance funds, processing card transactions is like extending credit, as acquiring banks rely on a merchant's cred-itworthiness to pay for potential chargebacks. In circumstances where a merchant is unwilling or unable to pay for chargebacks, the acquiring bank would be on the hook for these amounts. A credit check typically weeds out businesses that are at risk.

TRANSACTIONAL RISK

Transactional risk occurs when there is a potential breakdown of the fulfillment of a good or a service. Simply put, if someone buys something, they should expect to receive it. This type of risk is more common with card-not-present transactions. In some cases, transactional risk arises from a consumer purchasing the rights to a future deliverable that cannot be fulfilled. Nobody wants to book a hotel, purchase a concert ticket or pre-order their favorite author's upcoming novel, only to later find out that the business cannot fulfill that order, for whatever reason.

REPUTATIONAL RISK

Reputational risk arises from the potential loss of capital resulting from damages to a business' reputation. Financially, a poor reputation can damage the company's brand image resulting in lost revenue, increased operational or regulatory costs, or loss of shareholder value. At Nuvei, we use a variety of sources that automatically crawl the public web and other databases to alert our Risk Department if certain businesses in our portfolio come up as a potential threat. Once the flag is raised, we investigate to determine our exposure. It's important to note, with words that spread like fire on social media, it doesn't take much to smear a company's name. With a single tweet that goes viral, a company with an otherwise sparkling image can be dragged through the digital mud, with real world consequences.

All it takes is a single bad actor such as a disgruntled employee or competitor to do the deed. Having these automated systems allows us to quickly avert any potential danger and, in some cases, our monitoring provides us with this information long before the actual merchant realizes that there is anything negative being said about them. Risk management is vital for every business.

OPPORTUNITIES ABOUND

Businesses placed in a high-risk category need to work with sophisticated organizations to be able to provide high risk merchant processing. As an ISO, being able to provide this service can help open incredible revenue streams. At Nuvei, we consider these "hard to place" accounts and try to avoid the label "high-risk".

As an agent or ISO, finding that right partnership is like striking gold. Business types often considered high-risk process a large amount of transactions or greater transaction volumes than standard merchants. Out of the gate, a business designated as high-risk pays more for their processing services. Depending on your reseller agreement, this can mean more money in your pocket at the end of each month. Let's explore these possibilities.

High transaction volumes

If a business is processing an unusually large number of trans-actions per month, say above $10,000, it usually raises a flag, especially if that business exceeds its approved monthly volume limits. Companies like affiliate or network marketing, direct sellers, memberships, magazine or other recurring subscriptions would fall under this category.

Processing limits act as a fail-safe for fraud, therefore the mer-chant's funds may be placed on hold, reserves increased or worse, the processor shuts down the account due to the risk factor involved. As a reseller, you may think this is counter-intuitive to the growth of the business. A processor that understands the nature of businesses with high volumes can work with you to help the merchant rather than hinder their growth.

Large ticket items

Luxury items, electronics, high end furniture, automobile repair, business to business (B2B) or business to government (B2G), credit repair agencies or travel and tour operators typically fall under this category. A single transaction can end up being thousands or tens of thousands of dollars. In these cases, the underwriting process requires special checks to ensure the business has a clean history, low chargebacks and a stable revenue stream.

Due to the financial risk involved with large ticket items, monthly transaction volumes may be capped for new merchants. However, by continuing to have a clean record, volume caps can be increased to accommodate for more credit card transactions.

eCommerce businesses face fraud due to the distance online trans-actions entail, but for big ticket items, reversals for fraud can create significant chargeback problems. Even beyond fraud itself, customer dissatisfaction with a product or service can lead to chargebacks.

WHAT IT MEANS TO BE HIGH-RISK

Unfortunately, payment processing risk does not include a spectrum of categories; merchant accounts are either high-risk or not. And regardless of how sound a business may become when it falls into the high-risk category, it will receive less favorable terms. Both the rates and the fees it is charged will be higher, and in some cases, it may mean difficulty in getting merchant services at all.

Not every processor is prepared to take on what amounts to riskier customers, and those that do may charge at very different levels to do so. However, for some of these business types, depending on their circumstances and goals, a high-risk designation may create advantages for the bottom line.

Pros: Higher top end for revenue & greater operational freedom

For some high-risk businesses, the processing services can provide benefits unavailable with traditional payment processing. Depending on the circumstances and the business goals, a high-risk label can create advantages for their bottom line.

The freedom to earn more is only part of the equation. High-risk businesses also avoid some of the intense monitoring that lower risk businesses face. Because risk categorization comes largely from chargeback potential, companies deemed low-risk must be careful to avoid problems that can shift them into the higher risk category. More than one percent of transaction volume being charged back can lead to a higher risk designation that sends fees higher or even forces a company to shop for a new payment processing provider.

High-risk businesses, while still needing to be careful to avoid the costs of chargebacks, do not face this ongoing challenge. They are already placed in that category and can instead focus on driving transaction volume. More transactions may create more chargebacks, but the result is higher revenue without fees increasing along the way.

A business that avoids risky transactions or industries will be charged less for payment processing. Still, that hurdle may prove small for high-risk businesses with models that maximize sales volume and generate high revenue. Over time, the high-risk designation should not prevent solid companies from processing transactions and operating successfully.

Cons: Higher reserves required & higher fees for services

Beyond the start-up costs and fees, high-risk businesses often face higher reserve requirements than more traditional, low-risk companies would face. This comes at a different inflection point than the fees, because reserves are money that still belongs to the business in question. But the reserves typically roll over time, with the funds not accessible for the company for months on end. While ordinarily the money represents profits a business owner can either pocket, use to pay employees raises or bonuses, or use to invest back into the organization, reserves must remain untouched as a buffer against default or chargebacks.

Of course, one potential upside here is that it forces the company to manage finances in a way that provides more margin. Over time, these reserves do become available, essentially working as a savings line for high-risk businesses. Liquidity is usually better, but it does build in a need to manage finances carefully for these companies.

High-risk businesses include companies with a risk of defaults and chargebacks for a variety of reasons. Online businesses, for example, carry greater risk of stolen payment methods from which funds must be reimbursed. And some kinds of companies like travel agencies have higher payment cancellations than others, placing the chargeback risks even higher. Payment processing providers often either refuse to work with companies at these risk levels or charge amounts to help cover the risk.

UNDERWRITING REQUIREMENTS AND APPROVAL PROCESS

Underwriters need to collect detailed information to determine whether the prospective merchant and its principals pose a risk to the processor and the payments ecosystem in general. This includes:

- Background checks to verify the validity of the business, ensure the application is being made by the principal business owners, and to determine the length of time the merchant has been in business.

- Government issued photo ID for all signers on the agreement.

- Financial details or tax returns, plus a credit check to measure the merchant's financial stability and ensure there are minimal potential credit challenges.

- Review of the business' operations including data security, chargeback handling, along with refund and exchange procedures.

- Proof of inventory on hand and fulfillment agreement or process.

- Business model documents and marketing materials, including live website URL.

NO DEAL LEFT BEHIND

Let's examine some business types that are considered high-risk that represent great opportunities for both merchant account resellers and the processors that accept these accounts.

Example 1: Nutraceuticals

Nutraceuticals are beverages and food that contain a functional medicinal element. The industry is already huge, and growing rapidly; products like sports nutrition PowerBar, with annual sales of $130 million, and Balance nutrition bars, with annual sales of $100 million, have mainstream footholds in the United States. These are just scratching the surface of the potential for an industry expected to achieve a CAGR of 11.95% from 2018 to 2023.

The opportunity that nutraceuticals present is huge. Consumers looking to gain medicinal benefits from drinks, food, snacks, and supplements have more options than ever. Grand View Research estimates that by 2025, the market for these products will reach $578.23 billion. As consumers become more health-conscious, demand for nutraceuticals will continue to surge.

Even so, there are risks that come with these kinds of products. Any time a company makes health-based claims, it faces regulatory scrutiny from the United States government. If a nutraceutical is found to be making fraudulent or unfounded claims about what it does, it risks being pulled from the market. Further, because many of these products are sold directly online, they face higher risks of returns and identity theft, which put in danger the payments they receive and the fees they generate for the processing.

Because payment processors categorize customers at times based on market space as much as individual credit concerns, the nutraceuticals industry for most companies falls into the high-risk merchant processing category. This broad brush prevents some processing providers from serving the industry at all. For others, it means requiring higher fees or establishing other protections against lost fees. The nutraceuticals industry provides a key example of where opportunity and risk tolerance collide. Payment processing companies and sales professionals who find flexible and creative approaches can generate high revenue by serving these and other clients in the high-risk merchant processing category.

Example 2: Network marketing

According to some experts like Erik Christian Johnson, the network marketing industry already encompasses nearly $180 billion. This number may seem shockingly high if you've never heard of network marketing before, but it has spread its wings rapidly, and it is quickly becoming the second easiest way to get a business up and running – nipping at the heels of the franchise movement.

You can find network marketing opportunities that cover a wide spectrum of products and services from cosmetics and nutrition supplements to custom bath products and food storage. When it works, network marketing gives entrepreneurs a strong sense of stability with residual payments appearing in their account every month. Instead of working for one-time sales or a single commission payout, most of these new business owners can build portfolios of clients that pay overtime, and easily ramp up their business via online networking tools and strategies.

The one thing that many entrepreneurs love about network marketing is that it requires very little cash to get started. Unlike purchasing a franchise, most of these opportunities do not require a minimum net worth or a significant payout of cash up front. There is no time or money spent on building a location or infrastructure. Therefore, the risk involved is minimal for the agent. Instead, most of the risk falls on the side of the banks and payment processors who are handling the financials behind the scenes.

There have been some major cases of fraud within the network marketing industry in the last several years, and it is not uncommon for customers to report their purchases as fraudulent or to ask for refunds after they have bought in. This has led to excessive chargebacks and fees for some network marketers and has left payment processors to evaluate what level of risk they are willing to take with those in the industry. Nevertheless, with so much money on the line, somebody must be responsible for processing those payments and proper vetting is usually enough to minimize risk to the financial institutions involved.

The payment processing sector has initiated several safety precautions to protect against fraud in this industry as well. For instance, ensuring that the company, the agent and the bank account are all within the US helps reduce fraud. In addition, keeping a rolling reserve protects against unexpected spikes in chargebacks and other issues. For entrepreneurs, getting started with network marketing is easy and fun. It can open a whole world of possibilities while exposing them to minimal personal risk. In the meantime, they are still counting on payment processors to help them manage their finances as they build their customer list and start earning regular payments.

Example 3: Debt collection

Some companies face more difficulty than others in setting up payment processing services. In some cases, the business owner's personal credit or the newness of the business itself places it in a high-risk category. But for others, the placement comes strictly due to the industry in which they operate. Debt collectors are one such example. While these companies generally work carefully to perform a service critical to lenders, they generally fall into the high-risk merchant accounts category. Due to the nature and reputation of the business, debt collectors face some difficulty establishing processing services.

Some bad actors undoubtedly exist in the debt collection industry. One need only perform a cursory search online to find horror stories of people receiving harassing calls every day for debts that may or may not exist. While these represent the minority of collection companies, they also lead to the loudest voices of protest and to a reputation that most debt collectors do not deserve.

As a by-product of the reputational concerns, debt collectors face a litany of regulations that affect whether and how they can do business. These shifts, depending on politics, timing, and other factors, lend uncertainty to the entire business model collectors use. This uncertainty makes some financial institutions wary of doing business with them and pushes the collection agencies into high-risk merchant accounts when they can find service providers.

Beyond reputation, the nature of who pays debt collectors creates problems as well. A merchant operating a retail business can typically establish a regular revenue flow, with an expectation of a certain number of customers and a sales average that holds over time. For debt collectors, though, the entire business consists of collecting on payments from debtors who have had difficulty paying what they owe.

It is not unusual for a debtor to make and then cancel payment arrangements, block or revoke payments from their own banks, and dodge additional collection efforts. This creates difficulties in three ways. First, it makes the revenue stream for the debt collectors irregular, and at times unreliable. Collecting on any individual accounts takes time and may prove impossible. Doing this for every account makes the business model too unstable for some banks. Second, it leads to chargebacks and transactions that may have to be canceled, reversed, re-submitted, and run through multiple paths.

The administrative costs add to the collection uncertainty to push banks into requiring high-risk merchant accounts, even if they do approve them. Finally, collection work provides a high-stress environment. Collection agents often deal with unhappy or angry debtors, creating work conditions that lead to high turnover in the position. Many collection agencies struggle to keep a regular staff and may have trouble maintaining enough employees to remain in business. The uncertainty leads to an assumption that this kind of company is unstable.

The factors that go into the rating debt collectors ultimately lead some financial institutions and underwriters to refuse the accounts altogether. For others, they get automatically slotted into high-risk merchant accounts. Even so, some institutions and service providers are willing to take a chance on debt collection agencies.

Working with an organization willing to look at the individual agency beyond the industry stigma allows debt collectors to obtain payment processing services and run their businesses properly.

Example 4: Travel & tourism

When we think of high risk merchant processing, the industries that come to mind are typically gambling, adult content, and services, businesses based on subscriptions and start-ups that haven't been in existence for long. Travel and tourism are also very often considered high-risk merchants, however, partly because it's so easy for customers to dispute credit card charges.

- *Reason #1: Companies go out of business* – Most travel purchases are made in advance of delivering the product, and this creates a substantial time window in which a chargeback can occur. Travel operators are often small companies with short histories in business. If a customer pays for a trip a year in advance and then the travel operator goes out of business, the customer files a claim and the merchant provider is required to refund the payment.

- *Reason #2: Disappointed customers* – When clients purchase a product or service without being able to actually "see and feel" it, there's always a risk of disappointment when they finally receive it. There's no way to predict a client could be affected by an airline strike, for example, or experience cancellation of that tour of Rome they purchased with the credit card. When this happens, the client demands their money back from the operators, which incurs a chargeback on the account.

- *Reason #3: The fraud angle* – Travel options such as event tickets and tourist attractions are a popular scam for fraudsters. Tickets are bought with stolen credit cards and then resold at a discount for cash. When the cardholder discovers the fraudulent purchase, he is likely to demand a refund of the amount, resulting in a chargeback that could take weeks to resolve. Airlines already face a substantial risk of losses from chargebacks caused by "friendly" fraud.

Some payment processors accept travel and tourism merchants despite being labeled high-risk. Companies that show stability through bank statements and a sound credit history have an advantage, as do travel businesses that have a risk-management policy in place. This mostly applies to companies opening their first payment processing account, because there's no record of previous performance.

Travel operators that are switching processors are less likely to be refused an account because they can show a prior chargeback record. In some instances, processors accept high-risk merchant processing provided the merchants pay higher fees. These can be reduced later once the merchant has shown evidence of lower-than-anticipated chargeback risks.

FINDING THE RIGHT PAYMENT GATEWAY

When it comes to finding the right processing partner that accepts hard to place merchant accounts, matching up your clients with the right payment gateway provider is important. There are many gateway features to consider, but the ones below should be your minimum requirements.

Multi-currency acquiring capabilities

The right international banking relationships can provide lower costs and greater acceptance when processing payments globally. Multi-currency acquiring benefits merchants by allowing them to capture and settle in multiple currencies without requiring them to open a foreign bank account or set up foreign infrastructure such as an office or distribution center. In evaluating a payment gateway, look for one that has optimized or smart transaction routing. This can reduce risk and costs associated with international sales.

Multi-currency pricing

A global payment gateway can help open more growth possibilities when selling products and services in different countries and regions, plus it provides the added benefit of minimizing costs and improving authorization rates. Another factor is integrating a multi-currency solution into the payment mix. Providing online shoppers with pricing they can understand can improve client satisfaction by offering a "local" shopping experience and reduces chargebacks by avoiding currency exchange surprises.

ACH Payments

Automated Clearing House (ACH) or eCheck (electronic check) payments offer a secure, reliable and fast way to transfer funds directly from a client's bank account. It's an ideal, cost-effective alternative to credit card payments that can also help to reduce transactional risk. Compared to a wire transfer, ACH transfers are also more cost-efficient. Gym memberships, magazine subscriptions and network marketing companies who rely on recurring billing benefit from the ACH option.

Integrated risk management

Every company has a different risk management need depending on the business model. However, a processor with an in-house risk management solution can empower businesses with more customized fraud screening adapted to their specific needs. Regardless of merchant type, addressing fraudulent activity and chargebacks is vital.

KEEPING YOUR MERCHANTS' NOSES CLEAN

Regardless of the risk analysis and risk mitigation put in place by the processor, it's always important to ensure that your merchant has a handle on PCI compliance and the chargeback management process.

It is in your best interest to help your merchants maintain a PCI Compliant status. This helps to reduce risk of a data breach which may lead to the compromise of sensitive cardholder information. Merchants that do not comply with PCI DSS may be subject to fines, card replacement costs, costly forensic audits, brand damage, etc., should a breach event occur. For a little upfront effort and cost to comply with PCI, you greatly help reduce your risk from facing these extremely unpleasant and costly consequences.

Becoming PCI compliant

You need to complete a Self-Assessment Questionnaire (SAQ). The SAQ consists of 60-100 questions that will help you understand correct PCI processes on intuitive level management programs. Finding a processor that provides a managed PCI compliance process is important. All this is done in order to safeguard against data breaches that could expose sensitive information and lead to serious repercussions, both in monetary damages and in reputation.

Chargeback management

Being organized is crucial in fighting chargebacks successfully. Below are a few basic suggestions to provide to your merchant in order to reduce potential chargebacks.

- Provide excellent customer service. It will help prevent unhappy customers from filing chargebacks. If the issue is resolved quickly and efficiently, the customer will have no reason to file the chargeback.
- Pay attention to technical aspects of the process. Promptly void or refund duplicate transactions, use correct expiration dates, and process refunds for returns and cancellations on time.
- Describe products and services in detail on your website.

- Track and keep proof or confirmation of deliveries for each sale. Invest in chargeback management training for your employees who process payments daily.

- Submit documentation within the time period indicated on the chargeback notification. This is very important because if it's not done, the chargeback case is automatically lost by the merchant.

The chargeback mechanism is great when it comes to protecting cardholders. The unpleasant part for a business owner is when a fraudulent transaction takes place or an unethical cardholder uses the chargeback process to get a refund or to game the system, the liability is on the merchant. Having an effective chargeback management program in place is a must to reduce revenue loss and keep a company's chargeback rate well under 1%.

In the end, servicing a diversified range of merchants, some who fall under the low-risk category and some who can be considered high-risk, can be a measure of a healthy portfolio. Building and maintaining the right processing relationship is paramount to long-term success. It is also beneficial to help every one of your customers leverage best payment processing practices and fraud reduction tools. It not only improves the client experience but can help reduce attrition.

CHAPTER 24
PAYMENT FACILITATORS

CONTRIBUTING WRITER TODD ABLOWITZ

The payments landscape is transforming rapidly, fueled by factors such as globalization and technology that are changing how people expect to shop and pay. Disruptive providers such as software-as-a-service (SaaS) companies, marketplaces and commerce platforms have stepped in to upend the legacy payments system, using technology to connect buyers and sellers in new and innovative ways.

The experiences consumers have had with companies like Amazon have increasingly led them to expect a seamless buying experience in any environment, and this expectation is driving change across the entire payment ecosystem. This evolution in what consumers want is leading many providers to re-evaluate the way they do business. It has even reached B2B software companies and SaaS providers across every imaginable vertical and/or category that touch the payment function.

These companies have dabbled in payments for many years through partnerships with integrated payments companies, driving significant referral revenue. Meanwhile, since 2011, companies like Shopify and Toast have been gaining far more substantial revenue and enormous valuations by becoming payment facilitators (PFs). As these case studies virally propagate through the tech community, more and more of these companies are becoming PFs, not only extending payments to their merchant customers, but offering quick and easy boarding and simplified pricing along the way.

What's more, these companies are discovering the improved customer experience and many new ways to deliver more value to their users to drive millions of dollars in new revenue through offering payments.

PF TRANSACTION VOLUME

IN $US BILLIONS. EXCLUDING PAYPAL, STRIPE, & SQUARE.

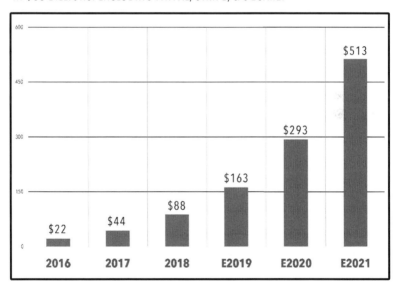

PF REVENUE

IN $US BILLIONS. EXCLUDING PAYPAL, STRIPE, & SQUARE.

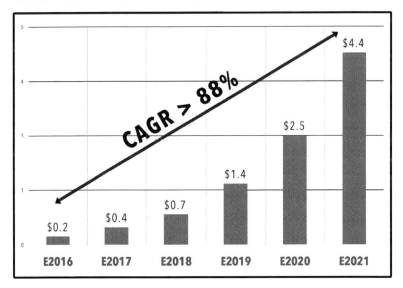

WHAT IS A PAYMENT FACILITATOR?

Traditionally, merchants have accepted payments through relationships with merchant acquirers, which are typically banks or bank-sponsored firms such as independent sales organizations (ISOs) that specialize in offering payment acceptance services.

Acquirers receive the merchant's card transactions, pass them to the appropriate card networks for processing and facilitate settlement of the transactions between the merchants and the card-issuing banks.

For merchants, obtaining accounts through traditional acquirers could be a complex, time-consuming process; it could take weeks to obtain an account. Underwriting was an extensive process geared to the needs of large merchants. Applications contained the same questions whether you were planning to process hundreds of thousands in sales a month, or were a small startup hoping to process a few thousand in a year or two. Contracts were detailed and complicated.

The ancestors of the PF model emerged in the 70s and 80s in floral delivery and petroleum as centralized merchants with accounts who managed the card acceptance, collecting settlement centrally through a single merchant account and then passing funds to each location. Then on the internet in the late 1990s, companies leveraged this model to assist small to medium-sized businesses in more easily accepting online payments; however, this model was against card network rules at that time. The first rules started to emerge in the early 2000s with the creation of the Internet Payments Service Provider (IPSP) – a precursor of the PF model we have today.

Today, PFs eliminate the need for individual merchants to establish their own merchant accounts. The business seeking to become a PF applies for an account with an acquiring bank and a processor, which will be referred to collectively here as a sponsor. Typically, the PF is underwritten by the sponsor, and when approved completes a contract and integrates into the sponsor's technology stack. The PF then uses this merchant account to facilitate payments on behalf of its sub merchants – sellers that use the PF's account to send transactions to the card networks rather than seeking their own.

The PF model provides several benefits for those involved. The sponsor benefits from processing the PF's aggregate payments volume. The PF collects the discount rate from the sub merchant, and then pays a wholesale rate on payment processing. Of course, fees are also charged on ancillary items such as returns and chargebacks, but often PFs go to market with a very simple pricing approach, which has proven popular with sub merchants.

The PF benefits from overall control over the experience it provides for its customers. For example, an integrated software vendor (ISV) might decide that payments are such an integral part of the customer experience that it wants to own more of the payments value chain. This can ultimately lead to more control over the onboarding and overall processing experience, higher merchant conversion rates, an increase in addressable market, and the opportunity to earn more revenue from credit card processing.

Because providing a fully seamless payment experience through the PF model improves a company's overall business fundamentals in these meaningful ways, it will necessarily also improve its market valuation. Typical valuations for PFs range from 18 to 22 times EBITDA, but some examples have gone far higher, as evidenced by the purchase price of Braintree, the private valuations of Stripe and Toast, and the public valuations of Square and Shopify.

And of course, for many small and medium-sized businesses, the PF model makes accessing payments services easier and more streamlined. They can begin accepting payments within an hour of applying, rather than days or weeks. Their payments are integrated into other business processes, eliminating the need to look to multiple providers and cobble together multiple systems to suit their needs.

WHAT ARE PAYMENT FACILITATORS RESPONSIBLE FOR?

PFs operate in cooperation with their sponsor(s), card networks, and the regulators who oversee the payments system. All these entities share a responsibility to protect the security and safety of the payment ecosystem, and PFs are a unique operating category with their own associated requirements.

The greatest challenge for a PF is the level of responsibility it must assume as part of enabling its sub merchants to access this system. This includes liability for fraud and chargebacks incurred by its sub merchants. Each sponsor has at minimum a set of requirements for the PF to follow the legal and regulatory framework, plus each sponsor's unique set of requirements. On top of that, the PF may choose to be even more restrictive, for risk mitigation or other business reasons. The best example is the list of merchant types the PF chooses to serve. Many PFs dramatically reduce their risk by serving a single vertical or a few verticals that are inherently low-risk and that they understand extremely well.

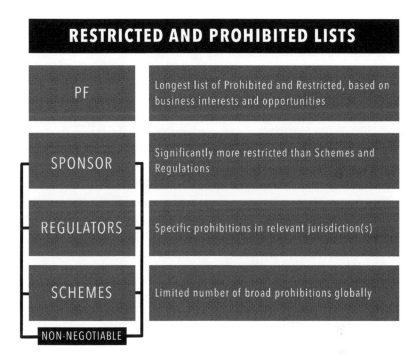

RESTRICTED AND PROHIBITED LISTS

PF	Longest list of Prohibited and Restricted, based on business interests and opportunities
SPONSOR	Significantly more restricted than Schemes and Regulations
REGULATORS	Specific prohibitions in relevant jurisdiction(s)
SCHEMES	Limited number of broad prohibitions globally

NON-NEGOTIABLE

The PF must also protect the payments system against data breaches by maintaining a secure environment and ensuring that its sub merchants are meeting their security responsibilities. It must comply with card network and regulator rules, and it must be certified as a PCI Level 1 or Level 2 service provider. It must maintain the resources it needs to build or buy appropriate payments technology.

Card brand rules require the sponsor to monitor the PF's compliance with operating rules and regulations and ensure due diligence when boarding and overseeing sub merchants.

Government regulations laid out by the Bank Secrecy Act and the USA PATRIOT Act require businesses to follow certain practices to avoid facilitating criminal activity, even inadvertently. Together, these regulations form the backbone of anti-money laundering efforts in the U.S.

The government regulations are supported by card brand rules that provide direction on PFs' specific roles and responsibilities. In September 2018, the Electronic Transactions Association (ETA), along with Double Diamond Group, published the Payment Facilitator Guidelines, a comprehensive set of operational guidelines helping clarify and formalize many of the important roles of the PF. These roles fall primarily into a few categories:

Onboarding

When onboarding sub merchants, PFs must perform the underwriting needed to verify that their customers are who they say they are, they are in the business they claim, they are not listed on the card networks' Member Alert to Control High Risk Merchants (MATCH) and they are not sanctioned by the Office of Foreign Asset Control (OFAC) for ties to crime or terrorism. "Know Your Customer" (KYC) practices and OFAC screening are critical practices for PFs.

Transaction monitoring

Once the sub merchants are onboarded, the work isn't over. PFs are responsible to implement systems they can use to monitor their sub merchants' transaction activity to watch for suspicious behavior and report it if needed.

Payouts

Depending on the business arrangement, the PF may also be responsible for paying the sub merchants and reconciling every day. Many PFs seek to control sub merchant funding in a bid to better manage that experience. PFs who wish to put themselves into the process must be prepared to take on the risk and compliance aspects of doing so. They must put appropriate processes and procedures, as well as accounting and compliance teams, into place.

This requires PFs to adhere to banking regulations, comply with card brands and government agencies such as FinCEN, abide by state-by-state licensing and regulations, and deal with tax and insurance implications. It also opens the potential of needing to adhere to money transmitter laws.

However, best-in-class sponsors have put together a payout structure to allow PFs to more easily comply with their responsibilities. For example, the sponsors often have payout APIs and/or an underlying banking structure to prevent the PF from owning the settlement funds, simplifying the process greatly. This is an essential part of the process.

Technology and Tools

While the many responsibilities of a PF may appear scary and certainly daunting, especially for a software company that has never owned payments operations, there are many tools that can help, including a new class of technology that has sprung up to simplify and automate these functions. PFs can leverage a wide variety of payment gateways and tokenization providers that reduce PCI scope and provide rich functionality for almost any vertical focus.

Much like how payment gateways originally bridged the technology gap between ecommerce merchants and processors starting in the nineties, a PF middleware platform like Infinicept automates operations functions, without requiring the PF to spend 12-18 months developing custom tools. The key components of a PF middleware platform include a flexible new account onboarding system that should have a white-labeled sub merchant application, instant automated KYC, OFAC, MATCH and underwriting, a dashboard for manual review of exceptions, and provisioning of the processor and the gateway. These platforms must have an effective and compliant transaction monitoring system. The PF needs a back-office system for performing fee calculation, reporting, funding, chargeback and funding exception management, as well as a user-friendly sub merchant portal for communicating all these activities with the sub merchant.

PAYMENT FACILITATORS VS. ISOS — WHAT IS THE DIFFERENCE?

Before the advent of PFs, acquirers often relied on ISOs to sell and sometimes service small merchants. While both models serve as an extension of the sponsor and provide merchant processing services on the acquirer's behalf, they're not the same thing. Here are a few of the ways they are different:

Agreement	2 Party Agreements Allowed (PF <-> Sub merchant)	The sponsor must be on the agreement. The ISO is sometimes also a party to the agreement (3-party agreement).
Funding	The PF may perform funding from a bank account owned and/or controlled by the PF.	The ISO is not allowed to touch funds. Settlement must be directly from the sponsor to the merchant.
Liability	PFs usually have liability for the merchant risk.	Wholesale ISOs have liability for the merchant risk. Retail ISOs and agents do not have liability.
Ownership of Portfolio	PFs own the portfolio of sub merchants.	Varies by contract.
Portability	PFs have portability (they can move their portfolio from one sponsor to another at will).	Varies by contract.
Merchant Application	PFs create the sub merchant application within parameters set by the sponsor.	Varies by sponsor, but most ISOs must use the sponsor's merchant application.
Onboarding	PFs perform the tasks required for underwriting and onboarding based on broad requirements as agreed with the sponsor.	Varies by sponsor, but most ISOs have strict requirements for how onboarding must be performed.
Ongoing Risk Monitoring	PFs perform ongoing monitoring and oversight of sub merchants.	Varies by ISO.

WHO ARE PAYMENT FACILITATORS?

There are only a few hundred businesses that are registered with the card networks as PFs in the United States. Businesses that choose to become PFs often fall into one of two categories, software vendors or commerce platforms.

Business-to-business software vendors

Business-to-business software providers, often known as ISVs, sell a wide range of software to businesses. These might include enterprise accounting and billing systems or specific vertical market applications such as medical practice, nonprofit, or hospitality solutions. ISVs have an opportunity to capitalize on trends and generate new revenue streams by embedding payment acceptance into the software they provide to their clients.

Commerce platforms

These platforms enable payments acceptance through their proprietary technology on a white label basis. The platform owns the sub merchants, performs the underwriting and oversight, controls the payment flows and is responsible for paying out funds to its sub merchants directly.

CONCLUSION

The massive growth of software and SaaS platforms has attracted enormous investment, and the large valuations that result from incorporating the PF model into those platforms has been fueling tremendous attention to the PF model since 2016. The payments industry has reacted by evolving the sponsor and third-party ecosystem to provide the essential knowledge, structure and tools that have turned that attention into adoption and growth beginning in 2018 and 2019. Experts expect that evolution to accelerate in the next few years, resulting in tens of thousands of PFs around the world, which will lead to hundreds of millions of new acceptors of electronic payments.

CHAPTER 25
SURCHARGING

CONTRIBUTING WRITERS MICHAEL TOMKO AND EVAN WEESE

America's payments marketplace is home to many "firsts"—including the first card networks established and the largest card volume processed. But there is one superlative American merchant would prefer to change: The United States has the single most expensive interchange pricing in the world.

Despite increasing economies of scale, and decreases in interchange in other countries, the cost of card acceptance continues to rise for businesses in the U.S. From 2012 to 2018, the total interchange fees levied by Visa and Mastercard in the U.S. went up by a shocking 77%.

Globally, reductions in interchange fees have largely been driven by *direct regulatory intervention*—whether in the form of new laws, regulatory threats, or government-led industry agreements—an approach that many believe is ill-suited to American free market principles.

Yet the landmark 2017 case in *Expressions Hair Design v. Schneiderman*, coupled with modifications to merchant contracts with the card brands, have created a market-driven option for cost reduction: credit card surcharging.

HOW SURCHARGING WORKS

Credit card surcharging has seen significant adoption within the U.S. in recent years. This model, in which a fee is added to credit card transactions to offset the cost of payment acceptance, allocates the costs associated with a payment to the cardholder who chooses to pay by credit.

To understand the surcharging model, consider a hypothetical purchase of $100.00 in goods.

If the customer chooses to use a credit card for convenience or rewards, the costs associated with that choice are added to the transaction, typically as a percentage fee (e.g., 3.5%). On the surcharging model, the customer would pay the costs created by the choice to use a credit card (in this case $3.50) and the merchant would receive the full sale amount of $100.00.

If the customer instead chose to pay by cash, check, or debit card (which is generally much less expensive to accept than a credit card), there would be no fee charged. Rather, the merchant would pay the cost of cash or check handling, or the relatively low cost of debit card acceptance (as required by the card brand rules).

PRICE PRESSURE AND PAYMENT ACCEPTANCE OPTIONS

The primary motivation for businesses to pass on their credit card fees to customers is simple: they need to manage costs.

When reviewing the list of top verticals for credit card surcharging, which includes auto repair, wholesale distribution, law, medicine, accounting, insurance, recurring membership billing, and home contractors, a clear pattern emerges: businesses in industries with low margins and high average tickets have embraced this option.

Each business faces different challenges in managing card processing costs. In wholesale distribution, for example, profit margins are often in the single digits and, if a customer chooses to pay by commercial credit card, the distributor's profits may be eliminated entirely. Auto repair shops often voice frustration that their customers receive insurance checks to cover repair costs yet demand card payment options that may result in hundreds of dollars of fees. Law firms are accustomed to charging clients for all of their quantifiable expenses, such as printing materials or sending documents by courier, and payments costs are no different.

In each case, however, the businesses face the same fundamental choice. They can (1) absorb the cost of credit card acceptance and suffer reduced profitability; (2) raise prices across the board, which affects all their customers, not just the customers choosing to pay by credit card; (3) refuse to accept credits cards at all; or (4) pass on credit card fees to their customers.

Businesses are choosing the fourth option—credit card surcharging—for many reasons: they are unwilling or unable to reduce profitability to accommodate their customer's preferred method of payment; raising costs across the board is likely to make them less competitive; and they risk losing customers if they don't provide the option to pay by card, especially as an *increasing share of customers use cards as their primary or sole method of payment.*

CONSUMER FAIRNESS

In addition to helping businesses reduce costs, the introduction of credit card surcharging has been lauded by consumer fairness advocates. This support may be surprising to many observers, who are more accustomed to seeing added fees as profit centers for business, but the reality is that surcharging allocates existing costs, rather than creating new ones, and does so within a framework that ensures consumer protection.

In the U.S., credit card surcharging is governed by a robust set of rules designed by the card brands to make this payment model straightforward and fair to cardholders. Businesses that surcharge must register with the card brands, must apply surcharges across the card brands on the same terms, must charge fees only to credit cards (and not to debit cards), must make all the necessary disclosures, and must comply with a number of other requirements. These rules ensure the customers are not surprised by the surcharge, that the surcharge fees do not become an additional profit center for the business, and that customers continue to have a "no-fee" card payment option in the form of debit.

The card brand rules ensure fairness at the level of individual transactions, and the overall market shift towards credit card surcharging creates more fairness for consumers overall. A Federal Reserve Bank of Boston study found that the average rewards card user is subsidized by over $1,100 per year by other consumers paying by cash, check, or debit, who are often using those payment methods because they are underbanked or do not have access to credit. In this sense, the conventional merchant-absorbed payments model in the U.S. is a regressive tax.

This fairness concern has rallied support across the political spectrum for the surcharging model. Conservative think tanks like the Cato Institute advocate for free speech and open communication about pricing, while liberal consumer protection advocates like Elizabeth Warren criticize the merchant-absorbed model in which *"first-class upgrades from frequent flier miles are subsidized by food stamp recipients."*

Surcharging ensures businesses don't have to raise costs for all of their customers to cover the costs of those choosing to use credit cards, while still ensuring that their customers are able to pay in as many ways as possible. This model, while new in the card payments space, is a key feature of emerging payment methods, including Bitcoin and the majority of blockchain technologies, in which the party initiating payment bears the costs associated with making that payment.

MARKET EVOLUTION AND MOMENTUM FOR CHANGE

The rules for credit card surcharging were first introduced to the American market in 2013, and momentum for passing on transaction fees accelerated in 2017 when the *U.S. Supreme Court ruled 8-0 that state "no-surcharge" laws restrict constitutionally protected speech*. This momentous decision led California, Florida, New York, and Texas, four states in which over 40% of the U.S. population lives, to allow surcharging for the first time, leading to even more merchant adoption of this model.

The payments industry has eagerly responded to these regulatory developments, as passing on the credit card fee provides a differentiated and higher-margin alternative to conventional "interchange-plus" pricing models. With surcharging, acquirers are able to offer payments solutions that increase their profit margins without the risk that their merchants switch to a competitor who promises to lower their rates, since the merchant is already accepting credit cards at no cost to their business.

Amidst the enthusiasm for passing on credit card fees, many payments providers have been insufficiently attentive to the rules. Credit card surcharging has been introduced to the American market through the adoption of new rules, and the market continues to be shaped by compliance demands. Many payments providers who attempted to evade the card brand rules and add illegitimate fees (often fallaciously marketed as "cash discount") soon found that the card brands and processors are paying close attention, swiftly shutting down merchants who violate the rules. In October 2018, Visa issued a bulletin reinforcing that merchants that add a fee at the point of sale must comply with Visa's contractual requirements for surcharging, regardless of what merchants call the fee.

The rules for credit card surcharging ensure consumer fairness, but also create a set of requirements that merchants, and acquirers are almost universally unable to meet without the assistance of a technology provider that automates compliance. As the market for passing on fees has continued to expand, many payments companies have recognized that the best strategy for long-term compliance and sustainable growth is partnership with established technology companies focused exclusively on surcharging, as they are able to automatically manage all of the regulatory requirements and provide a turnkey solution for payments professionals to sell to merchants.

THE AMERICAN MODEL

The model for credit card surcharging adopted in the U.S. both responds to the unique demands of the American market and provides a strong model for global leadership going forward.

At a time when other markets are struggling to *encourage electronic payment adoption*, seeing banks reintroduce various fees to compensate for excessively stringent interchange caps, and attempting to improve the consumer friendliness of their card acceptance methods, the U.S. has introduced a transparent, market-driven, and pro-competitive approach to cost reduction.

As credit card surcharging continues its explosive growth within the U.S., it will transform the American market and set an example for the payments market worldwide.

CHAPTER 26
SELLING CASH DISCOUNTING

CONTRIBUTING WRITER JAMES SHEPHERD

I distinctly remember my first month as a merchant sales professional. I recall walking into one merchant location after another, asking for statements and closing deals. What stood out to me was how merchants believed credit card processing was important. But to them, it was important in the same way their electric service was important. It needs to work, but they don't want to think about it unless there is an opportunity to cut costs.

I quickly learned how I could leverage technology to change the nature of my value proposition for some merchants. However, no matter how hard I tried, I could never eliminate cost reduction from my pitch for every merchant. The truth is that even in today's world of payments technology and ISV's for every vertical, merchants still want to save money. They consider "match or beat" a prerequisite to any conversation about their payment processing solution.

Another lesson I learned very early was that a focus on savings for merchants also means slim profits for me. Whether a minimum pricing requirement on a bonus or lower fee revenue that didn't leave much room for residual profits, seemingly every dollar I saved the merchant was coming out of my pocket. I realized there were two things I wanted to do: save merchants money and grow my margins. The problem for years has been that I couldn't do both simultaneously. Cash discounting has changed this reality and created a win/win for merchants and merchant salespeople.

This chapter will be focused primarily on selling cash discounting. However, by way of introduction, I feel I should explain some basics about how cash discounting works and what program options currently exist.

The concept is actually very simple, but recent compliance instructions have complicated implementation. A cash discount means that a person paying with cash will pay less than someone who is not paying with cash. Although cash discounting has been around a long time, especially in the fuel industry, the Durbin Amendment is considered by many as the founding document of the current programs.

The Durbin Amendment established three important things to note about cash discounting programs. Let's cover each of the three before diving deeper into how cash discount programs are implemented.

1   Cash Discounting cannot be inhibited by the card brands, banks, or anyone else. The exact language states, "A payment card network shall not, directly or through any agent, processor, or licensed member of the network, by contract, requirement, condition, penalty, or otherwise, inhibit the ability of any person to provide a discount or in-kind incentive for payment by the use of cash, checks, debit cards, or credit cards..."

2   discount means: "a reduction made from the price that

customers are informed is the regular price; and does not include any means of increasing the price that customers are informed is the regular price."

3   In lieu of a discount, the Durbin Amendment also protects the implementation of an "in-kind incentive" to encourage consumers to use a different form of payment. Unfortunately, the term "in-kind incentive" is not mentioned in the definitions section of the Durbin Amendment. What could this term mean?

I am not an attorney, and this is not legal advice. But when reading this language from the Durbin Amendment, we can assume this term does not mean a discount. If it meant discount, it would not have been mentioned since the term "discount" was already used. So, it is some sort of alternative to a discount that encourages a consumer to use another form of payment.

So, where does this leave us? We are left with three possible approaches to creating a cash discount program.

Option #1 – Implement a true cash discount. This would be a discount that complies with the definition above, which is, admittedly a high bar. Merchants could adjust their pricing to a higher level and then provide a discount when a consumer pays with cash. This method would require merchants to change their pricing prior to implementing the discount. This is a great approach for professional services and other invoicing services, because these documents can be easily adjusted. However, for a retail store with 10,000 SKUs, it is not practical.

Option #2 – Implementing a service fee with a separate cash discount. There are still companies who have worked with the attorneys general from many states to create signs that adjust the "regular price" of all in-store sales at the counter using a service fee. Then with a different section of the sign, they offer an immediate discount for those paying with cash. This method has the added benefit of being easily implemented in physical location businesses. However, staying compliant can be tricky, as we will see in the Visa bulletin below.

Option #3 – Working with a merchant to create a "non-cash adjustment" or other "in-kind incentive" to encourage the customers to pay with cash. While the definition of this term is a bit vague in the Durbin Amendment, it seems logical that adding a fee for non-cash payments would be an "in-kind incentive." Many ISOs have taken this path.

The last document I will discuss before moving on to sales techniques is a bulletin released by Visa in October of 2018. Contrary to what some in the industry have stated, this document does not discourage cash discounting. Rather, it states, "discount offer programs should be evaluated to ensure compliance with the Visa Rules."

In my opinion, the only option this bulletin document affects is "Option #2" above. Here is the relevant language from the bulletin, "Models that encourage merchants to add a fee on top of the normal price of the items being purchased, then give an immediate discount of that fee at the register if the customer pays with cash or debit card, are NOT compliant with the Visa Rules and may subject the acquirer to non-compliance action."

There are two schools of thought among ISOs who offer "Option 2" about this language. The first thought is that the Durbin Amendment should preclude Visa from taking any action. Keep in mind that the language above from the Durbin Amendment singles out the Card Networks, such as Visa, and specifically limits them from inhibiting a merchant from implementing a cash discount. Obviously, Visa's argument is that because of the definition of the word "discount" in the Durbin Amendment, these programs would not fall under the protection of the amendment in the first place.

The second school of thought is that this bulletin, taken together with the discount definition from the Durbin Amendment, makes programs which add a service fee to all non-cash payments and then offers an immediate discount non-compliant. Thus, those programs should be avoided. These ISOs have either switched to surcharging programs or implemented a "non-cash adjustment." They hold the firm belief that surcharging or "non-cash adjustment" pricing systems are protected under the Durbin Amendment's "in-kind incentive."

One thing is clear. Visa will continue to monitor these programs, especially among the larger ISOs. There is a strong desire in our industry for a level playing field, and Visa seems to have the desire to enforce compliance rules that will create an environment where everyone is on equal footing. There have already been acquirers who have been fined for non-compliant programs. So, this is something you should consider carefully as you design a cash discounting program or choose one to represent.

Now that I have covered the basics of cash discounting program implementation and compliance, let's move on to the fun stuff! I'll explain how you can leverage these programs to close more deals and grow your profit margins!

DISCOUNT SELLING TECHNIQUES

In many ways, selling cash discounting requires an opposite approach from that of selling traditional processing. This can throw off many experienced agents. How ironic that many brand new, inexperienced agents will be able to sell cash discounting while their more experienced colleagues will be convinced it can't be sold.

The fundamental difference is that traditional processing is predicated on convincing merchants there is enough value to switch providers. So, the primary objection to traditional processing could be summarized as "not good enough."

"These savings are not good enough."

"This POS System has features that will not make a huge difference."

"Your service is not going to be that much better than what I have."

With cash discounting, the savings are usually 80% to 95%. This leaves the merchant thinking, "What is the catch?" or, "I will probably lose business when customers see the price increase. That will cause me to lose more than I am saving." or, "I have never heard of this program; it sounds too good to be true." or, "Why don't I know any other business owners doing this?" We could summarize all of these objections as "too good to be true" which is the opposite of traditional processing.

Before I talk about how to overcome these objections, let's understand the facts about merchant implementation and consumer behavior. Numerous studies have been conducted by ISOs in the industry. (Sadly, none that I am aware of have been made public.) Of the studies I have seen, two facts seem to be consistent. First, less than 1% of consumers even notice the increase in price for non-cash payments. Second, 95% of businesses who try cash discounting do not see a negative result from this program and stay with it for more than ninety days.

What do these facts tell us? We can sell cash discounting with confidence, knowing that in most cases the merchant will see significant savings with minimal negative push-back from customers. This program, when implemented correctly, has a 95% chance of saving merchants almost all of their processing fees. And there is only a 5% chance of merchants converting back to what they had in the first place. What a deal! How do we help merchants make the right decision for their business? How do we overcome the preconceived notion that this offer is simply too good to be true?

I am going to split the sales process into three short segments. The opening, the presentation, and the close.

THE OPENING

The goal of the opening pitch is to grab the prospects' attention and get them to ask, in one way or another, "How does it work?" If you can accomplish this, you have yourself a good opening pitch for cash discounting.

The simplest version of an opening that accomplishes this objective is a simple flat-fee approach. Let's say that your program includes a $49 monthly fee and that the extra revenue from the consumer covers the rest of the processing costs. You might approach the merchant like this, "Hey (Prospect Name.) How are you doing today? I wanted to stop by and drop off a brochure for you. Our company is offering a true flat-rate payment processing program. The monthly charge is $49 with no percentage or per item fees. Whether you process $5,000 per month or $100,000 per month, the charge is just $49. Have you heard about our program from any of our other clients in the area yet?"

Another one of my favorite approaches includes a short survey. The pitch might go like this, "Hey (Prospect Name.) I'm introducing a new program for small business owners and need to see if it is a fit for this market. So, I'm taking a three-question, thirty-second survey. Do you have thirty seconds to help out a fellow business owner?" The questions then center around processing - how much volume, how much spent on processing last month, average ticket size, etc. At the end of the survey, thank the prospect for answering the questions. Let the merchant know that based on the answers given, the new program would be a savings of roughly X amount per year and is clearly a fit for the merchant's particular business type. I can assure you the prospect will ask for more information at that point.

Regardless of the approach you decide to use, the key is to grab their attention with the simplicity of this model and the amount of potential savings. Then lead them towards asking you a question about how the program works.

THE PRESENTATION

Once you get them to ask how the program works, be ready with a good answer. Remember, merchants are already thinking "too good to be true." So, the key here is to make the program seem realistic, simple, and something that would fit into their existing business processes. If you make it seem like a HUGE CHANGE, they will say "No" almost every time.

My favorite approach is what I call the price increase presentation. Here is how it goes:

Prospect: How does this program work?

Sales Professional: The best way to explain it is for me to ask a question. I am sure that from time to time as your rent or electric bill or other costs have gone up, you have implemented price increases. I'm sure you try not to do them very often and to keep them small, but this is just part of doing business. Am I right?

Prospect: Sure.

Sales Professional: As I am sure you have noticed your payment processing costs have been steadily rising for years. The banks and card brands like Visa and MasterCard offer more rewards to consumers. Implementing a price increase to cover these costs would make sense. But unlike the rent or electric bill, these costs only affect your non-cash sales. What we have developed is a program that runs in our terminal which identifies non-cash sales and implements a small price increase affecting only those transactions. As with other price increases you have done in the past, less than 1% of consumers even notice the price increase. Within a few weeks you'll be back to business as usual. What we do is capture that tiny bit of extra revenue from each non-cash transaction and use it to pay all your processing fees except a few monthly fees to operate the program for you.

You may or may not use this exact pitch. The point is to normalize the program and relate it to something with which the merchant is already familiar. There are many ways to present cash discounting; the only thing you must avoid is hype. Don't hype a service that already seems too good to be true.

THE CLOSE

Closing a cash discount deal can be tricky. The most important word to keep in mind is "risk." This is the word in the mind of prospects keeping them from moving forward. Every merchant wants cash discounting to work, but most merchants don't believe it will. They are worried about the risk of losing business or hurting their local reputation by adding a fee to consumers that their competitors are not currently charging. Here are a few ways to lower risk.

First, you can offer a trial period. Let merchants know they are not locked into anything long term. Rather, tell them you would like for them to try the program for a week and see how it goes.

Second, make a smooth path back to traditional processing and be honest with them about the 5% of merchants who are not a good fit for this program. Tell them they have a 95% chance of saving a lot of money, but there is a 5% chance they will choose to switch back to traditional processing. Explain how easy this process will be.

Provide them with two quotes. One quote should show the extraordinary savings from cash discounting. The second one should show them modest savings on traditional processing. Give them a choice between the two in order to close more sales. Here is how this closing pitch might sound:

"Susan, it has been such a pleasure speaking with you today. Let me get your thoughts on two different options I have for you based on our conversation. The first option would be to give cash discounting a try. As we have discussed, you would save over $10,000 per year on this program. And, of course, if this program turns out not to be a good fit, you already have a proposal showing that I can still save you a little over $1,000 on our traditional processing program. We can flip the switch with as little as one day's notice if you decide the program isn't working out. The other option would be to go with our traditional program, knowing that your terminal is ready to activate cash discounting once you decide it is time to give it a try. Which of these two approaches do you feel would be the best fit for your business?"

There have been a lot of changes in the cash discount landscape in the last few months, and there will continue to be changes. There are two things I believe in strongly. First of all, I believe the concept of passing the cost of processing on to the consumer is here to stay. Second, I believe that five or even ten years from now we will be able to pass the cost on to the consumer for all transaction types, including debit. I don't know exactly how it will be structured. It might be as a surcharge; it might be as a non-cash adjustment; or it might be a cash discount. But this concept is here to stay, and it is a huge opportunity for agents and ISOs. Hopefully this chapter has given you some insight into these new programs. I wish you great success as you build your book of business.

CHAPTER 27
POINT-OF-SALE FINANCING

Today's landscape of offering point-of-sale (POS) financing options to consumers is rapidly evolving. Being issued a revolving line of credit, installment loan from a financial institution or financing from a favorite retailer was a standard practice for buyers looking to purchase large ticket items or make upgrades or repairs to their homes and/or vehicles. But according to a recent TransUnion study (Generation Revealed: Decoding Millennial Financial Health), POS financing is evolving to meet the needs of today's consumer.

In the study, data showed that while millennials still use credit cards for purchases, they tend to utilize them less often, own fewer cards, and carry smaller balances. Instead, millennials rely more on debit cards for smaller purchases, and they prefer the ease of online loan origination, such as pay-over-time loans, to make larger purchases.

Digitization and eCommerce have helped younger consumers comparison-shop to find an item or service at the lowest price, as well as find the best rate when purchasing something over time. With consumer demands rapidly evolving, especially as younger generations gain purchasing power, it's essential for merchants and service providers – both in the brick and mortar and eCommerce space – to be proactive in meeting the demands of today's new credit market.

WHAT IS POS FINANCING?

POS financing is an instant-approval loan offer, whether online or in-person, that is typically presented to the purchaser during the sales process, before the transaction takes place. It provides financing options and enables customers to buy high-ticket items without having to worry about having the cash up front. Like traditional loans, loans financed through the point of sale will offer a range of interest rates, monthly payments, promotions and repayment periods, based on the creditworthiness of the consumer and the terms set by the provider.

TYPES OF POS FINANCING
Revolving credit

Revolving credit is when a lender extends a credit line to an individual that has a credit limit which remains the same amount month over month. The individual is free to charge within that credit limit every month and is sent a statement for the balance at the end of billing period. If the balance isn't paid in full, an interest rate is charged on the remainder of the balance which is then carried over to the next billing cycle.

Installment loans

Installment loans are typically for a fixed amount, fixed interest rate and fixed term. Installment loans can be bundled with a zero percent promotion or offer. For instance, a consumer may purchase a piece of furniture at zero interest for twelve months. If the furniture is not paid off within the twelve-month period, the loan converts to an installment loan with interest.

In-house financing

In-house financing is a type of seller financing in which an organization, such as a medical or dental practice, automotive, or furniture and appliance store extends a term-limit loan to the buyer, allowing them to purchase its goods or services. In-house financing eliminates the organization's reliance on banks and credit unions, allowing them to provide competitive financing to the customer, as well as to keep the interest earned in the organization's own financial accounts. There is a significant risk and servicing component to any business wanting to conduct in-house financing.

Lease-to-own financing

Lease-to-Own financing involves a contract or purchase agreement between the business and the borrower. This type of financing allows the borrower to purchase the property, typically furniture or electronics, at the end of the lease term. Lease-to-own financing is a great alternative to a traditional loan, especially for consumers with little to no credit history or those with poor credit history and is more budget-friendly for consumers with short-term needs.

eCommerce financing

Online businesses can integrate a customer finance program into their online shopping cart, presenting financing options during the sales process, so by the time the consumer is at the end of the checkout process, they'll know what finance options are available and can complete the transaction successfully.

WHICH VERTICALS ARE BEST TO TAKE ADVANTAGE OF POS FINANCING?

- Consumer goods
- Dental
- Ecommerce purchases
- Orthodontics
- Hearing aids
- Cosmetic or elective surgery
- Chiropractic
- Med spa, laser hair removal, body sculpting
- Any elective procedure, like stem cell injections
- Home improvement
- Patios/Decks
- HVAC
- Plumbing
- Flooring
- Roofing
- High-risk business
- Jewelry
- Club memberships
- Time shares
- Debt consolidation
- Treatment centers
- Legal fees or criminal defense
- High ticket coaching or consulting
- Vocational/Trade schools
- Veterinarian
- Weight loss surgery

WHO ARE THE INDUSTRY LEADERS?

POS financing is nothing new; it's technically a new application of an existing financing solution that provides more flexibility and more control than traditional credit card purchases allow. POS financing appeals to not only store-based merchants and service providers, but to online providers looking for more ways to close the sale while the striking is hot. So, it's no wonder that players emerging in the field of POS financing range from large financial institutions, credit card issuers and large retailers, to FinTech start-ups and merchant service providers. Here are a few of the innovators that are emerging in the market as industry leaders.

Surv Credit, a consumer finance platform, partners with agents around the US to provide B2C, POS financing to merchants primarily in the home improvement, consumer goods, medical and eCommerce industries. The Surv Credit platform integrates multiple lending products for a quick approval at the best possible rates.

Synchrony has more than 85 years of lending expertise. Synchrony works with national retailers and small businesses, online retailers like Amazon, manufacturers and service providers across a wide variety of industries and markets to offer POS financing. Through their customized credit card programs, Synchrony partners can offer private-label financing like CareCredit or Synchrony CarCare which are tailored towards healthcare and auto, respectively.

Affirm is a leader in the POS financing world. Affirm partners with over 2,000 merchants, including online giants like Shopify and Walmart.com to give shoppers the option to pay over-time during the checkout process. Unlike payment options that have compounding interest and unexpected costs, Affirm shows customers exactly what they'll pay each month – prior to the completion of the transaction.

GreenSky is another dominant player in POS financing. Their loan application platform allows merchants to offer straightforward payment options to consumers. Financial institutions also leverage GreenSky's "apply and buy" technology to provide loans to super-prime and prime consumers nationwide.

JPMorgan Chase launched its new pay-over-time product, My Chase Plan, in August 2019. This feature allows Chase cardholders to choose among past card purchases of $500 or more and to finance them for longer periods for a flat, monthly fee. Chase has also added My Chase Loan to enable creditworthy consumers to slice off a portion of their card's approved credit line and treat it as a personal loan for larger purchases.

American Express launched the Pay It, Plan It program in 2017 offering creditworthy cardholders the ability to use its online app to change an existing purchase from a one-time charge to an installment loan with the term of their choice.

Vyze was acquired by Mastercard in April 2019. Vyze is a point-of-sale technology platform which allows merchants to offer a selection of different lenders' credit programs. Vyze works in both in-store and online environments.

Square offers Square Installments. With the flexible payment option, consumers can apply in-store or online via their smart phones and choose the payment plan that fits within their budget. Approved customers will see the total cost clearly spelled out up-front, with no surprises like deferred interest or early payment penalties.

PayPal Credit, formerly named Bill Me Later, offers POS financing to consumers on any website that takes PayPal as a payment form. Once approved, PayPal Credit is automatically added to the consumer's PayPal account.

Numerous other providers are in or entering this space. Among them are Klarna, Bread, Blispay from Visa, SuperMoney, and lease-to-own financing with Acima.

WHAT ARE THE BENEFITS TO THE CONSUMER?

In a 2018 study, Citizens Financial Group found that 76% of consumers surveyed said that "they are more likely to make a retail purchase if a payment plan – backed by a simple and seamless point of sale experience – is made available." The study also found that two-thirds of the consumers are looking to build a credit history, which doesn't equate to opening more credit card accounts or traditional bank loans.

The bottom line is that consumers want a simple and easy experience when they make a large purchase; financing that fits within their budget and payments that won't impact their wallet or jeopardize their creditworthiness.

WHAT ARE THE BENEFITS TO THE MERCHANT?

Contractors and service providers (both online and in-store) interested in growing their client base and seeing an increase in their financed sales are looking for a flexible financing provider to help make it happen. By offering payment options to sell the product or service, POS financing can help make the sales associate's job of closing the sale much easier. It also increases the customer's purchasing power, incenting them to upgrade their selection or expand the scope of the original project.

The flexibility of POS financing allows customers to apply for financing earlier in the sales process, knowing upfront whether the product or service they're shopping for can be financed over time. With the ability to pre-qualify at the start of the purchase, and in a matter of seconds, customers are less likely to walk or click away and more likely to complete the transaction.

In a nutshell, the benefits of POS financing for merchants are:

- Increased sales – PayPal showed an aggregate increase of 32% by offering pay-over-time financing*
- Increased transaction amounts – PayPal showed a 75% increase in average order value*

- Improved cash flow – in many cases customer payments are deposited directly into the merchants account, allowing merchants to keep more revenue
- Attract and retain loyal customers
- Increased positive word-of-mouth and company reputation

*Forrester Study: Total Economic Impact of PayPal Express Checkout for Web and Mobile (2012).

WHAT ARE THE COSTS ASSOCIATED WITH POS FINANCING?

Depending on the service provider, POS financing can come with a single cost. Some providers charge only a percentage of sales financed through the provider or offer discounted rates. Other providers may have more monthly fees, disclosed upfront or hidden within the contract. Monthly maintenance fees, setup fees, training, compliance and minimum monthly quotas can be an additional expense added to the base cost of services. It's important that each merchant compare providers to make sure that both the one-time and monthly fees are easy-to-understand and are aligned with their business goals.

HOW ARE ISOS AND AGENTS USING POS FINANCING IN THEIR PRODUCT MIX?

Consumers want a simple and easy experience when they make a large purchase. Multiple studies show that new generations of consumers are looking to retailers and service providers to modernize their payment models by moving away from the co-branded store credit of the past.

As merchants look to meet the needs of their customers, they'll also look for ways to receive their payments faster and with bigger profit margins. By adding POS financing to their suite of services, ISOs and their agents can ensure that the merchant has a full-service solution to attract and retain consumers. The results are compelling; according to statistics published by SURV Credit, businesses that partner with them to implement a POS financing solution can expect to see a sales increase of 20% over time. Combined with experienced customer service, these businesses are poised to offer a seamless service experience for in-store, online or mobile purchases.

ISOs are using consumer financing as a tool to prospect and generate interest with business owners. Merchants are much more open to a conversation about increasing sales, average transaction and floor traffic than saving basis points. In addition, ISOs are also bundling card processing services with consumer finance to create a bundled service approach, helping to reduce merchant attrition.

Consumer finance products are just a no brainer for ISOs and agents alike.

CHAPTER 28
ALTERNATIVE LENDING

CONTRIBUTING WRITER JIM FINK

In this chapter we will review short-term commercial financing. Specifically, the focus will be on "working capital financing (aka alternative lending) and the benefits to the ISO/ISA by adding it to their sales arsenal. This type of lending is typically known as non-traditional financing. Whereas traditional financing is commonly referred to as bank financing. Non-traditional financing started in the late 1990s with the birth of the merchant cash advance (MCA). It was not until the mid-2000's when key players entered the space along with the introduction of a broader product offering. Here are a few key players that make up the working capital landscape today – Rapid Finance, OnDeck, Kabbage, Funding Circle, and Blue Vine.

WHAT IS "WORKING CAPITAL" FINANCING

Working capital financing typically consists of short-term loans, merchant cash advances (MCA), and line of credit (LOC). The target market is small to medium enterprises (SME). Underwriting is based on the ability to tap current cash flow of the customer. Repayment is through the assignment of future credit card receipts, or a direct ACH from the customer's business bank account on a daily, weekly or sometimes monthly basis.

THE STORY

Since the financial crisis hit the US economy in 2008 lending to the SMB community significantly declined. According to the Wall Street Journal, business lending decreased 38% from 2006 to 2014. The shift in bank lending practices have created a pent-up demand for capital in the SME marketplace. The lending gap that traditional banks created left millions of small businesses in the U.S. without adequate access to capital. That demand created a significant opportunity for alternative financing companies to step in and fulfill the capital needs of main street America. The same businesses you are speaking with every day. According to a 2017 Bryant Park white-paper they estimated the market for small business non-bank loans and merchant cash advances to be $15.3B. The prediction for the foreseeable future is the SME market and demand for short-term financing will continue to grow year after year. It is time for the ISO/ISA to participate in this lucrative revenue stream.

DELIVERING VALUE TO THE SMB.

Alternative lenders open the door to main street American businesses that have been overlooked by banks, and help them obtain much needed capital to grow and improve their operations. Non-traditional lenders evaluate non-traditional data when underwriting applicants. Todays, sophisticated risk models and fintech platforms create a higher applicant approval percentage and the ability to deploy capital to the business owner within 24 hours or less. That would never happen walking into a local bank branch and applying for a traditional loan.

Benefits of Alternative Lending.

- Fintech platforms make the end-to-end process simple and transparent
- Easy application process
- Higher approval rates
- Fast funding – same day vs. weeks or longer when applying for traditional funding
- Flexibility

Leverage the power of capital and close more merchant accounts.

In my 20 years in the payments, leasing and working capital industries I have never come across a "value-added" product that complements merchant services, generates more income for the ISO/ISA and delivers maximum benefit to your merchant.

In today's processing environment margin compression is not going away. This is caused by legacy competition, industry consolidation and disruptors, like Square, and Paypal. All are negatively affecting residuals and making it harder to retain customers. Stop the bleeding and change the conversation. Use working capital to help you close more accounts, reduce merchant attrition and deliver real value to your merchant. Elevate your value in your customers eyes and make it easy for your merchant to access much needed capital.

Don't settle for less. There are many working capital providers out there to partner with. Do you want to partner with a direct lender, or a cash broker? Whichever way you decide to go my advice is to select a partner that offers multiple products, will close transactions on your behalf with no reduction in commission, understands the merchant acquiring industry and has a proven track record of working with ISO/ISA/Processors. A partner that understands what is important to you, and the importance of the merchant/ISO relationship is paramount to your success.

WORKING CAPITAL OPTIONS

Merchant cash advance (mca)

A merchant cash advance (MCA) is a form of financing based on a company's future credit and debit card sales. The borrower pledges a fixed holdback percentage of their future credit/debit receivables until the lump sum and financing fees are paid back to the lender. The fixed holdback percentage is determined on a transaction basis and typically falls between 8%-25%. Initially most clients were retailers and restaurants, but that has changed.

For the right business and the right circumstance, a merchant cash advance offers certain advantages over many other financing solutions:

Key Benefits:

- Fast approval
- Bad credit doesn't have to hold back the business from applying
- Flexible and affordable repayments, rather than a fixed amount
- Lower risk than a traditional loan because no collateral is required, and repayments are deducted from actual sales
- No need to manually keep on top of repayments or face late payment fees
- No restriction on the use of funds

Short term business loan

Short-term business loans are lump sum loans that are designed to be paid back in less than 24 months. These loans have less restrictive requirements, which makes it easier for the small business to secure the funds. Repayment frequency is daily, weekly or monthly and done via direct ACH from the borrower's business bank account. They can be a flexible financial tool, best used for financing short-term needs—including managing cash flow, dealing with unexpected needs for extra cash, bridging larger financing options, paying off expensive debt, or taking advantage of unforeseen business opportunities.

Key Benefits:

- Fast approval
- Set payment structure
- Doesn't require collateral
- Limited documentation required
- No restriction on the use of funds

Line of credit (LOC)

A working capital line of credit offers a company the flexibility to withdraw funds up to their approved credit limit and repay debt when needed. Businesses can borrow up to a certain amount and only pay interest on the amount withdrawn. Rather than going through the sometimes-lengthy process of securing a traditional LOC, with a line of credit, businesses know that they have a certain balance available to borrow quickly as needed.

Key Benefits:

- Doesn't require collateral
- Access large sums of funding quickly
- Easily withdraw funds when needed
- Businesses can quickly access their line of credit by using a business checking account, a small business credit card, or a mobile banking app
- Lower interest rates: Interest rates on a business line of credit are usually lower than a business credit card, which can have rates of 20%+ APR, or a cash advance
- No restriction on the use of funds

TARGET INDUSTRIES

Here are industries and business types that frequently use working capital financing to supplement their cash flow.

Auto repair & body shops	Health clubs	Sports leagues & camps
Florist	Manufacturing	Golf courses
Miscellaneous retail	Car washes	Medical practices
Restaurants & bars	Self-storage facilities	Transportation / trucking
Lodging (hotel/motel)	Seasonal businesses	QSR /fast food
Construction	Grocery / liquor	Veterinary offices
Transportation	Franchises	Wholesale
Plumbing / HVAC / electrical contractors		Business services
Spas & salons (includes nail salons, tanning salons		Dry cleaners

QUICK RECAP
ISO benefits:

- new and meaningful revenue stream
- close more merchant accounts
- merchant retention tool
- provide merchants an in demand, high value product
- high frequency of merchants renew for additional funds
- each renewal is commissionable
- new talking points allows you to change the conversation

As you evaluate value-added products that will differentiate you from the competition, deliver real customer value and meaningful revenue you should consider adding a working capital solution to your sales arsenal. Partner with a capital provider that is transparent and delivering a positive client experience is their top priority.

CHAPTER 29
MAXIMIZING PORTFOLIO VALUE

CONTRIBUTING WRITER ALEX DAILY

"Why would anyone sell their most valuable asset?" is the question I asked myself when I first learned about residual buyouts in the payments industry. A myriad of answers followed, from paying for the medical bills of a loved one to fueling hypergrowth for a new business venture, to establishing an exit strategy. I've seen motives across the board. Regardless of the reason, salespeople in the payments industry have great flexibility with the ability to leverage this asset.

There is a disconnect in the payments industry today as it relates to values of residual buyouts. Many agents receive offers for their portfolio where they are disappointed because of the cost and work effort put into building it. However, the price that a buyer offers is usually reflective of the true value of the portfolio. This chapter is focused on how to build value into your portfolio from the perspective of the buyer. I will be speaking from personal experience and occasionally reference how my company Cutter, views the topic, as processes can vary among buyer companies.

THE PROCESS

Before we get started, let's take a minute to review the process of selling your book of business. If you are choosing to sell to a third-party purchaser (a buyer other than your ISO), first check with your ISO to see if they have right of first refusal (meaning they have the first right to purchase your book of business) and if they want to exercise that right. A potential buyer will typically want to see the historical performance of your book, proof of ownership and the terms you agreed to with your ISO. Be prepared to have these items available:

- Months of Residual Reports
- 2-3 Recent Bank Statements
- Signed/Dated Agent Agreement

Based on these documents and some conversations about the portfolio, a buyer should be able to give you an offer. If you accept the offer the next step is a purchase agreement followed by a reassignment of residuals. If purchased by your ISO, they will stop paying you your residual split listed in your Schedule A. If purchased by a third party, the ISO will start paying the residuals to the buyer. The seller is typically paid the purchase price at closing after the reassignment of residuals is agreed upon and signed by buyer, seller and ISO.

In this industry, your valuation format is typically in a multiple of monthly revenue as opposed to a multiple of EBITDA. So, if John Smith's portfolio averages $5,000 per month and he gets 25X, he'll receive $125,000 in total ($5,000 times 25). Many buyers will offer trailing earnout payments in addition to the closing price to give a higher total offer price. This structure is to mitigate the buyer's risk. These payments are usually contingent upon the performance of the portfolio.

VALUE OF YOUR PORTFOLIO

In the eyes of a buyer, there are six main driving factors that affect the value of your residual income stream: attrition, size, age, residual apportionment, products, and agent agreement terms. Each of these areas may directly affect the risk associated with the purchase, therefore changing the value of your portfolio.

ATTRITION MITIGATION IS THE KEY TO VALUE.

Separately attrition is the biggest driving factor in the valuation of a residual portfolio. The other main factors can play a role in the attrition rate. Across the industry we've seen differing opinions of how to calculate attrition. Attrition may be calculated in two ways, by merchant count and separately by volume.

In short, we take the original merchant count from the first month's residual report and see how many of those original merchants are still processing in the most current residual report. For example, if there were 100 merchants in month 1 and 83 of those original merchants remaining in month 12, the annualized attrition by merchant count is 17%. Next, we look at the residual volume of the remaining 83 accounts and compare it to 1st month's residual. The residual volume attrition can be higher if larger residual merchants stop processing. Both numbers are used in the valuation to predict the future income of the portfolio. Note that any new accounts added are not calculated into the equation. This calculation is utilized by buyers who require agents to work for them, post-acquisition. We'll talk about the different types of offers later in this chapter.

HAVE YOU EVER BEEN TOLD "SIZE DOESN'T MATTER?", IT DOES IN THE PAYMENTS INDUSTRY

The size of your residual not only affects the risk factors, but supply and demand as well. There are many buyers willing to take the time to do valuations on a portfolio yielding $10,000 per month or more, but almost none that will take the time to look at anything below

$2,000 per month because for most, it is not worth the time and effort. Needless to say, because of the demand, larger portfolios typically sell at a higher multiple. Another aspect is the risk. If there are only 10 MIDs in your book, and one leaves, there goes 10% of the portfolio by merchant count.

WINE ISN'T THE ONLY THING THAT GETS BETTER WITH AGE

Typically, merchants are most likely to leave for another processor in the first 6 months. The older the accounts, the more valuable they are. You would be hard-pressed to find a buyer for your portfolio if all your accounts were boarded in the last few months. A more realistic scenario is when you are looking to sell a portfolio you have built over the last 2 plus years. Assuming you signed up the same number of merchants each month and none left, 25% of your book would have been boarded in the last 6 months. This is usually factored into the purchase price.

THE BIGGER THEY ARE THE HARDER THEY FALL

A few massive residuals can spell risk in your portfolio. Residual apportionment is what makes a portfolio balanced or top-heavy. If the top 20% of your merchants bring in 20% of the revenue, your portfolio would be considered perfectly balanced. However, there are always merchants that bring in more revenue than others. The typical agent portfolio in today's climate has 50% of its revenue coming from the top 20% of merchants. Let's use an extreme example to showcase a top-heavy portfolio. John Smith's book has 100 merchants and brings in $5,000 per month. His top 10 merchants bring in $4,000 per month. So, his top 10% brings in 80% of the revenue. This is extremely top-heavy and adds risk. What's even worse about John's situation is that 7 of those 10 merchants are different locations for a car dealership with the same owner. This is a major risk for any buyer. No one is asking you to pass up on large revenue opportunities. A large residual income portfolio is more valuable than a smaller portfolio. However, understand that the risk associated with one or two large accounts will change the valuation.

YOU DON'T WANT TO BE IN THE BUSINESS OF SELLING COMMODITIES

What has been sold to the merchants in a portfolio directly correlates with attrition. Payments alone are a commodity product. It is the integration with other valuable services that give some portfolios low attrition. Ideally, you sell services that a business cannot operate without and is integrated with payments. For example, restaurants using a POS system that manages their inventory, staff schedules, accounting, reporting, etc. will typically stay with that product for as long as possible. It's not until something much greater, or much more cost effective comes along before they switch because of the headaches and possible costs that come with changing their process. Other products can deduct from the value of the portfolio. An over-priced terminal lease, merchant cash advance, or outdated technology are three common products or services that typically lead to attrition. The bottom-line is to sell payments with some sort of value-add, and your portfolio becomes entirely more valuable.

IT'S IN THE FINE PRINT

Terms of your agent agreement can vastly change the value of your portfolio. Your ISO knows exactly what is in your contract, so this mostly applies to third-party buyers. If you receive bonuses and have a large number of outstanding claw backs, it could repel potential buyers as they don't want to pay back the bonuses if your new accounts leave. If you get a split increase with higher volume, a buyer will pay less. As the attrition brings the residual volume down, the revenue split is decreased. Some contract terms state that if the residual drops below a certain amount, the ISO will stop paying the agent all-together. Depending on the size of the portfolio and monthly minimum, this could affect the valuation as well.

Although many more variables come into play, the aforementioned major risk factors are what buyers look for first, because it affects the long-term performance of the portfolio. Build your business like you are selling tomorrow, regardless of your intention, and your portfolio will yield far more revenues.

VALUE OF THE OFFER

When considering the value of a proposed offer look not only the purchase price but also closely review the terms. If the terms require you to meet possibly unreasonable attrition numbers, or require you to commit to boarding new accounts, or have penalties for not meeting minimums, and this makes you uncomfortable then it's not the right deal for you. Let's use some detailed examples to show how companies may structure their agreements to align with the needs of the seller.

We've got three salespeople looking to sell their book of business; Steve, Emily and Larry.

SINGLE PAYMENT FULL PURCHASE

Steve is 30 years old and looking to start his own ISO. He's been selling for 7 years and he's ready to become his own boss. Steve has a $5,000 residual income and is looking for upfront capital to jump start his business venture. Steve truly cares about his current clients; he sold to friends and family and worked from referrals.

I would structure this offer as a single-payment full purchase. We would offer a large lump sum at closing with no trailing earn-out payments. Our company would handle customer service needs so Steve can focus on his business. Steve was comfortable with this because his merchants are never moved to other processors and not offered products they don't need.

MULTI-PAYMENT FULL PURCHASE

Emily is 40 years old, married, with kids. She has a $7,000 per month portfolio with an annualized attrition rate of 5%. Her son just got into one of the country's top universities but needs help paying for it. This offer is structured as a multi-payment full purchase. Emily gets a sizable payment at closing with trailing earnout payments at month 24 and 36. This way she can get a higher total price.

Emily was apprehensive because she has sold a portfolio before and the last buyer structured the deal so it was highly unlikely for her to meet the requirements for her trailing earnout payments. I walked her through our terms; if your portfolio exceeds the agreed upon attrition annually by volume, (not merchant count), you will not earn your trailing payments. However, we always allow you to assign accounts to make up a shortfall if one exists in the event her portfolio exceeds the allowable attrition. She was comforted at the fact that we designed terms for sellers to have the means to receive all their payments.

PARTIAL PURCHASE

Larry is 65 years young and he is thinking it is time for retirement. His grandchildren all live in the area, and he wants freedom from work to spend time with them. His portfolio brings in $10,000 per month, but in December his residual spikes to $17,000 due to annual fees he built into the merchant agreements. His annualized attrition is 10%. Larry has about 100 merchants and he handles all customer service personally. He's been wanting to sell but his portfolio is extremely top-heavy and hasn't received an offer anywhere close to his expectations. Larry has no need for a large lump sum of money but wants the most value for his portfolio.

I would structure this offer as a partial purchase. We would purchase $7,000 of his residual and Larry keeps the overage. In this scenario, Larry receives a sizable upfront payment with some large earnout payments in future months. We handles all his customer service to give Larry time with his grandkids, and because Larry keeps the overage, he has cash flow every month.

Steve, Emily and Larry's deal structures represent a few common types of offers that companies may make. There are other types of deal structures with different values altogether.

FULL PURCHASE + MINIMUMS

Another deal structure that is common in the industry is a full asset purchase with terms that also purchase your time by requiring you to add a specific number of new merchants. If you fall short, you are penalized and may be required to pay back some of the purchase price or not qualify for an earnout payment. Some buyers will offer higher valuations in exchange for your time. Keep in mind you could be building another portfolio to sell later if you did not commit to handing these accounts over to the buyer.

TAKING OUT A LOAN AGAINST YOUR PORTFOLIO

Most banks consider lending against credit card processing residuals as a risk, so they don't accept it as valid collateral. Instead, there are lenders in the merchant services industry that cater to the lending needs of agents and small ISOs. The interest rates are drastically higher than prime rates but the value in loaning capital against your residual is that you still have your residual income at the end of the term. This can be a good option under the right circumstances, and you can get funded quite quickly. However, you should never borrow against your residual stream if you aren't using the money to grow your business.

So, let's recap:

If you are looking to sell your residual income portfolio, first speak with your ISO to see if they will exercise first right of refusal. You'll need 12 months of residual statements, a couple of recent bank statements, and your original agent agreement with any addendums.

To maximize the value of your portfolio, ensure you build it in a way that the attrition rate, size, age, residual apportionment and products add to the value. If and when you do sell, fully understand the terms of the agreement and ensure you are getting the full value of your portfolio.

Lastly, understand the value of the offer you are considering. Think about your goals, the steps to get there, and how this purchase offer will help you get there. Understand the value of your time and work and compare offers with all these variables in mind.

SECTION 3

SALES TRAINING

CHAPTER 30
SELLING IN THE MERCHANT
SERVICES INDUSTRY

"Whether you think you can or that you can't,
you are usually right."

—Henry Ford

There is no other industry that offers the opportunities for income, long-term security, independence, and advancement that the merchant services industry does. Consider this: in most sales jobs you must hunt for prospects constantly and convince them that your service will be of benefit. In most cases, you have to create the desire and the need for the product.

In our business there are prospects on every corner. Business owners know that they must accept credit cards and alternate forms of payments to be successful. Ask any retailer or Internet company where their sales would be without accepting credit cards. The question then becomes not if they are going to buy, but from whom are they going to buy?

When you have an industry where the customers know they must have your product, it creates fierce competition. Selling in the merchant services industry is competitive to say the least. Standard bankcard services have become a "me too" or commodity product. The good news is that most of the competition is largely untrained and uneducated, and their major marketing strategy is to sell at the cheapest price.

As industries grow and mature this is a normal occurrence. In order to thrive in this business, you must be able to distinguish the value and uniqueness you provide to the merchant over the competition. There will always be someone "cheaper."

Remember, there are two types of people at any company:

- Those Who Generate Revenue
- Those Who Consume Revenue

Being in the sales profession puts you in the first category; just stay aware of the fact that nothing happens until something is sold. Without salespeople, banks have no merchants. Merchants don't have products to sell. Credit card processing companies don't have sales to process. Manufacturers have no way to distribute their product. Customer service departments have no customers to service. In short, the economy dies.

The salesperson on the street drives this industry. Become a merchant-focused salesperson – a master service provider – and you will be invaluable.

CHAPTER 31
WHERE THE MONEY IS

I bargained with Life for a penny,
And Life would pay no more,
However, I begged at evening
When I counted my scanty store;

For Life is a just employer,
And gives you what you ask,
But once you have set the wages,
Why, you must bear the task.

I worked for menial's hire,
Only to learn, dismayed
That any wage I had asked of Life,
Life would have willingly paid.

—Jessie B. Rittenhouse

There are multitudes of selling strategies; your immediate and long-term income will be directly impacted by your individual strategy and business plan.

There are several potential income streams to consider when selling merchant services:

- Application and Setup Fees
- Equipment Sales (cash or lease)
- Placement Bonuses
- Residual Income
- Value-Added Product Sales

Application, setup fees, equipment sales and bonuses keep the food on the table, so to speak. Residual income builds at a slower pace and continues to accumulate on a monthly basis as a merchant portfolio grows.

You need to be clear about your income goals and the actions required to reach them.

Let us look at the income potential from equipment sales or bonuses. Equipment commissions vary depending on several factors: sales price, merchant credit standing, monthly lease payment, cost of equipment and commission plan. In many cases you may be placing a free terminal that your ISO supplies, the ISO will normally pay some type of placement bonus on these types of accounts.

Commissions fluctuate depending on selling style. Some salespeople sell more terminals at lower monthly lease payments, while others will write larger leases with less volume. Today, many salespeople don't even lease any longer, most place free terminals. It all depends upon individual style and local market conditions.

A good figure to use is an average commission of $450.00 per lease or placement. This takes into account good credit, slow credit, and bad credit. Using a $450.00 commission, the income potential would look like this:

SALES WEEK	COMM.	MONTHLY	YEARLY
1	$450.00	$1,935.00	$23,220.00
2	$900.00	$3,870.00	$46,440.00
3	$1,350.00	$5,805.00	$69,660.00
4	$1,800.00	$7,740.00	$92,880.00
5	$2,250.00	$9,675.00	$116,100.00

As you can see the numbers can get rather large. Most full-time sales representatives will average between 8–12 new accounts per month depending on the market area.

RESIDUAL INCOME

Residual income is the most powerful way to create long-term wealth. In most companies the salesperson is only as good as his last sale. With residual income you are compensated monthly for a one-time effort. Many agents have adopted the "Free" model in order to focus solely on building a residual portfolio. Remember servicing your merchant is critical in order to maintain your residual income base.

There are many ways residuals can be paid; here are just a few:

- Above A Certain Buy Rate
- Percentage Split
- Per Active Account

Each organization pays residuals differently; make sure your pay plan is understood thoroughly. Residual income is paid monthly based on the profit generated on the merchant account.

A $30.00 residual per account per month (many accounts will yield much more) and 10 new accounts per month will earn the following on a monthly basis (Note this is just bankcard residuals; it does not take into account other residual streams from consumer finance, business lending, POS systems, checks, gift cards, etc.):

END OF 1ˢᵀ YEAR (ASSUMED 10% ATTRITION RATE)

120 Accounts Sold
12 Accounts Closed
108 Active Accounts @ $30.00 each
$ 3,240.00 Monthly Residual
$38,880.00 Yearly Residual

END OF 2ᴺᴰ YEAR

108 Accounts from 1st Year
108 New Active Accounts
216 Total Accounts @ $30.00 each
$ 6,480.00 Monthly Residual
$77,760.00 Yearly Residual

END OF 3ᴿᴰ YEAR

108 Accounts from 1st Year
108 Accounts from 2nd Year
108 New Accounts
324 Active Accounts @ $30.00 each
$ 9,720.00 Monthly Residual
$116,640.00 Yearly Residual

If you averaged just 10 sales per month, your total income at the end of year three would be:

New Equipment Sales	$54,000.00
Residual Income	$116,640.00
Total Yearly Income	$170,640.00

I know of very few jobs where you can work hard for three years and make over a $170,000 per year – do you?

Naturally this is just an example. Your income potential is unlimited; in this business you write your own paycheck. If you really want to accelerate grow focus on selling Cash Discounting or Surcharging program, your residuals will be 2-3 times higher on these programs!

Many agents have a strategy of building residual income only and sell existing high-volume merchants with little or no new equipment sales. These are called reprograms or rollovers. Many sales representatives can write 15–20 reprograms per month and build a significant portfolio in a relative short period of time, 18–24 months.

These projections are based one agent's efforts alone; they do not account for income that can be generated from recruiting and managing a team of salespeople.

In addition to residual income on merchant services, you also have the opportunity to earn commissions from value-added products, like consumer finance, business lending, POS systems, online ordering, gift/loyalty cards, ACH, and check processing.

Organizations are always looking for people who can hire, recruit, and motivate a good outside sales force. But in order to realize your income goals, you must have a strategy.

CHAPTER 32
WHAT'S YOUR STRATEGY?

"The best way to predict the future is to invent it."

—ALAN KAY

Now that you are aware of the kind of income you can earn; you've got to develop a sales strategy. The best strategy is to model one that is working. Don't reinvent the wheel if you don't have to. Your strategy should be fairly simple. Try this basic outline, and then ask yourself the questions below so you can start to define a strategy.

- Identify your market.
- Analyze your market – its needs, wants, and problems.
- Satisfy your market's needs, wants, and problems; they are your products and services.
- Market, Market, Market.

Who's your market? (New businesses, existing business, auto repairs, doctors, liquor stores, restaurants, etc.)

Are you targeting a specific vertical or niche industry?

What core products are you going to offer besides payments?

Is this a good candidate for cash discounting or surcharging?

Are you going to sell a bundled package or program?

How are you going to generate fresh prospects, appointments or leads?

What tools do you need to be successful?

What skills do you need to develop?

What sales and product training do you need?

What is your Unique Selling Proposition – why are you different?

What wants, needs, and problems does your product satisfy?

How do you find and eliminate their pain?

What benefits will your customers receive from your product?

CHAPTER 33
TARGET MARKETING

"I don't measure a man's success by how high he climbs but how high he bounces when he hits bottom."

—GEN. GEORGE PATTON

- Prospecting is Sifting Numbers
- Marketing is Building Relationships
- Target Marketing is Focusing on The Best Prospects for Your Product

Six key questions you need to ask when developing a target marketing strategy.

Question 1:   Who?   Who is my ideal prospect?

Who buys my products?

Who has a problem my product can solve?

Question 2:	Where?	Where do I find them?
		What areas have the highest business growth?
		Where can I locate this ideal prospects information?
		Where can I buy or locate leads?
Question 3:	What?	What does my prospect want?
		What challenges does my prospect face?
		What's in it for them?
Question 4:	Why?	Why should they buy from me?
		Why am I unique from the competition?
		Why do they need my products or services?
Question 5:	How?	How do I penetrate this market?
		How do I become a specialist or expert?
		What materials do I need to reach this market?
		What relationships do I need to penetrate this market?
Question 6:	When?	When do I begin? (How aboutNOW)
		What is the best time to approach these prospects?
		Is there a seasonal time that is best to approach this market?
		Is there a better time of day to solicit this customer?

Now that you have worked on your target market, let us consider the qualities required to be an extraordinary salesperson.

CHAPTER 34
THE EXTRAORDINARY SALESPERSON

*"Since most of us spend our lives doing
ordinary tasks, the most important thing is to carry
them out extraordinarily well."*

—HENRY DAVID THOREAU

The sales profession is ever-changing; it is dynamic. With the advent of the Internet, fierce competition, and the availability of information, merchants are much more sophisticated. The extraordinary salesperson must have the ability to adapt and change strategy accordingly.

Due to the high cost of selling, many firms are reducing outside sales forces and, instead, are relying on automation and inside salespeople to maintain and increase revenue. Instead of face-face contacts many companies and individuals are making their purchasing decisions directly via the Internet, direct mail, telephone, fax, radio and other means.

The exciting thing about the merchant services industry is that, as more and more complex products are brought to market, there will be an *increase* in the need for professional outside salespeople rather than a decline.

This new breed of salesperson must acquire skills that were not required of his/her predecessors. The new era of selling will be as a "partner, consultant, or counselor." Partnership or consultative selling means that salespeople will have to become actively engaged in their client's business. In essence, salespeople will work for their clients.

This new type of salesperson will be open to forgoing short-term gains in order to achieve long-term benefits. One-on-one relationships are built on a foundation of trust, respect, and performance. Extraordinary salespeople form these types of partnerships with their customers. They are considered an invaluable resource.

Many companies are cutting back vendor relationships in order to deal with fewer salespeople. Consultative merchant services professionals will have the ability to provide multiple solutions, benefiting their merchants and increasing streams of revenue for all parties involved. Win-win relationships will be the norm.

The days of the fast-talking, pushy, back-slapping, hard closer are almost extinct. This method may continue to work in used-car sales; in the merchant services arena, however, salespeople who use these techniques may have short-term success but are more than likely doomed to long-term failure.

Agents who have the ability to combine traditional closing methods with new sales paradigms, like value-based selling, will be able to write more business without having to use high-pressure tactics. Observe how successful companies market their products and services today. They focus on education, service, relationship-building, and added value to the end customer.

Partnership selling entails doing things for the merchant rather than doing things to the merchant. If they don't benefit from a particular piece of equipment or service, don't sell it. The goal is to build a long-term mutually beneficial relationship, much like those accountants, lawyers, and doctors have with their clients. Trust is being sold first.

The main skills for the extraordinary salesperson will not be closing, closing, closing, but will emphasize building rapport, analyzing customer needs, and asking the right questions to uncover dominant buying motives. If done correctly, gaining commitment will be a fluid and effortless process, not an event.

Salespeople will be required to demonstrate new qualities in order to meet the demands of today's merchant. Their makeup will include the following characteristics:

- **Integrity**
- **Authenticity**
- **Understanding**
- **Professionalism**
- **Customer Service**

Integrity is defined as a steadfast adherence to a strict moral or ethical code. The extraordinary salesperson understands that his/her future depends upon honesty in all business dealings. How you act demonstrates who you are much more than what you say. Integrity is demonstrated by doing what you said you were going to do, "Walking Your Talk."

Authenticity (being genuine) is the opposite of being phony. People have a second sense about whether salespeople are being real or not. Merchants know where there is a lack of a true desire to help. When being inauthentic, salespeople's words do not match their actions or body language; customers pick up on it immediately. Be authentic in all interactions with customers.

Understanding is the ability to walk a mile in the other person's shoes, to see the wants, needs, and concerns of the merchant from the merchant's perspective. There is an old saying that goes like this: "If you want to see why John Smith buys, look at the world through John Smith's eyes." This skill is contingent upon the ability to actively listen to the client's needs and then be able to step into the client's world.

By demonstrating a higher level of professionalism the extraordinary salesperson creates an environment that distinguishes him/her from the pack. Extraordinary salespeople internalize the meaning of professionalism, which is being prepared, organized, and knowledgeable about their services and products.

They are driven by a need to serve the customer; they are merchant-focused. It is understood that it costs much more to acquire a new customer than to keep an existing customer. Extraordinary salespeople also realize that every customer knows roughly 250 people and, if that customer isn't serviced exceptionally well, their reputation will suffer.

By demonstrating these key characteristics, the one-time sale will evolve into a lifelong partnership where all the participants win. At this stage you are a partner, and partners look out for each other. Your merchants will in turn look out for you by sending referrals, buying additional products, and continuing to process with your bank.

Wrap your mind around these ideas and demonstrate them, and you will be guaranteed success. Once again, the main qualities of an extraordinary salesperson are:

CHAPTER 35
7 REASONS WHY SALESPEOPLE FAIL

*"Defeat is not the worst of failures.
Not to have tried is the true failure."*

—GEORGE E. WOODBERRY

After working with thousands of salespeople, from lackluster performers to superstars, we have heard every reason in the world why they haven't or can't succeed. We have recognized a pattern in those salespeople who do not excel in the sales profession. Many share the following characteristics:

#1 Insufficient Product Knowledge

#2 They Don't Know Their Presentation

#3 Poor Time Management Skills

#4 No Marketing or Prospecting Plan

#5 They Didn't Research the Competition

#6 They Gave Up Too Soon!

#7 They Lack Clarity about Their Purpose or Mission in Life

It's scary that there are so many salespeople who don't thoroughly know their industry services and products. If you are going to be a professional salesperson, with the potential to earn a six-figure income, you've got to learn every facet of your product line. This is a foundational key to success.

In the merchant services arena, you are required to have a working knowledge of your products; services; future technologies; equipment capabilities; rates and fees; underwriting criteria; and customer service procedures. Commit to be a lifelong learner. Stephen Covey calls it "sharpening the saw." If you continually learn and improve your skills, you will soon be a master. Master salespeople control their own destiny.

Knowing about your product in and of itself is not enough. You must be able to present your product effectively. This begins with gaining rapport, asking the right questions, and discovering why your customer is buying and gaining commitment. Your presentation will require constant tweaking and improvement to perfect. Try new things; test different approaches until the right one is discovered.

Bad time management skills are one of the biggest killers of sales success. Poor salespeople don't manage their time; they let outside circumstances control their destiny. Time is the only finite resource we have; use your time wisely, prioritize, and spend time on those activities that generate revenue.

You've heard it before: "People don't plan to fail, they fail to plan." You must have a prospecting and marketing plan that is executed daily. *Guess what? Selling is a contact sport; you have got to suit up and show up every day.* It all begins with finding an interested party. Create a system that utilizes multiple lead channels; this will ensure you're never without a prospect to call on. One of the best buying signals is when a merchant will listen to you.

You must research your competition. Make sure you know who all your major competitors are: call and shop them. File a new business DBA and see what mailers you receive. Research their rates, their selling strategy, what sales tools they are using, and what promotions they are offering. Learn their strengths and weaknesses so you can capitalize on them at every turn.

*A Quitter **NEVER** wins – and a **WINNER** never quits!*

—Source Unknown

This is the worst one of all. You won't believe the number of salespeople who fold their tents up too early. Many of us have expectations of becoming successful but forget the work and persistence required to realize our goals. Give yourself enough time to learn your trade. Dedicate six months to this industry and you will never leave.

The final reason most salespeople, and people for that matter, fail is that they lack clarity about their life mission or purpose. A big part of a person's life is spent working. Your career should be a key ingredient in fulfilling your purpose on this planet. Alignment of values, mission, and goals is a critical step in achieving your destiny. If these factors are not in alignment, you're what is called incongruent.

"There is one quality which one must possess to win, and that is definiteness of purpose, the knowledge of what one wants, and a burning desire to possess it."

—Napoleon Hill

Many people divide their lives between what they feel they have to do to make a living and what they want to do to have fun or gain fulfillment.

For instance, you may have one goal of making $100,000 per year and a second of working 30 hours a week and spending more time with your family. This is a conflicting goal, initially, because you will have to spend more than 30 hours a week building your business until your business network grows. You are incongruent. It's been said to "work smart not hard" in the beginning; why not "work hard and smart?"

Do what you love and love what you do. Naturally, there are always elements, even in things we love, that we may not care for. Just ensure that this business offers you more of what you love to do than what you don't.

I can't urge you enough to explore how your business will help you accomplish your life purpose. It will help you gain clarity on where you are going and how you're going to get there. In order to explore your business mission and values, I invite you to complete a life design workshop. You may download the workshop at our Website free of charge: *www.surviveandthrive.biz/resources*

Remember what Nietzsche said:

"If the WHY is strong enough, you can bear any HOW."

CHAPTER 36
THE SALES PROCESS

"Do, or do not. There is no try."

—Yoda

The sales process is not an event. It is a fluid movement from one step to the next. It should be natural and unforced. Here are the steps involved:

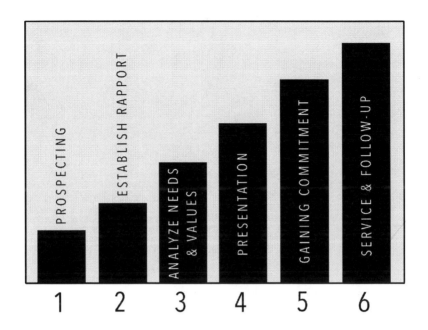

Let us review each step in detail.

CHAPTER 37
PROSPECTING

*"One who has a thing to sell, and goes and whispers
in a well, is not so apt to get the dollars,
as one who climbs a tree and hollers."*

—CHINESE PROVERB

I once heard it said, *"you can have the best story in the world, but
if you don't have anyone to tell it to – it's useless."* New business
development is paramount to your success.

Your marketing and prospecting plan should outline the steps that
need to be taken to generate sufficient leads to reach your sales
targets. Make sure you develop a prospecting strategy that fits
your personality and individual style. If you know you are not going
to cold call, don't lie to yourself; develop an alternate strategy.

Here are several tactics to generate solid prospects:

- Cold Calling
- Telemarketing

- Niche or Target Marketing (i.e., restaurants, doctors, car dealerships)
- Direct Mail
- Referrals and/or Joint Ventures
- Lead Companies
- Search Engines
- Social Media
- Association Endorsements
- Chamber of Commerce Meetings
- Lead Exchange Groups
- Civic Groups
- Seminars
- Print Media
- Free Newsletter
- Automated Dialing
- Trade Shows
- Local Picture
- Picture Business Card
- Dream 100

Let us review each in detail.

TACTIC #1 – COLD CALLING
Cold Calling – New Businesses

Cold calling is still one of the most effective ways to reach prospects. The advantage of marketing to new businesses is that they must accept credit cards and they need equipment. The disadvantage of marketing to new businesses is that every merchant service provider is going after this market. The new business market is huge; according to the Small Business Administration, over 600,000 new businesses start each year.

If approaching new businesses, you will need to acquire a new business list. This can be accomplished through a list company or the local county courthouse. Just inquire about the new business list, corporations list, or assumed names; the wording varies by state. Many agencies will give you access to download the new business list or email the list daily or weekly for a fee.

Another source for new business owners is new licenses issued, many states issue permits and licenses for:

1   Liquor

2   Electrical/HVAC contractor

3   General contractor

4   Cosmetology

5   Insurance

6   Certified Public Accountants

7   Appraisal Services

8   Home Inspection Companies

Once the list is acquired, target only those merchants that require your product or service (use some common sense). Sort them by zip code so a route can be developed. While on the road look for signs like "Grand Opening," "Under New Management," and "Coming Soon."

If your list has phone numbers, the most effective approach is to call and set appointments; this will save time and money in your prospecting efforts.

If you would like to figure out how many cold calls you need to make to reach a certain annual income, complete the *Income Goal Worksheet located at www.surviveandthrive/resources*

A good beginning ratio for cold calling is a 10% presentation ratio and a 20% closing ratio. If you make 50 cold calls a day, you will get 5 presentations and close 1 sale.

Cold Calling – Existing Businesses

Existing business are always on the lookout to improve the bottom line. Rather than leading with traditional merchant services, you may want to lead with another product. Try opening the door with one of the following:

- Cash Discounting or Surcharging
- Point of Sale Systems
- Working Capital
- Consumer Finance (POS financing)
- Gift Cards/Loyalty Cards
- Payroll/HR Solutions
- ACH Processing
- Check Services
- Ecommerce Processing
- Website or Graphic Design
- IT Services

Another tactic is to make a service call. You can open a dialogue with a merchant by giving him window decals, free paper or by cleaning the heads on his credit card terminal.

The best plan is to decide the night before which area you will target. If targeting existing businesses work the areas that have the most businesses. North, East, West, and South: it doesn't matter; there are merchants everywhere.

Target those businesses that use credit cards the most, such as auto repair shops, carpet stores, furniture stores, restaurants, retailers, car dealerships, doctors, dentists, repair centers, brick and mortar businesses and service companies.

TACTIC #2 — TELEMARKETING

Telemarketing is a great source for generating qualified prospects. More people can be contacted in less time on the phone than face-to-face. Another great strategy is to hire a part time telemarketer on commission, websites like *www.upwork.com* and *www.outbounders.com* are a great place to start looking for telemarketers. Get a list, develop a script, and have your telemarketer hit the phones.

Many people today want to work from home, this is a win-win situation for everyone. Good telemarketers are worth their weight in gold. Call the new business list yourself unless your telemarketer is experienced. New business leads are valuable; however, inexperienced telemarketers can burn through a lot of good leads until they get proficient on the phone.

Remember when telemarketing that the appointment is being sold, not the product. Once the appointment is set you may want to qualify your prospect in more detail, such as making sure they have their business banking set up, and that all decision makers will be present at the appointment.

You may want to offer an inducement or ethical bribe for meeting with you, like a free business planning software package, a free eBook, a free report, a waiver of all application or setup fees, free trial, try several different promotions.

Telephone surveys are another great tool to determine merchant interest. Conduct a one-minute survey and call those merchants later in the week who expressed an interest in saving money.

Here are some basic tips for successful telemarketing:

1   Before placing a call, have a clear, specific objective of what you are trying to achieve. Know the purpose of your call in advance.

2   To stay on track and meet your objective, prepare a list of questions that require answers prior to your call. Have a prepared script that includes all possible answers to objections until you get comfortable on the phone.

3   Calling into multiple departments in a company or organization cannot only provide the information or person sought but

can also give a unique overview of how a company's internal processes work. This can be useful information if further calls are required to the same or similar companies. Human resources, purchasing, investor relations, or the president's office are all good examples of places to begin the initial foray.

4   By starting at the top of an organization such as the president's office, the president or the president's assistant will know the correct source of information or the individual who can provide what is needed to meet the objective. As these individuals are usually very busy, having a short concise statement prepared such as "who is responsible for..." enables them to provide a quick answer.

5   When being referred from a higher-level person (such as the president or the president's office) to a lower-level person, use the higher person's name or office to lend credibility and importance to the request. For example: "Mr. Smith's office referred me to you regarding <the nature of the call>."

6   After briefly introducing yourself and your company, ask for permission to speak before explaining the reason for the call.

7   If the person sounds busy, make an appointment by asking when a good time would be to schedule a call.

8   Use the optional choice methodology. Ask, "Which is better, Monday or Tuesday? Morning or afternoon? 10:00 or 11:00 a.m.?" The result will be a person who is expecting the call.

9   Listen to what is going on in the background. If a call or distraction occurs in the background, politely inquire whether or not that situation needs to be dealt with and offer to be placed on hold. This shows respect for the other person and is greatly appreciated.

10   Practice the Q/A/F/Q technique. Ask a question. Wait for an answer. Feedback what was said to you to be sure you have a clear understanding of what was said. Finally ask another question to direct the conversation into the area where you

want it to go. The person asking the questions controls the direction of the call.

11   Finally, and most importantly, be persistent in your quest. If you remain persistent, you will most likely find the person who has the information you seek.

Need help developing the right telemarketing script? Go to Developing a Telemarketing Script located at *www.survivandthrive. biz/resources*

TACTIC #3 — NICHE OR TARGET MARKETING

Many successful salespeople specialize in niche or target markets. For instance, you may want to specialize in just restaurants, healthcare providers or home improvement contractors. If you're in a niche market, you need to possess deep knowledge of that vertical market and how your products will uniquely benefit the merchant. Review the chapter on target marketing for ideas.

Get involved with local associations, write free articles, advertise in their newsletters or publications, and speak at their meetings. Try to get involved at the national level and create a special merchant program for their association.

Have your merchants write testimonial letters or provide videos. Align with key suppliers who work with that market. If you are selling to restaurants get with other equipment vendors, consultants, food service providers, menu designers and develop cross-referral relationships.

Become the expert. Make sure you service these customers above and beyond. A niche market is a double-edged sword. Merchants know each other – if you don't service your merchant the word will get out.

TACTIC #4 — DIRECT MAIL

Direct mail is still a fairly good source for leads. If you filed a DBA as I recommended earlier, you will know who is actively mailing in your market area.

Make sure you are getting a good return on your investment. For example, if you are mailing 4,000 pieces per month the postage alone is $1400.00 plus printing, labels, list cost and time. The average return is a .05 – 1% response depending on the area, offer and sales copy.

That means that a 4,000 piece mailing with a 1% response will generate 40 calls. The presentation ratio should be much higher with call-ins, usually around 30%–40%. A good representative will get in front of 16 people and close 30%+ of those appointments.

Another tactic is a pre-approach letter. Send out an introduction letter before you call your customer. This works well when targeting niche markets, but the cost is high.

Always track responses and closing ratios in order to determine if your return on investment.

TACTIC #5 – REFERRALS AND JOINT VENTURES

Referrals continue to be one of the best sources for leads. Offer customers and business associates a referral fee for each sale. If delivering and training on a new installation, always ask for five referrals before leaving.

Here are some great types of businesses to consider for referral partnerships:

- Advertising Reps
- Alarm System Companies
- Chamber of Commerce
- CPAs & Bookkeepers
- Consultants
- Financial Planners
- Food Service Companies
- Graphic Design Firms
- Hosting Companies

- Commercial Insurance Agents
- IT Companies
- Liquor Sales
- Local Banks
- Menu Planners
- MLM Distributors
- Newspapers
- Office Equipment Reps
- Office Supply Reps
- Payroll Sales Reps
- Printing Companies
- Restaurant Sales Reps
- Sign Companies
- Software Sales Companies
- Telecom Sales Reps
- Trade Journals
- Website Designers

If you build a referral network big enough you will never have to make a cold call again.

TACTIC #6 – LEAD COMPANIES

A lead company's job is to generate the appointment or lead for sale. Lead companies help salespeople focus their efforts on selling. The drawbacks of using a lead company are expense and often quality. Let expense varies drastically depending on the criteria of the lead and human interaction required, I've seen leads as cheap as $5.00 and as high as $225.00 for a double verified lead with volume parameters.

There are also telemarketing centers that will pre-set appointments. They usually work on a set amount of appointments per week and require prepayment. Prices range from $25.00–$100.00 for each appointment. Some will work out a fee arrangement for a lower appointment fee with a bonus per sale or a joint venture agreement.

The most affordable option is to hire you own telemarketer via a service like *www.upwork.com* or *www.outbounders.com*

TACTIC #7 – SEARCH ENGINES

The Internet is a great source of advertising. Competition on the Internet is fierce. In my opinion, you need a fairly sizable budget to advertise successfully on the Internet. Pay-per-click (PPC) is the fastest way to begin generating traffic to your website, but keep in mind that the cost per click and ultimately your cost per lead will be extremely high in the merchant services niche. The two largest players in PPC are Google – *www.ads.google.com* and Bing – *www.ads.about.microsoft.com*.

You must have a Website, a hosting company, and an email address before getting started. Always check with your ISO or sponsoring bank; there may be design guidelines and disclosure requirements that need to be met before placing ad copy.

Make sure to offer an affiliate program. Affiliate programs offer other Website owners or businesses a commission to send you a potential buyer.

TACTIC #8 SOCIAL MEDIA

Social media is a great way to target prospective merchants. Platforms like Facebook, LinkedIn, Twitter, YouTube, and Instagram all offer unique ways to target potential customers. These platforms are constantly changing their targeting options, rules, and data availability. You will want to do extensive research or hire an advertising agency to manage these campaigns to ensure you get the most bang for the buck.

Research social media advertising:

www.facebook.com/ads/manager (Instagram as well)

www.business.linkedin.com/ads

www.ads.twitter.com

www.youtube.com/ads

LinkedIn has a great tool called Sales Navigator that lets you segment potential leads based on a host of search criteria. With over 600M plus users LinkedIn is a great resource for potential clients.

With the rise of privacy concerns, the rules on how you can market and who you can market to on social media is in a constant state of refinement as companies adhere to new regulations. But no matter what changes, taking time to build your own personal brand on social media, especially locally, is always a good idea.

TACTIC #9 — ASSOCIATION ENDORSEMENTS

Association endorsements are about the best lead source available. If you are selected as the vendor of choice for a large association, success is pretty much assured.

The only challenge is that larger associations have agreements in place and the sales cycle to land these types of accounts is very long.

Only spend 5%–10% of your time dealing with associations or trade groups; but if you get one, that business can produce tremendous income.

TACTIC #10 — CHAMBER OF COMMERCE MEETINGS

Chamber of commerce meetings are a great place to meet business owners. Join your local chamber, attend all meetings, and you will start to earn new referral business.

Members receive 2–3 minutes at each meeting to introduce their products and services. Most chambers also have social mixers where you can network with other members.

Chambers also publish periodic newsletters and journals featuring new members. Offer to write an article in your local chamber newsletter; it will give you great exposure.

TACTIC #11 – LEAD EXCHANGE GROUPS

A lead exchange group is comprised of non-competitive businesses that exchange leads. Lead exchange groups usually meet once every two weeks or so.

One of the top lead exchange groups is BNI; they are located at *www.bni.com*.

Check your local listing there are quite a few local groups available these days, *www.meetup.com* is a great place to locate local groups.

If you don't have a lead exchange group in your market area, start one.

TACTIC #12 – CIVIC GROUPS

There are many civic groups and organizations available that will benefit you personally and professionally. Here are just a few:

Toastmasters	Rotary Club
PTO/PTA	Lions Club
Kiwanis Club	Optimist Club
Professional Associations	VFW
Red Cross	YMCA/YWCA
Networking Groups	Church Groups
Elks	Sports Leagues
Habitat for Humanity	Charity Groups

TACTIC #13 – SEMINARS

Seminars are a great way to promote any business. The ideal situation would be to get a group of complementary companies together to share in the expense.

Many new business owners want information on starting, expanding, or growing their businesses. You may want to partner up with a Website company, hosting company, printer, banker, office equipment vendor, or CPA and offer a small business seminar.

Seminars may also be conducted at business expos and trade shows.

TACTIC #14 – PRINT MEDIA

Print advertising is a great strategy to generate leads if you have the budget. Some great sources for advertising are the local yellow pages, local magazines, trade journals, and newsletters.

Check circulation and readership numbers to make sure you are getting a good value for each advertising dollar. There are thousands of trade journals available at affordable rates.

A live person is recommended for answering the phone at all times when advertising in print media. Many people want information immediately and will not leave a message on a voice mail system. If you must use a voice mail system, have caller ID installed in order to track hang-ups.

TACTIC #15 – FREE NEWSLETTER

This one will take a little more effort and time on your part. Newsletters are a great way to introduce new products or services.

I would recommend an email newsletter. There are many software vendors like:

www.constantcontact.com
www.mailchimp.com

That offer great platforms to distribute your newsletter. You will want to sign up subscribers on your website.

TACTIC #16 – AUTO-DIALING EQUIPMENT OR VOICE BROADCAST

Almost everyone has been called by an auto dialer. 99.9% of the people called hang up, but the other .01% responds. Verify if auto dialers are legal in your state and what the requirements are before implementing.

An automated dialer can reach up to 40,000 businesses per day. Naturally, you need to be in a market area large enough, so the same people are not being called over and over. I would suggest a market population of at least 300,000+ people. Also make sure you check current state regulations concerning using auto-dialers, you also want to scrub your database against the do not call list.

FTC: *https://www.ftc.gov/news-events/media-resources/do-not-call-registry/robocalls*

TACTIC #17 – TRADE SHOWS

Trade shows are great places to find new customers and develop partnerships with compatible businesses. Hunt for local trade shows or business expos in your area. Chambers often put on a yearly trade show.

For a listing of trade shows nationally, go to *www.eventsinamerica.com*

TACTIC #18 – LOCAL NEWSPAPERS

Check your local newspapers, business journals, and weekly papers. Many will list new businesses just starting and businesses moving to the area.

Call all the businesses whose advertisements in the local papers and service directories lack credit card logos and offer your services.

For business leads, go to *www.bizjournals.com*.

TACTIC #19 — A PICTURE BUSINESS CARD

This tactic has served the real estate and insurance business well. The business card is your representation of who you are to the business community. Since most people are visual, they remember other people's faces. A business card with a picture has ten times the impact of a normal card.

Also, use the back of the card. Write out all the hot buttons or benefits of your product on the back of the card. Use your card as an advertising tool that moves your customer to action.

TACTIC #20 - DREAM 100

This is one of Chet Holmes core strategies on how to double your sales and capturing top clients in your market. If you haven't read the Ultimate Sales Machine by Chet Holmes I would highly recommend it, it's one of the best meat and potatoes, real life guides on how to succeed in sales.

The concept is to go after Dream 100 clients in your vertical with a vengeance. Create marketing, sales and follow-up campaigns that target your Dream 100 every 45 days. After delivering a consistent message you will gain name recognition and hopefully book a meeting and gain a new client.

Once you start to gain these Dream 100 clients, you can leverage these relationships into more referrals and start to build your brand in the marketplace.

You can also take this concept and expand it to the Dream 100 Influencers, Referral Partners or Association Endorsements, etc.

Leads are the lifeblood of any business, test these tactics and settle on the top two to three that yield the best results. You must and I repeat must have a steady flow of high quality leads coming into your sales funnel.

CHAPTER 38
THE SCIENCE OF RAPPORT

"If you would win a man to your cause,
first convince him that you are his sincere friend."

—Abraham Lincoln

Establishing rapport is the most critical factor in the sales process. Without a rapport the odds of making a sale are slim and none. Rapport is achieved when two people can see the other person's viewpoint, be on the same wavelength, and appreciate each other's situation.

One technology that has helped me tremendously is NLP – Neuro Linguistic Programming. NLP was originally the creation of Richard Bandler and John Grinder who, in the early 1970s, combined their computer programming and linguistic skills to develop a new model of how to produce positive change in human beings.

Neuro refers to the physiological processes associated with internal pictures, sounds, and feelings. *Linguistic* refers to the language associated with those internal experiences. *Programming* refers to the fact that we have choices; that once we understand our own (and others') internal maps, we can choose to change them or reprogram them and thus change the way we experience the world.

NLP is a model of excellence; it has provided a roadmap for successful therapists, salespeople, communicators, and business people. NLP is a kind of human "software" that can be used to organize your experiences in more productive ways.

Here's a great acronym for Rapport:

R	*eally*
A	*ll*
P	*eople*
P	*refer*
O	*thers*
R	*esembling*
T	*hemselves*

The standard definition of "rapport" is a relation of harmony, conformity, accord, or affinity. Rapport is the central organizing concept for any communication interaction. If you don't have rapport your customer they will not purchase. When you have rapport it creates an atmosphere of:

- **Trust**
- **Confidence**
- **Participation**

The benefit of rapport is the establishment of *SAMENESS*, which is moving together in a common direction. *DIFFERENCE* is the basis of poor rapport.

Notice when people are in rapport – there is a pattern or dance to their communication and interaction. Their rhythm, bodies, and words match each other.

Remember that, when they are communicating, people process the majority of the information they receive through three sense-based learning styles. People use all five senses, but primarily use one particular learning styles for processing information internally.

PEOPLE UTILIZE ONE OF THE FOLLOWING LEARNING STYLES:

Visual = Mental Pictures (Most People)

Auditory = Sound or Internal Dialogue

Kinesthetic = Feelings or Emotions

How do you tell if a person is visual, auditory, or kinesthetic? Listen to their language. Here are the most common predicates (verbs, adverbs, and adjectives) people use and the learning style with which they correspond:

VISUAL	AUDITORY	KINESTHETIC
see	sound	feel
picture	hear	relax
perceive	discuss	grasp
notice	listen	handle
look	talk	stress
show	call on	pressure
appear	quiet	smooth
clear	inquire	clumsy
pretty	noisy	rough
colorful	loud	hard
hazy	outspoken	grip
flash	scream	rush
focus	pronounce	firm
bright	remark	euphoric
scene	resonate	clammy

perspective	harmony	touch
imagine	shrill	calm
view	oral	dull
vista	whimper	burning
horizon	mention	stinging
make a scene tongue-tied		get the drift
tunnel vision	ring a bell	boils down to
plainly see	loud and clear	hang in there
eye-to-eye	idle talk	sharp as a tack
mind's eye	to tell the truth	slippcd my mind
bright future	word for word	pull some strings
in the light of	unheard of	smooth operator

Most people mis-communicate because they process information differently from the person with whom they are trying to communicate. By understanding how your customer processes information, you can use the words that work best for your customer to explain your products and services. This establishes rapport.

For instance, if I have a kinesthetic (feeling) merchant, I don't want to show him a picture of a terminal. I want to hand him a terminal so he can actually feel and touch the unit. If I don't have a demo unit, I might use phrases like "this is a really solid unit" or "its sturdy construction means less service problems down the road."

It may feel awkward at first; but trust me, it works.

Here are some other clues for determining a person's representational system:

VISUAL (SEEING)

| Eyes: | These people look up to their right or left, or their eyes may appear unfocused |
| Gestures: | Their gestures are quick, angular, and include pointing |

Breathing & Speech:	High, shallow, and quick
Words :	See, look, imagine, perspective, reveal
Presentations:	Prefer pictures, diagrams, movies

HEARING (AUDITORY)

Eyes:	These people look down to the left and may appear "shifty-eyed"
Gestures:	Rhythmic, touching their face (rubbing chin)
Breathing & Speech:	Mid-chest, rhythmic
Words:	Hear, listen, ask, tell, clicks, in tune
Presentations:	Prefer lists, summarize, quote, read

FEELING (KINESTHETIC)

Eyes:	These people look down to the right
Gestures:	Their gestures are rhythmic, touching their chest
Breathing & Speech:	Deep, slow with pauses
Words:	Feel, touch, grasp, catch on, contact
Presentations:	They prefer hands-on, do-it-yourself demonstrations, test drives

WHAT'S YOUR REPRESENTATIONAL STYLE?

For each of the following questions, go with the first answer that comes to mind.

1   When you think of your first car, what comes to mind first?

    a   A picture; i.e., you driving your car?

    b   A sound; i.e., the sound of the car starting up?

c   A touch; i.e., the way the car handled?

d   A smell; i.e., the smell of the interior?

e   A taste; i.e., food you ate in the car?

2   When you think about something funny, what is the first thing that comes to mind?

a   A sound; i.e., a joke you heard?

b   A smell?

c   An emotion; i.e., someone tickling you?

d   A taste:

e   An image or picture; i.e., a comic telling a joke?

3   When you think about your favorite restaurant, what do you think of first?

a   A picture; i.e., the furniture? The people?

b   A taste; i.e., your favorite dish there?

c   A smell; i.e., the aroma of the kitchen?

d   A sound; i.e., the owner saying hello?

e   A touch; i.e., how you feel when you are there?

4   When you think about your job, what comes to mind first?

a   An emotion; i.e., how you feel about your job?

b   A sound; i.e., people talking in the office?

c   A taste?

d   An image; i.e., you sitting at your desk?

e   A smell; i.e., something in the environment?

5   When you think back on your last birthday, what comes to mind?

a   A taste; i.e., something you ate?

b   A smell; i.e., the candles burning on the cake?

c   A picture; i.e., where you had the party? The balloons?

d   A sound; i.e., people singing "Happy Birthday"?

e   A touch; i.e., someone hugging you?

6   When you think about your next vacation, what do you think about first?

a   An image; i.e., the beach? Skiing? Scuba diving?

b   A sound; i.e., the family laughing or playing?

c   A smell; i.e., the food at the buffet?

d   A touch; i.e., the warm sun on your skin?

e   A taste; i.e., an ice cold drink?

7   When you think about a physically challenging activity, what do you think of first?

a   A sound; i.e., a conversation you have with yourself?

b   A touch; i.e., how the weights feel in you hand?

c   A smell?

d   A taste?

e   A picture or image; i.e., seeing yourself exercising?

8   When you think about a major challenge you have had in your life, what comes to mind first?

a   An image or picture; i.e., you going through the challenge?

b   A sound; i.e., someone speaking to you?

c   A touch; i.e., an emotion you felt?

d   A taste?

e   A smell?

9   When you think about your mother, what comes to mind first?

a   A picture; i.e., what she looks or looked like?

b   A touch or emotion; i.e., how she hugged you?

    c   A smell; i.e., her perfume?

    d   A taste; i.e., her cooking?

    e   A sound; i.e., her calling you in for dinner?

10   When you think about your favorite book, what do you think of first?

    a   A taste; i.e., what you were eating while reading?

    b   A smell?

    c   An image; i.e., the book cover? The characters?

    d   An emotion; i.e., how you felt while reading?

    e   A sound; i.e., you talking to yourself?

Review your answers and determine what representational system you lean on the most. Also determine the one you use the least; this will be the style that needs more work when you attempt to develop rapport with that type of person.

Another great tool for establishing rapport is called mirroring. This is when you mirror your customer's posture, gestures, tonality, and breathing (this is not mimicking – it is just flowing with the person).

Mirroring occurs naturally when two people are in rapport. Just go to a mall or nightclub and watch people in deep communication; they are already mirroring each other. They might lean in when speaking or have their legs crossed the same way, or they may be making the same hand gestures, etc.

Mirroring is not a gimmick; it is a valuable tool designed to help you enter your customer's world and get "in sync" with their wants, needs, and desires.

Studies show that during interpersonal communication a major part of communication is through body language and verbal tonality. Use every tool available.

Here are several tips on building rapport:

- Match the type of words clients use
- Follow their pace
- Listen for inflection; match their tone
- Mirror their posture, gestures, and breathing

Think back to a time when you were in rapport with someone, maybe a close friend or loved one, and examine how you were interacting. Weren't you both speaking at the same pace, using relatively the same movements and gestures?

People buy from people they like. Getting into rapport with your merchants is a critical step in the sales process. If you don't have rapport, stop, regain rapport, and continue. Practice rapport-building skills with everyone you meet; after a while it will become second nature.

CHAPTER 39

ANALYZING NEEDS AND UNCOVERING BUYING VALUES

"You can tell whether a man is clever by his answers.
You can tell whether a man is wise by his questions."

—NAGUIB, MAHFOUZ

During this phase you should be listening 80% of the time and talking 20% of the time. Top sales producers actively listen much more than they speak. The way we learn about our customer's needs and expectations is by asking questions. A conversation begins a sales dialogue.

Questions serve many purposes:

- You learn valuable information about your customers and their situation.
- They relieve pressure.

- By asking a question you can be sure that the customer understands your point, especially when dealing with a complicated issue.
- The answers you receive to your questions help you judge the progress you are making in your presentation.

Remember, you are on a fact-finding mission. Find out what *their* expectations are in a payment system, a new vendor relationship, or your service.

The initial questions asked are determined by the service or product you are marketing. Our goal is to get the initial information we need to recommend the right solution and then finish up with the three value questions in order to determine the customer's dominant buying motive.

There are many different types of questions you can ask:

OPEN-ENDED QUESTIONS: (INFORMATIONAL)

Who, What, Where, When, How?

CLOSED-ENDED QUESTIONS: (ANSWER IS USUALLY A YES OR NO)

Would you consider changing processors if I could save you _____ in fees?

Emotional:	How do you feel about...?
Preference:	Which do you prefer...?
Trial Close:	Is this what you were looking for?
Tie-Downs:	This is important to you, isn't it?

Make sure you know all the questions you are going to ask during the initial interview stage.

If you can't remember them, create a client questionnaire (there is a sample one for you in Appendix D). Naturally your questions will be determined by your sales call goal.

By really listening to your merchant's answers, you are demonstrating the qualities of an extraordinary salesperson. This is your greatest tool to establish rapport and trust. Who do people like to talk about the most? You guessed it – themselves. Get them talking about their plans and aspirations.

Once you have investigated their business plan, work your way into the three value questions. These three value questions will determine the customer's dominant buying motive.

Use your own language style to ask these value questions; these are just examples.

1   Mr. Merchant (first name), what is *MOST* important to you when considering the purchase of a payment system (whatever product or service you're offering)?

    OR

    Mr. Merchant, what is most important to you when considering a new vendor?

2   How do you know when you have _____?

We want the merchant's definition of what is most important. Don't assume you know what service, price or quality means; have them define it.

3   If I could show you a program that gives you _____, and make sense for you, not me, would you consider doing business today?

    OR

    If I could give you _____ would you feel comfortable moving forward?

    If the client responds "No," ask, "What else is important to you when purchasing a payment system?" and repeat the cycle.

By asking these questions you are uncovering your customer's dominant buying values. Now you know what is important to your customer, make sure you highlight the customer's buying values throughout the presentation.

EXAMPLE:

Salesperson: Mr. Merchant, what is MOST important to you when considering the purchase of a payment system?

Merchant: I would have to say service.

Salesperson: Mr. Merchant, how do you know when you have great service?

Merchant: Well that's easy; there is someone on the other end of the phone when I call. I don't have time to make 5 calls to get an answer to my question.

Salesperson: Mr. Merchant, let me ask you a question. If I could show you a program that offered great service and makes sense for you, not me, would you considering doing business today?

Merchant: Sure, I'd consider it.

By asking the value questions you already have your merchant moving in the right direction – towards a sale. Everybody is different use these questions as a template, work on the wording to fit your individual style.

Questions are the doorway to your customer's mind; take the time up front to explore your customer's world and you will eliminate most of the roadblocks before they occur.

CHAPTER 40
THE PRESENTATION

*"The path to success is to take massive,
determined action."*

—Anthony Robbins

Up to this point we have gained rapport and, hopefully, uncovered the most important factors in your merchant's buying decision process. Now is the time to demonstrate that you can meet the merchant's requirements.

Here are 6 keys to making successful presentations:

KEY #1 — BE ENTHUSIASTIC

The definition of enthusiasm is a source or cause of great excitement or interest. The quality that will lift your presentation above all others is the enthusiasm you have for your products and services. Without enthusiasm yours is just another sales story, the kind that merchants forget the minute you walk out the door.

Enthusiasm comes from a genuine passion about what you do and how you feel you will positively impact your customer. Transfer your enthusiasm to your customers; this is your only chance to make a lasting impression and win the sale with this merchant. Enthusiasm is contagious and it sells.

Think about it. Have you ever purchased a product or service because of the salesperson's sheer exuberance? Have you given your business to the person who genuinely wanted to help you?

People have a sixth sense; no amount of enthusiasm will work if you don't believe in the benefits of what you're offering. If you're sold on your company, services, and products, you will generate genuine enthusiasm.

KEY #2 — BE PREPARED

Make sure you know your presentation from start to finish. Video tape and record your presentation, then look for any flaws, gaps, or information missing.

Focus on benefits, not features.

- A feature represents an aspect of your product or service. A feature explains what your product does.
- Benefits represent what that feature provides, how it will make life easier for the merchant or its customer.

Tune into your customers' radio station, WIIFM, and answer this question for them:

WIIFM = What's in it for ME?

Work with an experienced agent in your sales office. Have other agents give you their presentations. Call your competitors and see how they sell their products.

Keep a notebook and take notes after every presentation. Analyze what went right and what went wrong. Always hunt for ways to improve your presentation skills.

KEY #3 – CREATE A POWERFUL OPENING INTRODUCTION

Most presentations begin with an introduction about the salesperson and the company you represent. This is your first opportunity after establishing rapport to really impact your prospect. *You won't get a second chance to make a first impression.*

Make sure you use your prospect's first name at least once in the introduction and throughout your presentation. Your opening introduction should be an attention grabber that demonstrates the major benefits or unique selling proposition of your company. The introduction may also be used to prevent a common objection before it is raised.

Here's a sample traditional introduction:

Mr. Merchant (use their first name), I'd like to start by thanking you for your time. I know it's valuable. I have been specializing in helping merchants reduce overhead and increase sales, sometimes up to 50%, for several years now. I feel like one of our unique benefits is that we are a local company representing one of the largest processors of financial transactions in the country. We offer one-stop shopping for all your financial services including check processing; gift and loyalty cards; and debit and credit card processing. I feel we are uniquely qualified to partner with your company and meet all your transaction processing needs. I'd like to start by asking you a few questions so I can recommend the right solution. How's that sound?

Low Pressure Model:

Mr. Merchant (use their first name), I'd like to start by thanking you for your time. I know it's valuable. The first thing I think you should know about our company is our method of working with merchants is a little different from our competitors. We don't use any high-pressure sales tactics, tricks, or gimmicks to force you to do business with us. Often traditional sales methods cause unwanted pressure on our customers and, quite frankly, on me. And a lot of times it turns into an adversarial relationship. So, I just want to begin by saying, "relax." I'm here to create a win-win relationship for both of us. I'm not here to sell you anything. But I am here to create an atmosphere where you can buy without being pressured. Does that sound fair enough? Great!

I'd like to start by asking you a couple of questions so I can get a clear picture of what you needs are, okay?

Try several different variations and see what works best for you. Make your introduction personal; if you have 15 years in the retail business or a unique background, emphasize it in your introduction and explain how that will benefit the merchant.

Memorize your introduction; it's got to be fluid and smooth.

KEY #4 – USE VIVID WORDS

Paint a clear and vivid picture for your merchant. Review the Chapter on – The Science of Rapport.

If you haven't figured out your prospect's learning strategy, hit them all. Work all three into your presentation. Remember a picture is worth a thousand words; don't forget roughly 60% of all people are visual.

Design a presentation book that you can refer to while speaking to your merchant. Use colorful graphics, charts, and articles to highlight major selling points. This method works well; it keeps the merchant's mind busy while you are speaking. It also ensures that you are giving the same general presentation each time. This lets you uncover any flaws or areas where improvement is needed. Drawing pictures on a note pad also works well.

Use your pen to highlight each point during the presentation.

Use Power Words. Yale University did a study and found that these were the 12 most persuasive words in the English language:

Easy	Results	Save
Discover	Guarantee	Safety
Health	Love	Money
Need	Proven	You

KEY #5 – TELL STORIES TO MAKE POINTS CLEAR

There are three reasons why successful salespeople use stories in their presentations:

- People enjoy stories. A good story is entertaining, informative, and instructive.
- Stories put the imagination to work. Stories allow merchants to engage their own representational system. It allows them to turn your words into pictures, sounds, and feelings within their own minds.
- Stories can be used anywhere in the presentation. A good story can get your presentation back on track, emphasize a strong point, strengthen rapport, be used as a closing tool, and much, much more.

The best stories are the ones that illustrate the benefits that other merchants have received from using your specific equipment or service. It's not always what you say, but how you say it.

Here is one I've used several times when selling pin based debit services. The customer is an auto repair shop using out-dated equipment and feels he doesn't need to upgrade his equipment.

"I have a customer just like you over at Midwest Tire Repair, what we did was upgrade him to a new machine so he could accept debit and check cards. I'm sure you have seen all the advertisements on TV about check cards. You've probably got one in your wallet from your bank. Well up to 30% of all the credit cards you are taking are more than likely check cards, sometimes more (have backup article or material). You see, when you process a check card through the terminal, you have to pay the full discount rate like a credit card, but when you process the check card through your terminal using the pin pad you only pay a small flat transaction fee. Midwest's average ticket was $400.00, and he was paying $7.05 per sale; with his new system, however, he only pays $0.50 per check card regardless of the ticket amount. So, if Midwest does a $1,000 sale on a check card processed as a debit transaction, he only pays $0.50 for that sale. It saved him enough to pay for all his new equipment. Not only that, but now when customers start to write a check he asks if they want to use their debit card. It cut his bad check losses in half, eliminated handwriting receipts, and saved his office manager a trip to the bank." (Use simple straightforward language.)

Make sure you have several true stories you can share with your customers about the benefits that your products offer. You may also want to discuss future technology and how it is going to affect your customers' business. Your stories should demonstrate how you remove pain from their current or future situation and add benefit.

Again, remember the golden rule. Answer this question for them.

WIIFM = What's in it for ME

KEY #6 – KISS: KEEP IT SHORT AND SIMPLE

Small business owners and corporate managers have limited time. Make sure you let them know that you appreciate the time given you and that it will be used wisely.

Remember when you are marketing to new businesses that they know very little about transaction processing; speak in simple terms. Don't use industry jargon that will confuse and frustrate them.

Before we get into preventing objections let us review why people buy.

CHAPTER 41
WHY DO PEOPLE BUY?

"The art of life is the art of avoiding pain;
and he is the best pilot, who steers clearest
of the rocks and shoals with which it is beset."

—THOMAS JEFFERSON

The reason people buy is simple. *People buy for their own reasons, not yours!* Until you discover their dominant buying motive you won't know why people buy. Realize that their buying motives are influenced by two powerful forces driving their decision making process.

- The Need to Avoid Pain or Fear of Loss

  (Moving away motivation)

  OR

- The Need to Gain Pleasure or Benefit

  (Moving toward motivation)

These two forces not only guide buying decisions but life decisions as well. Buying decisions are emotional. It takes a stronger emotion to overcome a weaker emotion. The only way to overcome the fear of pain is to make the desire for gain, or to be better off, more intense.

These emotions can be experienced in the context of several time frames.

PAIN OR PLEASURE IN THE PRESENT

"How many sales are you missing as we speak?"

"You could start making money today by accepting credit cards."

PAIN OR PLEASURE IN THE FUTURE

"At this rate how much in lost sales will you have over the next 3 months?"

"Just think, by this time next year you would not have had to worry about a single bad check."

PAIN OR PLEASURE IN THE PAST

"How would you like to never have to worry about turning away a credit card sale again?"

"How would you like to reach the sales levels you had in the past by offering our loyalty program?"

The most powerful emotions are linked to the present. Show them how you can help today and/or avoid fear of loss today, and you will get the sale.

The majority of people will do more to avoid pain than they will to gain pleasure. In fact, studies have shown that pain is a 2.5 times greater motivator than pleasure. These behaviors are genetically and culturally programmed. Think about it, how did your parents motivate you as a child? Usually we are threatened with some type of consequence (spanking, grounding, lost privileges). A very small number of parents use pleasure or rewards to motivate their children.

When do most people make a major life change or modify their behavior? When the pain gets too great! Sit down one night and watch the majority of TV commercials and you will see they are using pain to motivate buyers. Do any of these ring a bell?

"Are you experiencing gas or bloating?"

"Can't cure that achy head cold?"

"We're moving them out fast. Don't wait; they won't last long!"

"Mortgage rates won't stay this low much longer; refinance today!"

It goes on and on.

This is simple psychology; often the most profound insights are simple. Just make sure you not only show your customers how much your products will benefit them, but how they can also alleviate their pain today.

If you would like to explore this idea further, complete the exercise at *www.surviveandthrive.biz/resources*

CHAPTER 42
PREVENTING OBJECTIONS

"Take your life in your own hands and what happens?
A terrible thing: no one is to blame."

—Erica Jong

The best way to handle objections or roadblocks is to prevent them ahead of time. The extraordinary salespeople weave the answers to the most common objections throughout their presentations.

When merchants raise an objection, one of the following is happening:

- *They Have Questions*

  "I need more information."

- *Defensive Reaction*

  "I feel threatened; fear or risk."

- *Emotional*

"I am in a bad state."

- *They Need Help*

  "Help me make the right decision."

HERE ARE THE 7 STEPS THAT CAN HELP PREVENT OBJECTIONS:

1   Identify every conceivable objection. Most objections are pretty much the same regardless of what you sell.

2   Write them down.

3   Write down the answer to each objection and how to overcome it. (Prove it; put together visual aids, testimonials, articles, letters of reference, etc.) Work with other salespeople in your office to brainstorm ideas.

4   Practice. Practice. Practice. Role-play with people.

5   Test the solution in the field.

6   Make any revisions or changes.

7   Practice. Practice. Practice.

I have a preventing objection exercise you can download at: *www.surviveandthrive.biz/resouces*

CHAPTER 43
WHAT BENEFITS DO YOU OFFER?

"Great spirits have always encountered violent opposition from mediocre minds."

—Albert Einstein

Before we can work on converting objections, let us do a short exercise on the benefits offered by your products and services.

List 10 things about your product or service that benefits your merchant the most (What's in it for THEM):

1 _____

2 _____

3 _____

4 _____

5 _____

6 _____

7 _____

8 _____

9 _____

10 _____

List 5 things about your processor, ISO, or bank that benefits your merchant the most:

1 _____

2 _____

3 _____

4 _____

5 _____

List 5 benefits of the equipment you are recommending to your merchant:

1 _____

2 _____

3 _____

4 _____

5 _____

List 5 things about you that add value to your merchant:

1 _____

2 _____

3 _____

4 _____

5 _____

Now that you know what benefits you bring to the table, be ready to prove it. You must have visuals, articles, reports and material that substantiate your claims; without them, your claims are all just talk.

CHAPTER 44
GAINING COMMITMENT

"People are always blaming their circumstances
for what they are. I don't believe in circumstances.
The people who get on in the world are the people who
get up and look for the circumstances they want,
and if they can't find them, make them."

—GEORGE BERNARD SHAW

A great definition of gaining commitment is helping people make an educated buying decision. You've heard it before: "People don't like to be sold, but they love to buy." Your job is to create an environment where merchants want to buy. Let us consider the most common reasons why prospects don't buy.

- *Fear of making a bad decision*
- *No perceived need and/or value*
- *They don't have the means to purchase*
- *Comfortable with current situation*

- *Lack of rapport or trust with salesperson*
- *Had a previous negative experience*

The job of the merchant-focused salesperson is to create a win-win situation with every customer, period. By now you should have the responses for your most common objections and how to master them. One thing to remember is that merchants want and need our services, or you wouldn't be there.

Also keep in mind that many initial objections are conditioned responses, which means they are automatic. When someone in a retail store asks you, "May I help you?" how do you respond? Probably with "No thank you, I'm just looking." Many of your merchants are doing the same thing.

Remember, people buy for their own reasons. Objections give you a good idea about what is really going on in your customers' minds and the chance to re-verify what is really of true value to them.

Answering questions to objections should not be adversarial; it is an opportunity to consummate the sale. Don't get defensive; an objection is not a personal attack.

Here are five traditional steps to overcoming objections:

1   Listen to the objection. Really listen.
2   Acknowledge the objection. Empathize and/or feed it back to the client or ask a question to clarify the objection.
3   Answer the objection. It must be believable and practical to the situation. Use your "prove it" tools.
4   Confirm. Verify that the answer you gave is acceptable.
5   Advance the sale.

TRADITIONAL CLOSING TECHNIQUES

Many traditional closing techniques still work. If you have rapport, offered a solution that met the dominant buying motive, and presented your product well, this step should be a natural progression.

THE ALTERNATE CHOICE

This is a technique where the client is given several options to choose from, usually just two. Regardless of the answer, it will result in a sale.

- *Would you like to start with the unit with the pin pad for $59.00 per month or the basic unit for $49.00 per month?*
- *Do you prefer delivery on Tuesday or Wednesday?*
- *Do you prefer the 48-month term or the 36-month term?*
- *Mr. Merchant, we have two programs. Program A is a lease to own for $39.95 for 48 months or Program B is our cash program for $995.00 cash. Which do you prefer?*
- *Mr. Merchant, we have two programs. Our platinum business development program offers you check imaging, gift cards, debit, and credit for $89.95 per month or you may enroll in our silver program, which is debit and credit only for $49.95 per month. Which works best for you?*

The list is endless. Multiple alternate choice closes can be created based on your individual product offering.

THE ASSUMPTIVE CLOSE

This close assumes the merchant wants your equipment and services; you simply act by asking a question, then just start filling out the application. And why not, after the fantastic enthusiastic presentation you just gave?

Sample Questions:

- *What is the legal name of your business?*
- *Do you have a copy of your business license handy?*
- *What is your tax ID number?*

- *When did you want me to train your employees?*
- *Then I can assume we can move forward?*

As long as the merchant continues to answer the questions, continue to assume that they have bought and finish your paperwork.

FEEL, FELT, FOUND METHOD

This is a great close. It works with just about any objection raised.

The "feel, felt, found" method accomplishes three things:

- *Assures the merchant its feelings have been accepted*
- *Let's the merchant know those feelings are valid and shared by other merchants*
- *Shows the merchant that others have found those feelings to be unfounded because of one or more of the benefits of ownership*

I understand how you feel; I've had customers who felt the same way but what they found was that _____.

THE SUMMATION CLOSE

The summation or recap close does exactly what it sounds like it does. It is a quick summation of all the benefits stated during the presentation that the merchant responded to.

"Mr. Merchant, just to summarize, the following benefits were important to you..."

1   That our new terminal will take all the major credit cards and the new smart cards being introduced to the marketplace, right?

2   One of the most important benefits we discussed was the ability to accept debit cards at a 0% discount fee and only a small transaction fee, right?

3   The new terminal is more user-friendly than your current system and will decrease your checkout time, which will really help you in the Christmas rush, correct?

4   That we can set you up with our new gift card program to help increase cash flow immediately.

"Well, Mr. Merchant, considering everything, why don't we go ahead with the program? Or – considering everything – is there anything that would prevent us from moving forward?

Quit here and wait for a response. If positive, proceed; if negative, clarify the objection, and advance the sale.

THE THINK IT OVER CLOSE

This is one of the most common objections. This is the prospect that never makes a snap decision. He wants to sleep on it. When you hear, "I want to think it over," respond with:

EXAMPLE:

That's fine; I understand. This is an important decision and you do need to feel comfortable with it. I know you want to make sure you covered all the bases. But, just to clarify my thinking and answer any questions you might have while I'm here, what is it that you want to think over? Is there something I didn't cover or is it the _____ or _____? (Keep firing possibilities at them in order to find out the true objection; i.e., is it the equipment? Is it the lease term? Is it our bank? Is it the price?)

The price should be mentioned last because it is the most common reason. This process will uncover the true objection. Once the true objection is uncovered you can deal with it.

SPECIAL OFFER CLOSE

Everybody wants a special deal; they want to feel they are getting the best value for their money. The only thing that limits a special offer is your imagination. Many times, by building value in your sales presentation and by offering something the competition isn't, you can hold your price.

Put a time limit on special offers. You want to create a sense of urgency.

Here are a few samples:

Mr. Merchant, for setting up with us today, we are waiving the normal application fee of $95.00, and charging no installation fee.

As an incentive, Mr. Merchant, we are currently offering five years free supplies for all new merchants who sign up this month.

As a bonus, Mr. Merchant, we are setting up all our customers up with a free 3-page Website.

Mr. Merchant, we have partnered with a local Web design company and have arranged a special package for our customers. We can now offer you a custom 5-page Website for only $99.00; this is a 60% discount off our normal price.

Just for doing business with us today, Mr. Merchant, we are including three valuable reports: "How to Avoid Fraud," "How to Write a Business Plan," and "How to Keep and Gain Customer Loyalty."

Mr. Merchant, we have partnered with XYZ Communications, and just for doing business with us today we are including a month's free high speed business class internet service.

Mr. Merchant, we are currently giving all our new clients a free 1-hour consultation with a local accounting firm that we have partnered with. They can assist you with setting up your books and payroll system.

Mr. Merchant, we are currently offering a free small business accounting system called QuickBooks to our next 50 customers.

Use common sense. You can partner with many vendors who want to reach this business market, and often they will give you free product to give away.

WHEN ALL ELSE FAILS, JUST ASK "WHY?"

Here is one technique that works in almost any situation and avoids using any pre-packed closing responses. Just ask the customer "Why." You can phrase this in many different ways; here are a few:

Why do you say that?

I'm curious; why do you feel that way?

Tell me, why do you think that?

Why do you think my price is too high?

Why is that?

This will get down to the real objection very rapidly and you can work with your customer to eliminate their concerns.

CHAPTER 45
LET'S TALK ABOUT PRICE

Most salespeople make price a bigger issue than the customer does. Is price important? Of course, it is. But very few people buy on price alone. If people bought on price alone, they would be watching black-and-white TVs, driving compact cars, wearing nothing but Timex watches, and dressing in second-hand clothes.

There are dozens of factors that influence customers' buying decisions; price is just one of them. In order to overcome a price issue your customer must believe that value outweighs price.

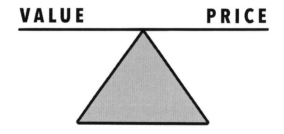

VALUE   PRICE

In order to tip the scales in your favor you must have an in-depth knowledge of the benefits you offer your merchant. You must emphasize your unique qualities and differentiate yourself from the competition.

Your terminal and rates may be the same as the next guy's, but your total offer may be completely different. You may have key differences in several areas. See where you are better or different from your competitor and you will distinguish uniqueness in your offering.

Let us do an exercise. Get a piece of paper out, create a column for each category below, and review your unique features and benefits (you may have multiple answers for each category):

For instance, one of the unique features you may include in the category "company" is that you provide local customer service and have been in business in this area for over 10 years.

CATEGORY
YOUR COMPANY

Size (small or large can both be a benefit)
Credibility
Awards
Locality
Time in Business
Breadth of Products
One-Stop Shopping
References
Special Partners or Alliances
Specific Expertise

SALESPERSON

Years in the Business
Life Experience

Special Training
Specific Expertise in Certain Niche
Testimonials
References
Credibility

BANKS OR VENDORS

Clients They Service Now
Funds Transfer
Custom Programs (tips, car rental etc.)
Size
Credibility
Awards
Locality
Time in Business
Breadth of Products
One Stop Shopping
Specialize in Certain Types of Customers
Reporting Capabilities
Online products or services

PAYMENT TERMS

Free Trial Period
Leasing
Special Terms (i.e., 3 payments same as cash)
No Money Down
Rental Program
Accept Credit Cards

SPECIAL OFFERS

45 Day Trial Period
Free Loaner Program
Free Supplies

Free Bonus Offering
No Down Payment
No Application Fee
Free Reports
Free Consultation
Referral Fee
Free Website
Free Training

RATES AND FEE

Discount Rates
Mid- & Non-Qualified Rates
Annual Fees
Cancellation Fees
Minimums
Statement Fees
Chargeback Fees
Investigation Fees
Batch Header Fees
Retrieval Fees
Transaction Fees
Application Fees

EQUIPMENT

Warranty
Ease of Use
Training
Delivery
Special Payment Terms
Future Capabilities
Current Capabilities
Upgrade Path
Size of Unit

CUSTOMER SERVICE

Hours of Operation
Average Hold Time
Size of Staff
Awards
Services Offered

TRAINING

Certification
Type of Training
Ongoing Training
Personal or Phone
No Charge

INSTALLATION

Time Frame (how quickly can they get it)
Shipment
Special Features about Installation
Personal Installation

Now that you have the ammunition to create value for your merchant and overcome the competition, choose 3–4 majors benefits in each category and be ready to use them in the sales process.

The sales professional must make the necessary changes to be successful in today's fast-paced market. By combining traditional closing techniques with new technologies, you will create a system that will yield consistently higher closing ratios.

The basics still apply! Sell yourself and your program, and then ask for the business. Selling is fun – enjoy it, be good to your profession, and it will be good to you!

CHAPTER 46
CUSTOMER FOLLOW UP

"We are what we repeatedly do.
Excellence, then, is not an act, but a habit."

—ARISTOTLE

Okay you did everything you could but didn't make the sale. Now you have to follow up; this is where the money is. Make sure that, before you leave the merchant, a follow-up time and date has been set.

This is where 90% of salespeople drop the ball. If you left the appointment and agreed to call the merchant next Tuesday at 2:00, then call him next Tuesday at 2:00. You will impress him with your ability to follow up on your commitments.

Make sure you maintain a database of your clients and utilize a CRM. Many CRM's have free versions so you can get started easily.

Here are some pointers to help close follow-up sales:

- *Send the merchant a handwritten thank you note.*
- *Send the merchant an industry-related article- (i.e., an article on EMV implementation, fraud, or debit cards).*
- *Call with a special limited-time offer to close the sale.*
- *Send a paper or e-card.*
- *Refer a customer to their company.*
- *Put them in your auto-responder follow-up system.*
- *Add the merchant on your newsletter list.*
- *Utilize SMS test messaging.*

CHAPTER 47

MLS 3.0 SELLING IN THE THIRD WAVE OF MERCHANT SERVICES

CONTRIBUTING WRITER DALE LASZIG

Through the years, merchant level salespeople (MLSs) have moved our industry forward, converting merchants from paper receipts to electronic processing and guiding them through ever-changing processing technology. MLSs were selling credit card processing when *How to Survive and Thrive in the Merchant Services Industry* was first published in 2003. By the time the updated edition appeared in 2009, processing had become a utility, like water or electricity.

As competition increased, ISOs and MLSs brought a diversity of point of sale (POS) products to market. Merchants, formerly limited to two or three styles of countertop terminals, could choose from an array of products and services. Some solutions were small and mobile or entirely virtual; others were big and complicated. All offered more than credit and debit card processing. These early value-added products and services may seem clunky by today's standards, but they were the precursors of present-day digital solutions.

Each era of the payments journey presents its own challenges, setting the stage for the next big thing. In the first wave, MLSs demonstrated the benefits of credit card acceptance. In the second wave, they upgraded merchants from basic POS to faster, smarter systems. This wave was approaching its peak a decade ago, when I wrote a chapter on selling technology for this book.

ADJACENT POS-SIBLE

If I were to rewrite "Ten Tips on Selling Technology," my first tip would be to stop selling it. Technology is just a toolbox. Like credit card processing, it has become a utility. MLSs did a great job of selling high-speed communications, battery-operated mobile devices, affordable integrated POS and chip-enabled card reader peripherals. These once revolutionary concepts are a mainstream, Main Street reality. What was once a frontier is now a baseline.

It's not easy to grasp technology's full potential, especially when solutions are unlike anything we have known. Innovation is iterative, each step leading to the next. Scientist Stuart Kauffman calls this the adjacent possible. When I wrote the chapter, I sensed adjacent, early-stage solutions that were still a few years out, without fully comprehending them. I brought an analog mindset to a digital game. Kauffman says this is normal. We work with what we've got.

Reading the ten original tips today is like opening a time capsule and seeing a way of selling that was right for its time. While some tips seem out of place in the modern digital playing field, each seems to sense something new, without always having the vocabulary to fully describe it. Let's take a look at what these tips reveal about payment processing, then and now.

Tip 1: Sell New *Never forget that the system you sell represents you and your company. Help merchants 'just say no' to old, non-compliant technology.*

When ISO and processor brands were displayed on countertop devices, MLSs could see who they were competing against just by looking at a terminal. Today's high-tech POS systems blend in with retail and hospitality settings; some are not even visible in upscale locales. Bring your own device (BYOD) is also an option for merchants who prefer to use their personal consumer-grade devices to accept payments.

Modern POS solutions are more affordable and easier to update than older analog machines. Fewer merchants are buying refurbished countertop terminals or reprograming old equipment. During the 2015 EMV migration, processors, card brands and service providers assisted merchants with POS upgrades and continue to provide resources and support to help them maintain secure, compliant processing systems.

Tip 2: Sell Security *Educate your merchants on industry security guidelines.*

The PCI Security Standards Council (PCI SSC) has produced *PCI Data Security Essentials Resources for Small Merchants* to help small and midsize businesses (SMBs) improve protections and assess security services. The downloadable guides are available on the PCI SSC website's Merchant Resource Page.

As predicted, when EMV technology decreased in-store counterfeit card fraud, criminals shifted their focus to card not present (CNP) merchants. It's crucial to educate ecommerce merchants about security best practices and EMV non-compliant merchants about their liability for fraudulent transactions.

Tip 3: Sell Value *Value-added solutions are cost-effective, easy to use and increase profits.*

Value can mean different things to different people. MLSs may think of value as ancillary products and services. Merchants may think of value as getting a good deal at a fair price. Successful MLSs know that value is not always a simple add-on; it's more about how they collaborate with merchants to solve problems and improve processing systems.

Tip 4: Solve a Problem *Consultative selling puts you at the black belt level of selling.*

Consultative selling, by its very nature, is different every time. MLSs who approach prospects with scripted presentations or preconceived notions of what to sell may miss clear buying signs and other nuanced, unexpected things that can happen on a sales call.

Tip 5: Multi-task *Sell solutions that give your merchants a single-access view of a variety of applications. Many countertop devices are "multi-app," which means that different programs can be added to the terminal.*

Before there were app stores, terminal manufacturers partitioned countertop terminals to support third-party applications while maintaining strict firewalls between payment processing and value-added services. This tip predates the Apple App Store and Google Play and seems to anticipate the gradual replacement of single-use machines by app marketplaces and solutions that work across multiple channels.

Tip 6: Customize *Logos can be added to gift cards, credit card receipts, virtual terminals and shopping carts, helping merchants advertise and build brand awareness.*

White label solutions enable merchants to improve brand recognition and provide a consistent customer experience across channels. Technology facilitates personalization at scale: it enables merchants to send unique offers to each customer and enables MLSs to create right-sized, customized services for each merchant.

Tip 7: Sell Services *Even if your merchant doesn't immediately decide to add services, you'll make a positive impression by showing a broad scope of offerings and pave the way for a future sale.*

In addition to implementing applications that improve their businesses and expand their reach, merchants can develop their own apps to make their services widely accessible to consumers and service providers on the app marketplace.

Tip 8: Sell Web-enabled Tools *With all the online banking and commerce available today, most merchants want more than a once-a-month paper statement sent to them by snail mail. Make them aware of online options that can help them track transaction activity in real-time and reconcile credit card reports with bank statements.*

Remember when help desks lit up every 30 days when merchants received their credit card statements? Today's merchants expect to view transactions from anywhere in real-time and communicate with customer service by email, phone, text or live chat.

Tip 9: Sell Maintenance *Overnight replacement policies, automatic supply renewals and other support services will give your merchants peace of mind and the freedom to focus on their core businesses.*

Merchant clubs, extended warranties and protection plans made sense in the early days of payment processing when merchants were learning authorization and settlement. Today's cloud-based subscription services frequently include overnight hardware replacement. Advanced sensemaking technologies monitor connected devices and generate alerts when they detect equipment issues and power failures.

Tip 10: Don't Overload the Apple Cart *You don't have to show all of your products and services on your first visit with a merchant. Ask questions; share ideas. When you understand a merchant's business, you're taking the first step in building a partnership and payment system that is strong enough for today and scalable enough for tomorrow.*

Merchant services will always be a relationship business. MLSs still focus on customers, despite how much their jobs have changed. As solutions evolve from standalone to integrated systems, MLSs help merchants of all sizes, from start-ups to enterprise brands, achieve objectives and remain relevant in the consumer-driven marketplace.

FROM ANALOG TO DIGITAL

Remember when we had to choose between fast and cheap or good and expensive products? In an April 2015 blog post, titled "Data-Driven Thinking, A Zero-Sum Game," Shelly Palmer, technology thought leader and CEO of The Palmer Group, wrote, "You can have it good, fast or cheap ... pick any two. If you want it good and fast, it won't be cheap. If you want it fast and cheap, it won't be good. If you want it good and cheap, it won't be fast."

While Palmer was describing data science, the same principle might apply to payment processing at a time when high-speed connectivity was scarce, and merchants paid top dollar for countertop terminals with Ethernet ports. Today's widespread and affordable communications technologies have made it possible for merchants to have good, fast and cheap products.

What do merchants want in the always-on, always-connected world? They want great customer relationships and partners who understand their businesses and can help them grow and scale. Today's merchants have a single-access, real-time view of operations and inventories and deliver personalized messages to their customers. They delegate mundane tasks to artificial intelligence, which frees them to focus on critical priorities. They use dynamic security solutions and threat intelligence to monitor, detect and eliminate threats, protecting their networks and customers.

FROM TRANSACTIONAL TO CONVERSANT

To fully appreciate how much the payments playing field has changed in recent years, consider the "click." What's the first thing that comes to mind when you hear that word? You might think of single-click ordering online or click-through rates that measure viewers on a web page, ad or email campaign. You probably don't think of credit card transactions, because advanced technologies have transformed simple transactions into complex conversations.

Transactions have come alive in the digital world and are no longer limited to a single device or channel. They don't always originate at the POS and they don't always end at checkout. Consumers want an easy, frictionless experience when they shop online, in apps and in physical stores. Customers may buy online and pick up in a store (BOPIS) or visit a store and buy online. If they're not sure about a purchase, they may share a photo on social media to solicit feedback from their friends. When they check out in a store, on their phones or online, consumers can combine a variety of payment types with points, coupons, discounts and instant incentives.

MLSs can follow the click's example by becoming less transactional and more conversational. The clarion call to be more consultative and vertically focused was eerily on point years ago, before anyone had even heard the word "omnichannel." Today we call it being contextual. Sales discussions are ideally framed by the context of a particular customer or problem to be solved.

In the third wave of merchant services, MLSs are selling to sophisticated buyers who have established processing relationships and already use technology in innovative ways. It makes no sense to lead with processing or technology. Research the prospect and understand the customer's customer, because customers hold the key. By asking research-driven questions and focusing on what merchants want, MLSs will spark interesting conversations and new adjacent opportunities.

SECTION 4

PROFESSIONAL
DEVELOPMENT

CHAPTER 48
TIME MANAGEMENT

"Time is life. It is irreversible and irreplaceable.
To waste your time is to waste your life, but to master
your time is to master your life and make the most of it."

—ALAN LAKEIN

Here are some interesting facts to consider:

- There are only 86,400 seconds or 1,440 minutes or 24 hours in our day – period. How this time is utilized will determine your success or failure in this life.

- The average person today receives more information on a daily basis than the average person received in a lifetime in 1900.

- Between 1900 and 1998, life expectancy in the United States increased from 51 to 80 for females and 48 to 74 for males.

- The life expectancy for females born in the year 2050 is predicted to be 87 years; for males, it is predicted to be 81 years.

- The average male's heart will beat 2,791,743,120 times during his lifetime, and he will take 581,613,150 breaths of air.
- The average human being has roughly 60,000 thoughts a day.
- The average person spends less than two minutes per day in meaningful communication with their spouse or "significant other."
- 28% of all households have two TVs, 28% of all households have three TVs, 20% of all households have four TVs, and 12% of all households have five or more TVs.
- On an average day 31% of all children will watch 1–3 hours of TV; 17% will watch more than 5 hours a day.
- 75% of heart attacks occur between the hours of 5:00 a.m.– 8:00 a.m.
- More heart attacks occur on Monday than on any other day of the week.
- 80% of people do not want to go to work on Monday. That number drops to 60% by Friday.
- There are 17 million meetings per day in America.
- The average person gets 6 hours and 57 minutes of sleep per night.
- The average person spends 35 minutes per day commuting.
- 1 hour of planning will save you 10 hours of doing.

PARETO'S LAW

Almost 100 years ago Vilfredo Pareto, an Italian economist, conducted a study on income and wealth patterns. He discovered a "predictable imbalance" that shows up in every area of life. This is now known as the Pareto Time Principle, or the 80/20 Rule. The 80/20 rule means that 80% of time spent poorly produces 20% of desired results, while 20% of time spent wisely nets 80% of the desired results.

Examples of the Pareto principle include:

- 80% of the sales that salespeople make come from 20% of their cold calls.
- 20% of the automobiles on the road cause 80% of the accidents.
- 20% of the producers create 80% of the production volume.
- 80% of the useful information on the Internet comes from 20% of the sites.
- 80% of what makes you happy comes from 20% of the people with whom you are close.

One of the secrets of success is to stay focused on the 20% of our lives that will help us reach our goals and mission. By devoting more time and effort to the 20% that matters, you gain tremendous leverage in your life.

Every 1% improvement in effectiveness produces five percent more in desired results! That's the power of Pareto's Law.

WHAT'S YOUR TIME WORTH?

"One thing you can't recycle is wasted time."

— ANONYMOUS

We all know we don't have enough hours in the day to do the things we want to accomplish. You've heard it before: "Time is money." But just how much is your time worth?

There are roughly 1,952 working hours in a year of 244 working days. This assumes you don't work Saturdays, which I would recommend doing at least once a month.

EARNINGS PER YEAR	VALUE OF AN HOUR
$30,000	$15.35
$40,000	$20.50
$50,000	$25.60
$60,000	$30.73
$70,000	$35.86
$80,000	$40.98
$90,000	$46.10
$100,000	$51.22

Now that you see how much each hour of your time is worth, you can understand the importance of time management. The most profitable hours are those that you spend in front of a qualified merchant.

If dedicated to being a professional, how efficiently you allocate your assets (your time, your skills, and your resources) determines your ability to deliver results to your customers.

We all start with the same 24 hours every day. Why do some people seem to effortlessly get their work done in the same amount of time while others struggle? The successful salesperson has learned how to manage assets around time. You always want the maximum ROT (Return on Time.)

Successful people utilized their time to its fullest by ensuring all their actions are targeted toward those things that mean the most with their individual goals and mission.

There are many great time management tools in the marketplace, select something that fits your personal style. If you work on computers get a software-based system like Act, Goldmine, or Outlook.

I recommend a software-based solution; this will allow you to create a database of your customers and continually keep in touch with them on a periodic basis.

REMEMBER, TIME IS A FINITE RESOURCE — USE IT WISELY.

"First I was dying to finish high school and to start college. And then I was dying for my children to grow old enough for school, so I could return to work. And then I was dying to retire. And now I am dying and suddenly realized I forgot to live."

—SOURCE UNKNOWN

ORGANIZING YOUR TIME

Develop a Daily Ritual (more on this in the next chapter):

- Review your goals or mission statement every morning before work
- Get started early
- Review your to-do list for the day and work your way down from the highest priority to the lowest priority
- Read or listen to a personal growth or motivational program daily
- Use the Daily Call Sheet posted on the resource website.

The Sales Hours:

Organize your time around the sales hours – the hours that you can be talking to prospects and customers.

Perform all non-revenue generating activities before or after your sales hours.

Prospecting Hours:

Dedicate a certain percentage of sales hours to prospecting.

Vary your time for prospecting and see what yields the best results.

Track your calls and results so you can create a sales formula for success.

Follow Up:

Create templates for your follow-up letters and correspondence for easy distribution.

Perform your follow up every day; this is where the money is!

Professional Development:

Continue 'sharpening your saw,' as Stephen Covey puts it; attend training at least 4 times per year.

Schedule exercise and personal growth activities during non-sales hours.

Listen to audiotapes while you're in the car. Create a rolling audio library to enhance your skills.

CHAPTER 49
THE 10 DISTINCTIONS

What makes one person with the same relative intellectual capacity, skillset and resources far exceed another? I've been observing salespeople, middle management and executives for over 25 years and have noticed several fundamental distinctions that separate the non-performers from the real producers. When I use the word *distinction*, I'm using it in the context of a demonstration of excellence that sets one individual apart from another.

I really wanted to share, at least from my perspective, what I felt were the driving mind sets and behaviors that, when diligently practiced, can set anyone free from the chains of mediocrity.

Mediocrity doesn't always mean underachieving; it means settling in and giving into inertia. Mediocrity comes from the Latin word *medius*, meaning middle and *ocris*, meaning a rugged mountain. Literally it means to settle halfway to the summit of a rugged mountain. It's a compromise of abilities and possibility; an arbitration between the drive to excel and the biological urge to settle for the most comfortable option. It's choosing the easier, softer way.

I've seen this mediocrity raise its ugly head in my life as well as almost every client I've had the privilege to work with. It's not whether it will show up in your life, but more importantly what will you do about it when you succumb to it?

Unless vigilant, mediocrity will creep up on you, it's akin to the boiling of a frog. What does this have to do with boiling a frog? As the story goes, 19th century researchers found that when they put a frog in a pan of boiling water, the frog just quickly jumped out. On the other hand, when they put a frog in cold water and put the water to boil over time, the frog just boiled to death. The hypothesis is that the change in temperature is so gradual, the frog does not realize it's boiling to death until it's too late. While the results of the experiment are in question it is a good metaphor for how mediocrity can slowly take over every area of your life.

These distinctions address the necessary alignment across six domains, which I believe are necessary to crush mediocrity, in order to realize a thriving business and awakened life. These domains are the foundation of what I share when working with any level of client, whether they are new to the industry or have been in payment processing for years. This is the foundation.

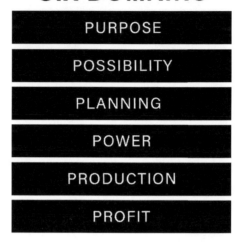

The six domains are meant to be worked on in order and applied across your life and business. To maximize each, we must align them appropriately. When I use the word alignment, I'm using it in the context of the proper positioning of the parts of your life. In order to fully experience the effects of the six domains, we must align them properly, these are the three alignments.

THE THREE ALIGNMENTS

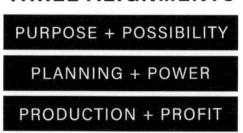

These alignments all work together, it's a process. First you gain clarity of purpose and a vision for where you want to take your life and business. Now that you have the vision, you plan the tactics to deploy; which provide clarity and power so you can produce the desired results. You are ready to launch into production, this is where *"the work"* is done. Then you reap the profits of your work by keeping yourself accountable and measuring your results. It's a design for living, providing anything you want out of life or business.

When these three alignments occur on a consistent basis you are now in the realm of self-mastery. Let me just stress this is not an event, but an ongoing process; you will be in alignment and out of alignment for the rest of your life. The idea is put yourself in a place of alignment and stay there for as long as possible.

Let's review the distinctions that exceptional producers share.

1   **They choose to take responsibility for their results.**

> *To decide, to be at the level of choice,*
> *is to take responsibility for your life*
> *and to be in control of your life.*

—ABBIE M. DALE

According to Merriam-Webster's dictionary - choice suggests the opportunity or privilege of choosing freely. The Key word being - freely. It's all about freedom – the freedom to pick one thing over another.

Are you freely making choices in your life?

You see, we all have the capacity to choose to take responsibility for our own results or live from an alternate place, the land of excuses, stories and reasons why we can't have the life we so desperately want.

The truth is that most of our decisions originate from the prison of the past. We make choices about the future but base our idea about what is possible on the past. We react out of old behaviors and past events that happened long ago. We carry these scars or stories of the past into present life, willing to tell anyone that asks, or doesn't ask for that matter, about the bad hand we were dealt or challenge we had to face. This bond to the past creates a prison in which we live, killing choice. We use these false beliefs or manufactured stories to justify our inaction here in the present. I call this the Doom Loop.

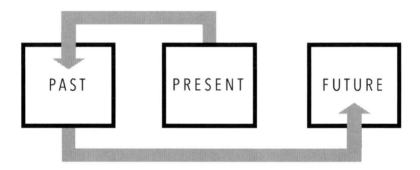

Release the past

The first step to true choice is knowing and internalizing that the past does not exist – it's over. The reason you get an endless loop of the same results, is that you are living from the same limiting stories you created from the past. I'm sure you've heard one definition of insanity is doing the same thing over and over again expecting different results. True choice is having the ability to make a decision based upon the here and now and the future you want to create.

Understand that you are a *"meaning-making machine"*. Your mind is constantly giving meaning to everything in your environment. The past is just that – the past. We assign a meaning or story to all the experiences of our life – you determine what that experience means. If you think you had a failed business venture – then you gave yourself the meaning of a "failed business venture" and vice versa. Remove the word failure from your vocabulary. There is no such thing as failure – only results. Learn from the results you create in your life. Tony Robbins puts it like this, *"Success is the result of good judgement, good judgement is a result of experience, experience is often the result of bad judgement."* Now that so called "failed business venture" can be recast as a learning experience.

I'm sure you've heard the story about how they catch monkeys in India. They build a small box, just large enough for the monkey to fit his hand through. They place some nice juicy bananas out for bait, these are no ordinary bananas; they are ripe and tasty, the kind of banana a monkey could hold onto forever. And we all know monkeys live for bananas (Just like many of us live for our excuses). The monkey smells the banana and hesitantly puts his hand in the box and grabs the banana, but his hand will not fit back thru the slot unless he drops the banana. Now he's got a dilemma, does he release the banana and go free or hold on and live a life of quiet desperation at the zoo for eternity? It's an easy choice for a monkey.

Guess what? If you haven't released the past – You're living your life like a monkey!

So, the first step to true choice is removing the illusion of the past.

Taking responsibility

Now let's go to step two of true choice – responsibility. The definition of responsibility is; being answerable, or accountable for something within one's power, control, or management.

Responsibility begins with the willingness to BE cause in the matter of your life. You are causing your life on a perpetual basis whether you are conscious of it or not. Let me state it this way, you are creating intentionally or by default, regardless you are the creator. Responsibility is taking ownership in the cause of your life.

Being responsible starts with the willingness to deal with a situation from the view of life that you are the generator of what you do, what you have and what you are. There is no middle ground in responsibility, you can't say, "I think I am responsible for my life" you either believe you are, or you choose to deny that you aren't.

Responsibility is not burden, fault, praise, blame, credit, shame or guilt. In responsibility, there is no evaluation of good or bad, right or wrong. There is simply what's so, and who you are willing to be in that area of your life. When you live from a context of being responsible you live from authentic freedom.

You are the cause in your life, so when you hear a cliché like *"If it's going to be, it's up to me"* it should ring true. All the successful or even above average producers realize and live from this place.

If you are having trouble being able to unravel the past and see how the power of your stories and beliefs are literally shaping every decision you make, I would recommend looking at *"The Work"* by Byron Katie. I had the privilege of attending a workshop with Katie many years ago, she really put the pieces together for me regarding honestly evaluating my thoughts and unraveling my false stories. I love what Katie says about arguing with reality: *"I realize that it's insane to oppose it. When I argue with reality, I lose - but only 100% of the time."*

Her website states: *"A simple yet powerful practice. As we do The Work, not only do we remain alert to our stressful thoughts—the ones that cause all the anger, sadness, and frustration in your world—but we question them, and through that questioning the thoughts lose their power over us. Great spiritual texts describe the what—what it means to be free. The Work is the how. It shows you exactly how to identify and question any thought that would keep you from that freedom."*

Katie offers all the training and material to do "The Work" free of charge on her website - *www.thework.com.*

So, here is the choice – you can decide to be a slave to your stories or the creator of your future taking 100% responsibly for your results. The truth is, in the end it's all up to you, no one is coming to save you.

2   They live in alignment with their values and purpose.

"If you don't know what you stand for
you will fall for anything"

—SOURCE UNKNOWN

The people that have gotten the results they were striving for, don't just know their values and purpose, they live them. In order to discover your purpose, you must first determine what your core values and ideals are. Let's look at values. Values are what we stand for, what guides us in our decision-making process. Our values are the compass by which we live. Every decision and action are filtered through our belief and value system. Knowing what you value most and living from those values will reduce conflict and indecision in your life.

Milton Rokeach, a well-known values expert, defines values as "modes of organizing conduct – meaningful invested pattern principles that guide human action. They are real determinants of behavior, acting as the criteria by which goals (and means) are chosen among alternatives...Values and their hierarchical arrangements thus are observable as choices; they provide a means of studying all human action in a way that culture in its strict normative sense cannot".

He also made five assumptions about the nature of human values:

- The total number of values that any person holds is relatively small.
- All individuals throughout the world possess the same values to different degrees.
- Values are organized into value systems.

- The predecessors of human values can be traced to culture, community, society, and personality.
- The consequences of human values can be manifested in almost every aspect of an individual's life.

Your values are sets of beliefs and convictions that let you know what matters most to you as a human being. These values are critical because they determine what actions we take along our path. By living by our own high ideals or principles it gives us a foundation and a sense of consistency. Knowing your core values opens the doorway to the mind.

Two types of values

There are basically two types of values: *ends values* and *means values*. Ends values are the deeper emotions that we want to experience in life such as love, security, independence, freedom, joy, etc. Means values are a way for you to trigger or realize you ends values.

For instance, if I ask you what does money mean to you? You might say "independence, freedom, security". Money is your means value, but your ends value is independence, freedom and security. The challenge that most people face in our society today is that they are so busy pursuing means values; that they don't achieve their truest desires: their ends values.

Abraham Maslow noted in his book Motivation and Personality that one of the key characteristics of a self-actualized person is, *"They are fixed on ends rather than on means, and means are quite definitely subordinated to these ends."*

Purpose

Okay, you understand the importance of values, now it's time to discuss the first domain of purpose. Many of us still struggle to find our true purpose let alone live it. The word purpose and mission are synonymous, but I prefer the word mission, it gives me a sense that I am here to do something big in this life.

You can also use words like; quest, grand purpose, philosophy, creed or calling, whatever resonates with you. Your mission has always been with you, you just may not have uncovered it yet. Or maybe you've known what your purpose is but let your limiting beliefs, thoughts and feelings about yourself stop you from pursing it.

You see, most people live a divided life. They spend their time between what they must do to earn a living and what they want to do to find joy or meaning. They are choosing to make a living rather than designing a life. Their business or career is not in alignment with their life purpose. This creates duality and unfulfillment.

People living their purpose do what they love and love what they do, there is no separation. They have a *"Mighty Why".*

> *"This is the true joy of life, the being used for a purpose recognized by yourself as a mighty one, the being thoroughly worn out before you are thrown on the scrap heap; the being a force of nature instead of a feverish selfish little clod of ailments and grievances complaining that the world will not devote itself to making you happy"*

> —George Bernard Shaw

Your purpose isn't work, a must do, a burden, a responsibility, – it is your life – your reason for being on this planet, the direction you are moving. Your purpose is your inspiration, motivation, and sense of who you are as a human being. The reason the creator brought you to this place at this time in your life.

Your purpose should excite and inspire you to action; it should make your heart beat faster, and your mind expand. It is the essence of who you are. Ultimately your purpose aligns around your individual pursuits and your loved ones, those people that mean the most to you. Those people that you would sacrifice it all for.

If you have walked through this process before, please access my life design workshop online at: *www.surviveandthrive.biz/resources*. This tool will help you gain clarity of purpose, values, goals and get present to the legacy you want to leave behind.

3 **They have clearly defined outcomes**

> *"You control your future, your destiny. What you think about comes about. By recording your dreams and goals on paper, you set in motion the process of becoming the person you most want to be. Put your future in good hands – your own."*

> —Mark Victor Hansen

This take us into the second domain of possibility, we are all creators, you are either creating intentionally or by default, I believe all things are created twice, first in the mind then in the physical world. When you are in the first phase of creation, discovering possibilities or vision casting, always start with the end in mind, where do you ultimately want to end up?

Why do the majority of business books address or discuss setting goals? Because goal setting works! If you don't know where and – more importantly – WHY you're moving in a particular direction, you'll never achieve the desired result. And after all, aren't we striving to produce a result in some area of our lives? And in my view, more importantly *consistent results*?

The long-term producers are not swinging for the fences, they are hitting singles, day in and day out. James Clears writes about this concept of the "aggregation of marginal gains" in his book *Atomic Habits*, which I would highly recommend.

He writes "It is so easy to overestimate the importance of one defining moment and underestimate the value of making small improvements daily. Too often, we convince ourselves that massive success requires massive action. Whether it is losing weight, building a business, writing a book, winning a championship, or achieving any other goal, we put pressure on ourselves to make some earth-shattering improvement that everyone will talk about.

Meanwhile, improving by 1 percent isn't particularly notable—sometimes it isn't even *noticeable*—but it can be far more meaningful, especially in the long run. The difference a tiny improvement can make over time is astounding. Here's how the math works out: if you can get 1 percent better each day for one year, you'll end up thirty-seven times better by the time you're done. Conversely, if you get 1 percent worse each day for one year, you'll decline nearly down to zero. What starts as a small win or a minor setback accumulates into something much more."

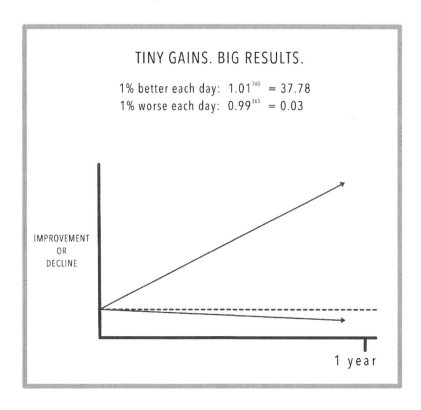

TINY GAINS. BIG RESULTS.

1% better each day: $1.01^{365} = 37.78$
1% worse each day: $0.99^{365} = 0.03$

IMPROVEMENT
OR
DECLINE

1 year

Jim Rohn puts it this way "Success is a few simple disciplines, practiced every day; while failure is simply a few errors in judgment, repeated every day."

The goal study

In 1979 a Harvard MBA study was conducted. The graduating class was asked a single question:

Have you set written goals and created a plan for their attainment?

Prior to graduation it was determined that:

- 84% of then class had not set goals of any kind
- 13% of the class had written goals but no plan to achieve them
- 3% of the class had written goals and plans to achieve them

The results? 10 years later, the 13% that had written goals but no plan to achieve them were making twice as much money as the 84% that had no set goals.

But astonishingly, the 3% that had both written goals and a plan to achieve them were making 10x more than 97% of the class.

Another study conducted by several well-known doctors demonstrated that goals are more likely to improve performance when three conditions are met.

A. THE GOAL MUST BE SPECIFIC AND MEASURABLE

Defining a goal as doing the best you can is as bad as having no goal at all. You need to be specific about what you are going to do and by when you are going to do it. It needs to be measurable and time bound.

B. THE GOAL MUST BE CHALLENGING BUT ACHIEVABLE

You will work harder for tough but realistic goals than for easy goals that pose no challenge or impossible goals that can never be attained.

C. THE GOAL SHOULD BE FRAMED IN TERMS OF GETTING WHAT YOU WANT RATHER THAN AVOIDING WHAT YOU DO NOT WANT

Approach Goals are positive experiences that you seek directly. *Avoidance Goals* are unpleasant experiences that you hope to avoid. People who frame their goals in Approach terms have much better results in accomplishing their goals.

I would recommend setting goals or targets for 1 year, 3 years, 5 years and a big vision at 10 years or further in the future, when we start to discuss execution, we will break them down even further.

Your goals and targets need to get your blood pumping, excite you and drive you in the direction of a compelling future. These goals and your mighty why are the fire that drives you to leverage yourself every day to take action.

4   **They have mastered the 90-day rhythm**

Having one year, three year and even 10-year goals are wonderful visions for you to create from, but where the real game is played and won is in 90-day (12 week) increments. I would encourage you to get rid of annualized thinking and start planning in 90-day frames. The human brain is limited in its capacity to focus for extended periods of time. 90 days is the perfect time frame to keep your brain engaged, motivated and focused on your desired outcomes. Each segment builds upon the next to help you drive toward the one-year target, which builds to the longer term vision.

As you continue to chunk it down, break your activities into monthly, weekly, and daily segments. This allows you to apply the principles of small incremental actions (hitting singles) and the aggregation of marginal gains.

I'm sure you've heard of the Chinese Proverb, *"a journey of a thousand miles begins with but a single step."* If you believe this to be true, then the wrong first step can begin a journey that could take you very far off course. So, it's important to make sure you take the appropriate first step and start your journey headed in the right direction.

In the book *The One Thing*, Gary Keller and Jay Papasan share what they call a focusing question to help you do just that, begin the journey headed in the right direction:

"What's the one thing I can do such that by doing it everything else will be easier or unnecessary?"

When planning, ask yourself this focusing question and build your actions around it. One integral tool to use to complete your "One Thing" is time blocking. Time blocking is the practice of setting aside specific scheduled time each week to work on your "One Thing".

For most people that is at the beginning of the workday where your brain has the most mental energy and focus. Remember no email. No phone calls. No interruptions of any kind. Just focus on the task at hand.

Cal Newport put it this way in his book *Deep Work*. Deep work happens when you get to have a period of uninterrupted time to focus on a single task or activity. Successful intellectuals do their best work when they go into isolation and get into deep work mode.

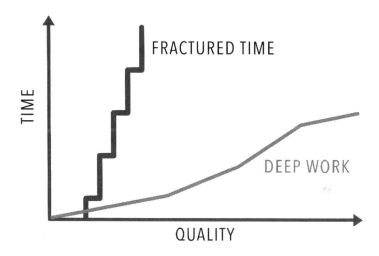

Brian Tracy so eloquently put it in his book *Eat that Frog!* "Throughout my career, I have found a simple truth. The ability to concentrate single-mindedly on your most important task, to do it well and to finish it completely, is the key to great success, achievement, respect, status, and happiness in life."

Define your outcomes, reduce them to a 90-day rhythm and time block and you will be all but guaranteed success.

5   They are creating a life not just building a business

Producers realize that just focusing on setting and achieving targets in their business omits most of their life. They know that in order to realize self-mastery they must focus on more than just money and business. I've been following Garrett J. White for quite some time and have been involved in the Wake up Warrior movement, if you haven't heard of Wake Up Warrior, visit their website wakeupwarrior.com and watch the documentary.

Garrett has created a movement for married businessmen, in order to help them actualize what he calls it the *"Have it All"* lifestyle.

Having consumed a mountain of Garrett's content, trained with him personally and completing Warrior Week (WW57), I would highly recommend listening to his free podcast, you will benefit immensely.

It's a no-nonsense approach to elevating your life to the next level. His training is built on a simple foundation of telling the truth, a simple concept, but not easy to practice, especially in areas of our life where we have fabricated intricate stories about events in our past.

High level achievers adopt a similar mindset, they're always striving to grow and expand outside just their business, areas like; body, mind, spirit, self-care, family, community, contribution and relationships. What I love about the payment processing industry, is that residual income provides the financial freedom to pursue growth in all of these areas. I've been fortunate enough to be able to focus on this type of lifestyle for 20 plus years now and I have zero regrets.

Remember, your business reflects you. If you're energy level is low, health is poor, your relationships with spouse or children is off or non-existent, you lack a spiritual connection, it will manifest itself in your business. I see so many people live from this story that they are building this business for their loved ones, sacrificing it all for them, yet their loved ones are the ones they sacrifice while they chase the almighty dollar or some artificial form of significance.

Looking good

When we get caught in this trap, we have the disease of "Looking Good" and guess what? Were all infected, it's unavoidable because it's part of the human experience. We try to look good by making money, acquiring things, getting advanced degrees, being pious or overtly spiritual, having the right relationship, being right all the time, joining the right political party or cause, wearing the right clothes, eating certain foods the list goes on and on. I would submit to you that this having to "Look Good" permeates every area of your life, whether you realize it or not. This looking good owns you and until you're aware of it and how it affects your actions, thoughts and outcomes it will continue to own you. When you can be present and aware of this need to look good, you can start to authentically create in your life, you're now aware, you're awake and ready to create out of what you really desire, not some pattern that keeps playing over and over again. It's ends values over means values.

The idea that you must give up one area of your life for success in another is a lie. Many have bought into this lie. Will every area of your life always be in balance? Of course not. There will be periods of imbalance, but you need to continually strive for balance, that way you will never get too far off track.

The odds of dying sit at around 100%, we are all going to experience death. I haven't seen many people on their death bed asking to see their stock portfolio, residual statement or sports car one more time before they die, have you? No, they want to see the people that meant the most to them, their loved ones. If you have fallen into this trap of producing just to look good, it's not too late to make a change!

The first step is to ask yourself, what do you really want? And keep asking until you go deep enough to discover what that is for you. Start taking a balanced approach across these four dimensions, to access true power:

FOUR DIMENSIONS

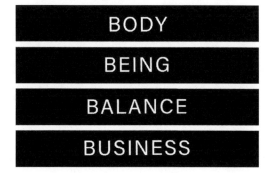

BODY

BEING

BALANCE

BUSINESS

These are the areas where we will create the possibility for a new way of living. When you work on all of it, your entire life combined with your business outcomes what do you think happens to your life, your family, your business when you start to produce within these four dimensions?

I'll tell you what, you step into a new level of clarity, peace, production and connectedness, a level that you may have had brief glimpses of in the past, but now experience on a consistent basis. The key word being consistent, through diligent work you're transformed from a mindset of scarcity to abundance. This is a simple concept, is it easy? Hell no.

We've covered a lot to this point, focusing question, weekly one thing, 90-day targets to support our long-term goals, but just how do we support all these targets on a daily basis? What do the elite producers do to pull this off regularly?

6   **They have installed powerful habits**

"Ultimately, people do not decide their future,
they decide their habits and their habits decide their future."

—John Maxwell

Habit creation is the hot topic these days. We are constantly running habits whether they are conscious or not. In fact, Duke university states that habits account for about 40% of our behaviors on any given day. Aristotle nailed it when he said *"We are what we repeatedly do. Excellence, then, is not an act, but a habit"*. Habits are what you repeatedly do; I'm not talking about what you're thinking about doing, rather what you actually do! Habits form the person that you are, from diet and exercise to personality and beliefs.

There are many great books covering habit's and their impacts on our lives, so I won't dig too deep here. The goal of any habit that supports you is to reach a stage of automaticity. How long does that take? Well there has been much debate over the time it takes to form a new habit, recent research from the University College of London has helped shine a light on how long it will actually take to reach the level of automaticity.

The study examined the habits of 96 people over a 12-week period. Each person chose one new habit for the period and reported each day on whether they performed the behavior and how automatic it felt.

Some people chose simple habits like "drinking a bottle of water with lunch", while others chose more challenging tasks like "running for 15 minutes before dinner." At the conclusion of the 12 weeks, the data determined that it took on average more than 2 months to create a new behavior – 66 days to be exact. Of course, this can vary by person and their individual circumstances. But the old idea that it takes 21 days to form a new habit was shattered.

DAYS NEEDED FOR AUTOMATICITY TO OCCUR IN NEW HABITS IN STUDY PARTICIPANTS

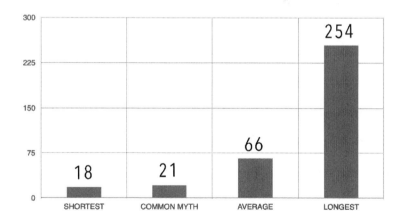

They also discovered that "missing one opportunity to perform the behavior did not materially affect the habit formation process." In other words, you can mess up every now and then.

Positive habits enable you to keep your commitments. The definition of commitment is *"the state or quality of being dedicated to a cause."* When you're working through your daily targets and morning ritual you must be present with what you're committed to achieving. Not what you think others want you to commit to, not what your parents or tribe told you to be committed to, but what you truly want to commit to.

What do you want for your life? What can you really take a stand for in your life? Not *TRY* to do, but really commit to. I'm not interested in your intentions; I'm interested in what you are ready to take a stand for.

Let me give you an example of an "All In" commitment. I'm not sure if you've heard of the "Marathon monks" of Japan, but they are known for their commitment to completing the kaihōgyō (circling the mountain) – it's an ascetic practice performed by Tendai Buddhist. It requires them to walk a route on Mount Hiei, the longest of which takes 1000 days to complete. The solo walking mediations are broken into 100-day hikes over the course of seven years.

In the first 100 days, withdrawal from the challenge is possible, but from day 101 onwards the monk is no longer allowed to withdraw; historically he must either complete the course or take his own life. Now that is commitment.

When we slowly give up on our commitments and easily justify why we can't live up to them aren't we experiencing the same punishment or taking our own life? I love what Jocko Willink says is his book *Discipline Equals Freedom*.

"NO MORE. No more excuses. No more 'I'll start tomorrow.' No more 'Just this once.' No more accepting the shortfalls of my own will. No more taking the easy road. No more bowing down to whatever unhealthy or unproductive thoughts that float through my mind."

The habit of a morning ritual

I hope I've established the concept that powerful habits empower you to live up to your commitments. The most important habit I've developed, by far, is creating a morning ritual, I've spent years crafting and practicing my morning ritual. I understand that either I create each day intentionally or by default; by practicing this morning ritual I'm almost ensuring that I'm going to be congruent with the three alignments. It's the power of this daily purposeful ritual that has helped me achieve more than I ever thought possible.

The key is purposeful practice as Anders Ericsson points out in this book *Peak*, he states *"purposeful practice has several characteristics that set it apart from what we might call 'naïve practice', which is essentially just doing something repeatedly, and expecting that repetition alone will improve one's performance."* Purposeful practice is deliberate, focused and is well-defined. Just as the body responds to exercise, the brain reacts to these new routines, it's called homeostasis. Homeostasis is a system's tendency to do what it needs to do to maintain stability. With deliberate or purposeful practice, you are challenging homeostasis – getting out of your comfort zone – and forcing your brain to adapt and expand.

The purpose of the morning ritual is to prepare you for the day ahead, get centered and set your intention, so you can perform at optimal levels when you hit-the-door to enter the world.

Your morning ritual needs to be just that – Yours! It may take time to develop the best ritual that serves you and of course routines may change as the rhythm of life changes. My routine today is much different than it was when my children were younger, and the demands of parenting were present. Be flexible and be open to trying new things that support your outcomes.

SO, THE QUESTION IS WHAT WILL YOU HAVE TO BECOME TO GET WHAT YOU WANT?

WHAT ROUTINES AND HABITS WILL YOU NEED TO CREATE TO REALIZE YOUR GREATNESS?

Checkout my resource website (www.surviveandthrive.biz/resources), where I post items to help you craft your morning rituals and discuss my system "The Framework"

7 **They keep score**

> *"In God we trust, all others must bring data".*
>
> —W. EDWARDS DEMING

What do I mean by keeping score? Whether you are a single sales agent or large ISO you must know your numbers, the data surrounding your business. You need to develop a scorecard or key performance indicators (KPI's) that drive results and help you manage the business.

What is a KPI? A KPI is a measure that helps you understand how you are doing against your targets or objectives. KPI's are:

- Specific and measurable (no room for interpretation)
- They drive results
- They are easy to understand
- They are tracked consistently
- They are visible

There are really two important types of KPI's:

- Lagging – Measures results
- Leading – Measures activities that drive results

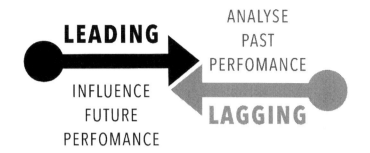

LEADING

INFLUENCE
FUTURE
PERFOMANCE

ANALYSE
PAST
PERFOMANCE

LAGGING

Numbers tell the truth, they expose reality. This concept has been around forever but very few entrepreneurs really know their numbers. If you are just relying on your profit and loss statement (P&L) to manage the business, you are typically too late, this is a lagging indicator. You need to be abreast of what is happening in your business today, so you can quickly respond to current market conditions.

If you are a small sales office most of your daily and weekly metrics will be around sales. Of course, this can vary widely depending on how you're running the business, here are examples of common data points to track:

Daily – Leading indicators

- New merchant applications
- Approval/Declines/Pending applications
- Installs/Activations/Deployments
- Number of incoming leads
- Number of appointments or presentations
- Pending closes or pipeline management (proposals out, statement analysis, hot prospects, follow-up, etc.)
- Customer service calls and disposition (larger ISOs)
- Technical support calls and disposition (larger ISOs)
- Risk Management Review and disposition (larger ISOs)

WEEKLY – LAGGING INDICATORS

- Closing ratio
- Appointments/Presentations set
- Lead source review
- Installs/Activations
- Pending activations
- Pending Merchant Applications
- Account closures
- Sales Pipeline

In the weekly review you will look back at the last week and plan for the coming week.

Monthly – Lagging indicators

- Total active merchants vs. year over year (YOY)
- Cost of acquisition (The cost of acquiring a new merchant)
- Total attrition (closed accounts) vs. YOY
- Merchant approval rates
- Average income per merchant vs. YOY
- Average BPS earned vs. YOY
- Total processing volume vs. OY
- Residual income vs. YOY
- Total bonus income vs. last month vs. YOY
- Your profit and loss vs. YOY (Revenue, Cash flow, Profit, etc.)

Quarterly

- 90 Day target review and outcomes
- Quarter over quarter growth
- Set new targets for coming 90 days

Naturally, KPI's will vary based on your business model, if you are running an inside sales team you will want to track more information on call activity. Maybe you have multiple distribution channels, like direct, partner and inside sales, then you would create KPI's for each channel.

If you are single agent in the field is this overkill? Sure, it might be. Maybe you focus on three to five core KPI's and start there. If you want to expand the business, you must know these numbers.

If you are a large organization you certainly want to assign metrics to each department like; operations, risk, marketing, recruiting, accounting, etc. Don't forget what gets measured gets done. Each department head can easily give you 3-5 metrics each week, that will give you the information you need to take the pulse of the business. Every department has a number, every department can be measured, every department must be responsible for their individual KPI or scorecard.

Regardless of size, you have no excuse not to use a CRM. There are many affordable CRM's on the market, like Pipedrive, Hubspot, Highrise and Zoho. There are also industry specific CRM's like IRIS, Instant Quote Tool and Clientvine that help analyze merchant statements and prepare proposals. My companies currently use Salesforce, but I would not recommend Salesforce for smaller offices due to its cost and complexity. All you need is a platform that will track sales activity, your ISO or processor should provide residual data, profitability, merchant metrics and revenue reporting.

An amazing thing happens when you install accountability within an organization. Stuff gets done! Accountability begins with clear communication and expectations. You cannot get any clearer than a number that your team leaders are required to provide daily or weekly. This creates an environment of clarity and commitment throughout the organization.

Your job as the leader is to set the expectations, communicate it and keep people accountable.

8 They surround themselves with the right people

"You are the average of the five people
you spend the most time with"

—Jim Rohn

If you are the sharpest person in your circle of influence, get a new circle of influence. You need to continue to challenge yourself and what you want to become, a great way to do that is to surround yourself with high achievers that push and encourage you to expand your boundaries. The people you spend the most time with affect your way of thinking, self-esteem, behavior and self-imposed expectations.

There are many ways you can improve your associations and inner circle. Join a mastermind group, a new community group, hire a coach, network in business groups, volunteer for a business committee or the local chamber, get involved with your church business ministry, the list goes on and on.

I play a lot of tennis and am considered a pretty high-level player, the only way I can really improve is to find someone better to practice with, someone that challenges and pushes me to think differently, to work harder, to focus more. It's the same in every area of your life.

Your employees and teams

Beyond your personal life, the next most important place to surround yourself with the right people is your business. All successful organizations have the right people in the right seats. Attracting and keeping the right people is paramount to the life of the business. If you ask any successful ISO, they will tell you they are the sum total of their employees. If you are lucky enough to have built a company large enough to hire employees, congratulations, many small players never grow that large or don't care to.

Hiring "A" players

Having made poor hiring decisions in the past I can testify that it can set your business back for years and cost you untold resources and potential income.

When building out a team or organization always hire "A" players at every level. Look at Steve Job's philosophy in the 1980's, he recruited people by dramatically unveiling the MacIntosh, and seeing how interviewees responded to the designs. He even unplugged an engineer's computer and forced him over to Macintosh from the Apple II team because Jobs recognized his "A" player status. You need to build your company with a collaborative hiring process where a candidate tours around the company meeting everyone that is relevant for hiring that candidate.

When Wozniak crashed his airplane in February 1981, he left Apple Computer. After the launch of MacIntosh in 1984, Scully merged the MacIntosh and teams with Jobs as their head. Jobs told the Lisa team that he was firing 25% of their team because they were "B" and "C" players. The management of the MacIntosh team would all gain top positions in the amalgamation. It was unfair, but Jobs latched on to a key management experience, that you had to be ruthless to produce an "A" player lineup.

"B" players always want to hire people who are inferior to them. "C" players hire "D" players. So, keep the best people on your team, and make sure that you keep the right people in your organization. Jobs believed that if you let any "B" players into your organization, they would attract other "B" players as well. "A" players love to work with other "A" players, by definition, they want to grow and be the best. That is what makes "A" players valuable.

Having the right people in your company and life is a big step to guaranteeing success.

9 They have processes, procedures and systems in place

Elite level organizations have invested the time necessary to develop their processes, procedures and systems. Every business function can be segmented into a process and/or sub process. Once you discover what processes drive a certain activity, it can be quantified, measured, and improved upon.

A process occurs in every area of business, whether it's marketing, appointment setting, sales calls, deployment, inventory management, risk management, data compliance, underwriting, technical support, customer service, training, recruiting, hiring or firing.

W. Edwards Deming who single handedly turned Japan into an industrial powerhouse after WWII developed what's called the Deming Cycle, which is, a continuous quality improvement model consisting of a logical sequence of four repetitive steps for continuous improvement and learning:

PLAN: Design or revise business process components to improve results

DO: Implement the plan and measure its performance

CHECK: Assess the measurements and study the results

ACT: Take action to standardize or improve the process

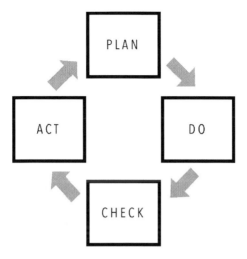

Start with improving your most important or core processes first, the ones that will have the most impact on your business if they are enhanced. This is the blocking and tackling part of any business, it's not glamorous or exciting but if you want to be able to scale or have the business operating independently, you need to develop documentable processes, procedures and systems.

Start with the low hanging fruit:

- Marketing (includes lead generation)
- Sales process
- Merchant boarding and activation
- Customer retention

Let's just look at marketing for a moment, this is an area where you have unbelievable leverage to create improvements. Think about it, if you are running a Facebook ad or pay per click (PPC) campaign you are spending a fixed amount each month, regardless if you generate 20 leads or 50 leads. If you have a salaried salesperson in the field the cost is fixed each month, you pay them the same salary whether they close 5 deals or 15 deals. If you have a call center, you are still paying a fixed hourly rate regardless of the number of appointments set and so on.

So marketing is one of the areas where you can realize the biggest leverage in your business. If you can increase those conversions ratios for Facebook ads or PPC campaigns, closed sales from salespeople, or higher appointment ratios you have just increased your revenue, sales, profits and portfolio value. Just small incremental improvements make a major difference!

Document each of these core processes, ask for input from team members, and keep it simple.

With technology where it is today, there is no excuse why you can't drastically improve your business in these four key areas. Once you get these four down, move to other areas like operations, finance or human resource related items.

Why do you think franchises are so successful? Because they have processes, procedures and systems in place, so the franchise in Houston, Tx is run just as efficiently as the one in Pittsburg, PA.

Systemizing your business gives you more power and control, you now have options; duplicate it in other markets, maintain it, sell it or turn it over to someone else to run. If you get these four perfected, you will be a long way toward building a massive residual stream.

If you want to grow and expand develop systems that allow you to do so.

10   They live like warriors

*"It's better to live one day as a lion,
than a thousand as a lamb"*

—ROMAN PROVERB

Every great civilization has fostered a warrior way of life and warrior legends. The Old Testament recounts the stories of a warrior people and a warrior God. In the ancient Mediterranean, the Spartans were probably the most legendary warrior. From birth,

Spartan society cultivated and trained their boys to become warriors, and that arduous training created men like Leonidas and his 300 soldiers that fought to the death. Japan had their courageous samurai warriors whose undaunted bravery came from living life as if they were already dead.

Today the warrior prototype continues in those who serve in the military and in modern media. General Maximus from Gladiator, William Wallace from Braveheart, King Leonidas from 300, all exemplify the classic warrior ideal.

Being a former Marine, I still embrace the idea of being a warrior, not on the battlefield, but in my life and for my family. I fight for them every day, it's what drives me, and I bet it's what drives you. Be assured, when you hit-the-door in the morning, you're going out in the marketplace to do battle, but the enemy is not the competition, it's yourself. The most difficult battle to fight is the one that centers in your mind. The warrior mindset will help you overcome this challenge.

In my opinion, there has been a societal shift away from this idea of the warrior man to a softer gentler type of warrior, certainly in many situations this is warranted. Our world has changed, for the majority here in the United States, we don't need to fight for survival, hunt for food and defend our cities from intruders any longer, we are relatively safe. The focus has shifted from physical survival to mental survival.

You see, there is an inherent conflict living inside many men. On one hand, we are expected to go out and make the money, provide for the family, "bring home the bacon", be aggressive, conquer the world, make it happen. Yet on the other hand, we are supposed to be calm, sensitive, not too pushy, and in touch with our "feminine side." The result is the nice guy; the man who will avoid confrontation and aggression even when confrontation and aggression are justified. This leaves men confused about the role they are supposed to be playing and it creates a lack of certainty in their lives.

Women don't get it any better, the expectations placed on them are just as severe, especially if they work. They are accused of not raising their children appropriately or being a good mother because they are pursuing a career and being selfish. Or the expectation of super mom is overlaid on their life and they are constantly struggling to live up to an image that is impossible to maintain.

The warrior in his fullness

What do you think of when you hear the word warrior? I remember when I first got off the bus for Marine Corps boot camp, the last thing on my mind was that I wanted to be a warrior, I was just looking to survive the first few days. But as time passed, they stripped me down physically, mentally and emotionally and rebuilt my mindset. My belief in what was possible for myself and my fellow Marines was transformed, we had become brothers.

Extraordinary achievers embrace the fact that they are living the life of a warrior. They embrace the warrior energy that comes with that declaration "I AM A WARRIOR". Fighting itself is not bad, the question is simply: *What are you fighting for?* The warrior's energy is needed not only in times of war, but on all the battlefields of life.

So, when I see elite performers, they exemplify the characteristics of warriors. You can define what a warrior or even "Bankcard Warrior" means to you but for me, I think of these qualities:

- Accountable
- Adaptable
- Aggressive
- Courageous
- Decisive
- Disciplined
- Honorable

- Loyal
- Masterful
- Persistent
- Powerful
- Tactical

Properly tapping into your warrior's energy provides an unsurpassable power source which will fuel you to reach your targets, provide for your family, fight for worthy causes, achieve greatness, and leave a lasting legacy.

SECTION 5

INDUSTRY INTERVIEWS

INTERVIEW WITH PAUL H. GREEN

(FOUNDER THE GREENSHEET)

Bio located at: *www.surviveandthrive.biz/resources*

Question: Since you've been in the bankcard industry, what major changes have you seen?

PG: I've been involved in the bankcard industry since the 1970s and founded the first Independent Sales Organization selling bankcard services in 1983. I've seen this industry move from knuckle-buster paper-driven processing to Web-based and wireless transactions. The evolution of bankcard acquiring, from BankAmericard and MasterCharge to Visa and MasterCard; from paper to electronic; and from the high-end merchant to "Everywhere you want to be," has been driven by the ISOs. All of the changes in this industry are a direct result of one decision: to move the merchant account sales from bankers to sales professionals.

Question:	What do you think the future looks like in the industry?
PG:	For the last 30 years, Visa and MasterCard (credit card) dollar volumes have shown positive year-over-year growth, and I expect this will continue. Even in the last two recessions, growth remained in the high single-digit to low double-digit range. The market for electronic payments is still wide open. In fact, I think that the dollar volume of card-based payments will grow at an average rate of 11% through 2010.
Question:	As a distribution channel, how important do you think the ISO and sales representative are to Visa/MasterCard?
PG:	The sale of payments processing services and the POS equipment that makes the transactions possible is dependent on the ISO sales channel. Without the army of independent sales professionals in the U.S., much of the growth experienced by Visa and MasterCard would never have happened. Banks are not sales organizations. If the bean counters and risk managers had maintained control over merchant account sales, I believe BankAmericard would still be a regional conversation piece for the wealthy.
Question:	What are the major challenges facing the industry?
PG:	There are several significant challenges facing the payments processing industry at this time, not the least of which is governmental investigation and possible regulatory statutes. The anti-trust action against Visa and MasterCard, FTC investigation of CMS, class-action litigation against the card associations, and statutory regulations affecting card receipts and tip reporting will all impact the economic strength of this industry. At this time it is not

clear if real growth is still possible in the bankcard acquiring market or if it has become a net-sum game, with merchants and revenue simply moving from one player to another.

With an industry built on residual payments the ultimate challenge is to develop the service infrastructure that will enable the sales professional to do what he/she does best: sell.

Question: What tools do you think are most important for field sales reps?

PG: The most important "tool" for any sales professional is a strong support team. Sales professionals are a special breed; their singular skill is that of selling. A team that enables the salesperson to sell and not to be distracted with support and service will come out on top. "Sales" is the most difficult of professions. Few have the ego-strength to withstand the day-in and day-out grind of proposal and rejection that the sales professional must withstand. Not just "withstand," but actually thrive on the challenge of making the numbers. Nothing happens in this industry until a salesperson sells.

Question: What would be your advice to a new salesperson entering the business?

PG: Winning in sales always results from the same simple process: hard work. Referrals or leads are nice and interested prospects that call you out of the blue can make your day, but they are seldom a steady diet. Regardless of whether you are knocking on doors or smiling and dialing, nothing replaces the hard work of starting all over again tomorrow.

Question: What skills are most critical to sales success in this industry?

PG: In all my years of sales and training sales professionals, I've found that the most critical skill is to
remember one thing: Ask for the sale.

INTERVIEW WITH BOB CARR

(FOUNDER & CEO, GET BEYOND, INC.)

Bio located at: *www.surviveandthrive.biz/resources*

Question:	I really appreciate the time today, so initially you were kind enough to do an interview with me in 2003 and I just want to get update on what you've been up to within the industry?
BC:	*Well, 2003 was a long time ago a lot has happened since then, I was CEO and founder of heartland payment systems in 1997 and when you were interviewing me that's what I was doing, focusing on building Heartland.*
	We were fairly successful, I would have to say, and we went public in 2005 on the New York Stock Exchange. We opened with a market value of about 600M, we started with a 2M valuation in 1997, so we did well getting on to the New York Stock Exchange at that valuation. Our stock price went for a dollar a share in

1997. When we went public, we sold a block of shares to the public for $16 and we opened the next morning for $21.50 and as you know our stock went up to $33.

Then the economy started faltering and we were breached Pretty much everybody in the industry learned about Heartland for the first time when we were breached because the Washington Post and other publications put us in the headlines; largest reach ever. We were accused of having 130 million card numbers compromised, which was not true, but it was still a lot of money; a lot of card numbers. It was a tough situation for us. We were almost shut down by Visa, but we were able to negotiate a settlement to pay $150M to the banks that were injured. We got back on our feet and got bigger and bigger and did lots of acquisitions. On April 16, 2016 we were purchased by Global Payments for $4.3B.

I had a one-year covenant not to compete and started a new company one year later and here we are today.

Question: What advice would you give to a new salesperson entering the industry?

BC: *First, decide your objectives. Is your objective to make big bucks in the short term and get out or is your objective to establish a long-term career? If your objective is to establish a long-term career, then find a role model. Find someone who has done the same thing successfully for a few years with the same company(s). Decide the value proposition you are going to offer your merchants. Do the math. How many merchants do you think you can deliver on the great service you will be promising? How will you make a living while you are building your portfolio and deliver what you promise all at the same time?*

| Question: | In your opinion what are the critical characteristics that salespeople in this industry need to possess in order to be successful? |

BC: *Successful salespeople need to have the same characteristics as most other entrepreneurs. They need to be tenacious, self-motivated, thick-skinned and smart to make it long term in our industry. If the position is commission based add the following characteristics: self-confident, willing to work very long hours, willing to study and study the technical and business details of the industry and the competition and be willing to accept the risk of failure.*

Question: I'm looking back at some of the things we talked about prior. Looking at the last couple years, what do you think are some of the major developments or major changes that you've seen in the payment space?

BC: *Well, obviously consolidation is the biggest thing sticking out. It's in our face right now with pending mergers of the giants. Significantly, after the mergers of First Data/Fiserv, FIS/Worldpay and Global/TSYS, there will be three survivors in the acquiring business. Out of that they will be the three biggest non-banks. Then we have the banks, Bank of America and Wells Fargo being the largest, along with some other decent size banks like US bank. When you take all the banks out of it and you take out the top three, the largest player left on the Nilson report is half the size Heartland was when we were purchased by Global. I think that is just stunning because it tells me it's an open playing field. The big guys are going to be tied up in their underwear for a couple of years doing their integrations and all the merger work that must be done, so that's one observation.*

The second is that I think margins are the highest they've ever been for merchant profitability to acquirers. For 20 years I have heard every year that margins are being squeezed. If you look at it on a per transaction basis that might be true, but because of the growth of the transactions and the overall profitability per merchant, I've never seen it higher than it is now. A lot of that is because there's still a lot of bad games being played by even the biggest players, tricking merchants into signing some really stupid agreements.

And then the third, are the ISV's as expected, there's no surprise here over the last several decades the industry is moving more and more to where a payment is part of the transaction and a lot of the data that's in the transaction now is being transmitted back and forth by the software companies and a lot of value is being created, valuable applications are being created for merchants that make payments more and more important all the time so those would be my three top observations.

Question: It seems like the integrated payments space and these ISVs is a market that all the big players are trying to tap into, so it's almost like a frenzy, would you agree?

BC: *Yes, I do. You know I've been accused a little bit of starting some of that because we made 34 acquisitions at Heartland. Many were over the last few years and it my new company has made a few acquisitions as well. So yes, I think that's true. The ISVs have a lot of influence. It's good to have a great relationship with ISVs but that's not new, that's been true since the 1980's.*

Question: With all the consolidation occurring, these big players are getting even bigger and with your comment on the accounts being more profitable than you've ever seen, I would assume that in your mind, this is still a great opportunity for ISOs?

BC: *I think it's the best time ever to be in this business. There are so many areas of opportunity that are out there, because these rich transactions can be used for so many things. There aren't enough entrepreneurs in the country to take advantage of everything that is possible right now in my opinion.*

Question: With the opportunities out there and ISVs we touched on, are there any products or new technologies you see that might change the face of the business in the in the coming years or make a major impact?

BC: *Well, I think "tap and go" will take over on a universal basis - all merchants, all locations, all verticals. The idea of having your chip or magstripe card read, frankly, reminds me of the sixties. When I was first in college, taking a computer programming class, the professor held up punch card, (which we called IBM cards back then), waved it and said, "Gentlemen you're not going to see these things in five years". Forty years later, he was right. I think that's partly what's going on with magstripe and chip cards, but I think the wave is going to be faster and a lot of us are going to be taking advantage of that. It's going to be a lot more functional and convenient for the consumers to pay with "tap and go" rather than the cumbersome method of handing over the card.*

Question: I guess with these new technologies and new software ISOs and agents must be more educated and prepared to offer these products. Do you think ISOs need to change their marketing approach?

BC: *Well to state the obvious, social networks and digital marketing are right at the top of the list. I think it's going to be a long haul for those of us who have the feet on the street sales organizations, but digital marketing is very effective for a lot of folks in this industry. I think the best solution is to do both. It's not cheap to have a feet on the street sales organization, but we're positioning to build both. We're probably going to be better at doing some of that in other parts, but we're trying to learn it and get better on all fronts.*

INTERVIEW WITH OB RAWLS

(PRESIDENT PAYSAFE NORTHAMERICA)

Bio located at: *www.surviveandthrive.biz/resources*

Question:	I'm excited to interview OB Rawls, the president of Payment Processing North America PaySafe. OB's has a wealth of knowledge and industry background from working with First Data and Hypercom and iPayment.
OB:	I'm looking forward to our discussion. We live in and work in a really exciting industry, don't we?
Question:	We sure do. I guess to get started you can share a little bit about how you got into the industry and then what you're focused on today at PaySafe.
OB:	I got into the industry while I was working for Bank of America in the Nations Bank days. As you know the bank grew through a series of acquisitions. I lived in Dallas when NCNB bought first Republic of Texas and built Nations Bank. We had

an accumulation of merchant acquiring divisions inside the bank and they were losing money.

I was challenged with moving to Norfolk Virginia where the company was headquartered and consolidating all the businesses that the bank owned into one and restoring profitability.

So, I started there. Along the way the bank ran into a real estate crisis in the southeast and wanted to sell some assets to produce cash. We came up with an idea that we should create a joint venture. It was kind of the rage in the industry at the time if you remember all of discussions with Roger Pierce and others at First Data. As the ISOs were talking and Deb Verossie was negotiating with First Data, we went down a path of discussing combinations and accommodations with Visa, with Discover Card and others and finally decided that we partner with First Financial Management Corporation, an Atlanta based company. I guess you could call them one of the first Fintech's even though we weren't very technologically ordered or structured at the time. For your reference FFMC, at that time owned both Western Union and NABANCO. And so, we built a joint venture putting all our sales business and the bank business together to form Unified Merchant Services. That was our first company. We were 50/50 owners in that joint venture with the bank and FFMC. Just as we closed, First Data bought FFMC. After the closing we became an even bigger joint venture because we put all the smaller businesses in one large enterprise.

Question: Today you find yourself at PaySafe. What are your marching orders there? What do you focus on today?

OB: It's all about growing the business. At PaySafe we're owned primarily by two private equity firms, Blackstone and CVC group, two of the most powerful private equity firms in the world. They have a pretty good portfolio of businesses in the Fintech space. It's a growth model if you just follow the traditional private equity model; trim your expenses, put money where you need to, invest in the growth areas, and head towards some kind of event, whether it's public or private. Wc can't talk about that today, but my task is all double-digit growth, expense control (if we can), leveraging the business and we've been doing that. We've had a fantastic first four months of the year with really good growth. We are refining the business and we're focusing very singularly, on the small businesses in America.

Question: That's excellent. My next question is, if you look back over the last say 5 years, 10 years or so, what do you think are some of the major changes that you've seen in the payments space? Any disruptors or changes that come to your mind?

OB: The first one is security. You know when you and I started in this business it was all about trust, right? We handed a merchant a plastic card, they swiped it in an imprinter, they looked in this paper magazine to see if our card number was good and we walked out of the store with a piece of merchandise. And then all this stuff happened in the backend— the merchant got funded 10 days later and everything was fairly simple. The first issue or the trend that's lasted the longest time is the move to security and the removal of trust from the credit card process. So many businesses are based on trust but now it's trust but verify. And we've had to, because the crooks have become so rampant in our business.

The second is the move to electronic payments, away from paper to electronic data capture, all the way to e-commerce today, or card-not-present and the invisibility of payments in apps like Uber and others.

The third thing is the change in the sales process. We went from banks being in this business selling terminals to clients or giving them away, trying to get deposits to distributed sales forces whether it be the ISOs growing by robbing the banks of their margins and their sales channels, because independent sales organizations could sell in the marketplace much more efficiently than banks could. And to the way we sell today, which is the digital environment with merchants self-selecting, to find their own merchant services.

Good examples are Square and Stripe and how merchants find them on the internet and buy first merchant services and then other services. We do the same thing. We have a well-oiled digital marketing environment where probably a third to 40 percent of the clients we have, find us themselves every month. They respond to one of our digital advertisements and then we sell to that market.

The old feet on the street payment activity is Jurassic and dying. There are still people out there to do it. But you know we're doing a really good job of covering the last mile, now in the selling environment.

Question: Things have changed drastically and I'm sure it will continue to change. Do you see any trends that really catch your eye, that are really affecting the industry, other than the three past things that have happened? Any major trends you see that you would want to discuss that's happening as the industry matures?

OB: The major trend would have been the fourth bullet point under your previous question, which is the whole arrival of Fintech; the amount of creativity that's centered in our area and the deconstruction of the bank and even ISO and third-party selling models by Fintech. I had a chart showing the deconstruction of Proctor and Gamble. It depicted P&G's verticals and it showed in this very graphic chart, all the singularly focused competitors that were just tearing into P&G's market with cheap innovations, fast time to market and all digital selling. That's happened in our space, Square started it.

Remember how we all laughed at Square (they're never going to get anywhere, they're losing money)? And they're still not making a lot of money on their credit card processing— but what they've done is they've filled the needs that were created by voids in other services.

With the bank, when we had the big banking crisis, they quit lending to small clients, even though they had lower cost of funds than they ever had before, zero cost of funds way into the future. These financial technology companies came in and filled the void. You look now at all the merchant cash advance companies, all the lending companies, all the financial companies that are creating products and solutions for the small businesses that weren't been solved by either their credit card company or by their bank or other lenders and now this whole industry is the most significant trend that I see. We're not a credit card acquiring business anymore, at least the smart ones aren't— we're a provider of small solutions to SMBs in the US and around the world.

When we sign a client, we talk to them about an advanced or smart terminal with apps and other things, that will help to run their business better. Time and attendance, we used to sell that but now there are fully complete scheduling programs out there that send notices to the workers and it's a really complete scheduling tool. There are very good payday tools, paycheck tools, merchant cash advances. We talk to our clients. A merchant, a pizzeria needs $40,000 so they can buy a pizza oven, how can they find that kind of money at the bank? The bank's not here to do that anymore.

If the guy has a home equity loan, he may be able to borrow the money that way, but he's incorporated as an SMB— they don't have the wherewithal. The risk of lending to banks and other small entrepreneurs is high. We can use their history of daily deposits to actually help them with working capital needs or buying a pizza oven or buying a recapping machine for a tire company. And that's how we are evolving. I really think that's the most significant trend that's impacting our industry right now.

Question: So, it's become more of a solutions sale.

OB: Yes. And that's really cool. But if you look forward to how we survive in the business today as ISOs and agents, I think that we're all better equipped to help our clients than ever before.

What we used to sell was "I can save you $10 a month and $0.10 per transaction" that was it. "And, by the way, would you pay $179 for this lease for 72 months? For a terminal that costs $300."

And we weren't doing anything back then, after merchants were convinced that they needed to move away from paper, we weren't doing anything but selling on price. We weren't really being value added salespeople. I'm watching our client base that we have today, sub ISOs, and we were early adopters of the clover device and smart terminals and we will sell over 18,000 of those devices this year through both our direct sales and indirect sales.

What we've spent a year and a half and are still doing today is part of our culture and our DNA itself, it's an evangelical type of training for our sub ISOs, let me help you learn how to make money differently. And you have to train your sales force differently, you have to expect that you will invest in the people that work for you — in their selling skills and teaching them how to sell solutions to small businesses. So today our ISO partners are very good at selling these solutions. They lead with a Clover; they lead with another smart device and they talk about the value of running a small business.

That sounds so cliché but it's really, really important because ISOs are figuring out by selling a smart terminal, they get $25, $50, to $125 a month in recurring revenue. You mentioned Bob Carr earlier, Bob figured this out when we all thought he was crazy buying all those cash register dealers.

Bob was really smart; he built a recurring revenue model that was unbelievable, and he got paid really well for it when he sold his business.

I looked at him when he was doing it and I thought WOW, how do we get that done? I was working at First Data and we were developing Clover, but as an organization we couldn't move as fast as Bob did in that selling model and now at iPayment and at PaySafe we can do that. We're nimbler. By teaching these ISOs and agents how to fish differently and by fishing differently ourselves, and we're able to fill the gap in our revenues that was being created by pricing compression in the marketplace by selling other products and services.

Question: I hear you saying the industry has changed, there are definitely some competitive pressures with Square and other people entering the market but on the flip side, by teaching them to add value and fish the right way, there's still an opportunity out there for ISOs and these subagents. Do you still feel like it's a great financial, residual growth opportunity for these ISOs and agents today?

OB: Yes, I think it is, if they're willing to invest in selling solutions.

If they're out there just selling on price, in the commodity market, and trying to deceive a merchant— do a flip of a terminal or something like that, then they won't survive. With smart terminals, once you sell those to a merchant, they can't be reprogrammed. That's something we've been smart about— when I sell a Clover, nobody else can come in and sell on price and take that merchant away.

With each device we teach how to sell a solution and you build all these recurring revenue models for things they buy every day— most small restaurants need payroll, scheduling apps, they need time and attendance, they need integration into QuickBooks, and they need IT solutions and other products and services. If we sell all of those in one bundle, then we tie that merchant up for a long time and we're not embarrassed to go back in the shop because we sold them something that's valuable to them.

This is a different business than what you and I grew up in.

Question: Yes, it is. I think you've answered a couple of the other questions that I had, but you mentioned Clover and these new apps and the solution selling that we discussed, but are there any new (and I know you mentioned a couple products) you see or technologies that might be in development now or maybe coming down the road that might have an impact to the industry or ISOs?

OB: Everybody points to the cloud, that magical atmospheric phenomenon that runs off a hard drive somewhere. People focus on the cloud, but it's not the cloud that excites me — it's the change in distribution, the change in the way products are sold. It's the disintermediation of these historical service organizations or product organizations like banks, like Procter and Gamble, things of that of that nature, people who have created this very intense singular focus on delivering one product to the marketplace.

I know about blockchain and all these other technologies that are out there, but I think it's a market focus on singular solutions that will help people win. That's the most exciting thing that I see coming.

Question: I was reading, and we've seen it in the news that PaySafe has made several acquisitions recently.

Any comments or do you have any thoughts on what's behind those acquisitions? I know you stated earlier kind of what the goal is, but are there any other points you want to discuss about the recent acquisition's you guys have made?

OB: That's the kind of question that scares me to death when I start answering it. But we're an acquisitive company. In the U.S. you look at the business and if you go all the way back to the roots of Optimal Payments in Canada, we're an acquisitive company. We look at a lot of opportunities in the marketplace. We're driven by our ownership and sponsorship by private equity firms who believe in acquisitions, so we will look and if it's the right time, at the right price, and has the right fit in our organization, then, yes we're shoppers. But we're not just on an acquisition growth scenario.

We're trying to be smart shoppers in the marketplace today. We're helping a lot of our small ISOs and agents. They build up these residuals and these portfolios but, how can they commercialize them?

How can they divest their revenue streams? Because they are just counting on us paying them. They sold a contract and it's owned by someone else. We can help them monetize their investment by buying their residuals sometimes or helping them with money to expand their businesses. But primarily an RBO helps an ISO or an agent become more financially secure and diversified. And it builds loyalty between us and our partners. So that's one of the ways we help our partners grow. For us, financially we stop paying the residuals and there's a time value calculation and a return to us because we have the capital to invest in these earnings streams.

Question: Well, OB, I really appreciate you being with us today. I think we got a lot of great input and feedback from you. I just want to give you one more opportunity, if there are any additional comments or thoughts or maybe something I didn't ask or something that you might like to comment on before we wrap up today?

OB: It's just a simple statement, this is an exciting business. I noticed that at Transact this year. You noticed how the crowd was getting older, and not changing, but now there are a lot of young people on the floor. The industry is changing and that tells me we've got a very bright future ahead of us in the provisioning of solutions for small businesses. We should all be happy about that, remembering the years where there were no changes, and nothing was exciting other than Visa or MasterCard giving us one more interchange code. I tell young people all the time in this business— it's bright and they should embrace it and find ways to grow in the business.

Question: Outstanding. Well, thank you so much, I really appreciate you spending some time with us today. Thank you so much, OB.

INTERVIEW WITH CHRIS LEE

(BILLING TREE, PRESIDENT ETA)

Bio located at: *www.surviveandthrive.biz/resources*

Question: In your opinion what is the state of the payments industry today?

CL: *I see a continued environment of consolidation. There has been a lot of merger and acquisition activity and I don't see that slowing down any time soon. The most important thing to consider in this industry is that things change fast.*

Question: What advice would you give to a new salesperson entering the industry?

Educate yourself via your processing partner and the ETA, or another organization you're aligned with. And attending regional industry shows is a must. If I were you, I would determine the type of merchants you want to sell to, then learn the products, regulations, pricing and approach for that industry.

Question:	What tools do you think are most important for the field sales reps?
CL:	*First and foremost, good customer service is extremely important. Once you've established that foundation, I would say it's simple items like your smartphone, LinkedIn and sales tools, such as demo decks and product collateral. Keep it simple.*
Question:	What do you think the future looks like for the industry?
CL:	*I predict that ISOs and agents will continue to look to sell their portfolios or get aligned with larger Super ISOs for product and service delivery. I also believe that the industry will shift to being all about integrations for merchants. Payments is a hot industry right now so consolidation will continue. We already see private equity companies as well as other players looking to get involved with the payments space.*
Question:	What do you feel are the top challenges ISOs are facing today?
CL:	*It's just as important to keep up on technology as it is regulations and compliance in the industry. It can seem overwhelming, but my advice would be to keep a close eye on the ETA in addition to regional shows to help keep your knowledge fresh.*
Question:	Are there any new technologies that you feel are game changers?
CL:	*I think there will be, but not nearly as many as we've seen over the past 15 years. Technology simply moves too fast with so many players in the market. In the last 15 years or so, a technology such as pay-on-plane was introduced, which was an absolute game changer for the airline industry—now nothing has that kind of 'wow' factor. I think 5G technology*

will help a ton with speed, data transparency and delivery, which are compelling benefits, but it's not overly dazzling.

Question: ISOs are facing competition from several fronts; do you think there will be a place for ISOs 5-10 years from now?

CL: *ISOs will always be around in some form or another, even if only acting as the sales arm for payments companies. Even if they look very different than they look right now, I don't see them going away.*

Question: What will be your major focus during your tenure at the ETA?

CL: *Looking ahead three to five years, I want to focus on growth of the ETA. A major revenue driver for the business is the annual TRANSACT show. We need a plan to bring significant revenue beyond that show. Overall, I want the ETA to remain relevant to all players in the payment ecosystem.*

INTERVIEW TODD ABLOWITZ

(INFINICEPT)

Bio located at: *www.surviveandthrive.biz/resources*

Question:	Tell us how you got into the payment business? And then what drew you the PayFac arena?
TA:	*I started as a merchant level sales person right out of college. A friend recommended the job to me.*
	What drew me to the payment facilitator model was that I saw an enormous opportunity very early when Visa and Mastercard changed the rules to allow payment facilitators. I immediately thought this was going to be one of the biggest things we've ever seen in the payments industry.
Question:	For those that don't know, what is a Payment Facilitator?
TA:	*A payment facilitator or PF is a provider of payment acceptance.*
	It is defined in the Visa and Mastercard rules, as a service provider that can sign up card acceptors,

directly service them, and pay them their transaction settlement.

What makes them unique compared to ISOs are that the PFs are allowed to have a two-party agreement with their submerchants, which means the PF does not need to include an acquiring bank on the agreement. Given the two-party agreement, they are also allowed to pay the submerchants directly, rather than relying on the acquiring bank. This eliminates an enormous amount of friction.

In return for having more flexibility and control over their submerchants, they are taking on most of the operations and directly taking on liability for their submerchants.

Question: What are the advantages for software companies to becoming a payment facilitator?

TA: *Software companies have a great opportunity in the PF model because in the first time ever, they have the ability to control their customer's (submerchant's) experience.*

In addition to that control, they get the lion's share of the payment revenue which dramatically increases their overall valuation.

Question: When does it make sense for a merchant to consider this model?

TA: *They have to have enough payment volume or have the ability to achieve enough payment volume in the future to make the ROI appropriate.*

Often times, this means over $50 million in payment volume going through the software company. The exact payment volume number where the ROI makes sense depends on a variety of factors.

Question: What is the process to become a payment facilitator?

TA: *The catalyst for the entire process is first the soft-*
                ware company must become educated on the
                benefits and responsibilities of the payment facil-
                itator model then ultimately decide to become a
                PF. To become one, the company must have all of
                necessary infrastructure and policies & procedures
                for underwriting and risk monitoring required to be
                approved by one of the sponsors.

                As there are numerous processors and banks that
                sponsor PFs you have the ability to select the one
                that is right for your company. Once you select your
                sponsor you enter into a contract and get approved.

                Once you get approved you must implement the
                process. Very often new PFs realize they need
                tools beyond what the processors or banks offer
                and building the necessary infrastructure in-house
                takes 12-18 months and often costs millions.

                This infrastructure would include application and
                onboarding needs like a submerchant application,
                automated underwriting tools, and a dashboard to
                review the submerchants that don't get automatically
                approved. It also includes software needed for when
                the submerchant begins accepting payments, such
                as, necessary software to provide reporting on trans-
                action data to both the PF and submerchant, creating
                deposits to pay your submerchants, risk monitoring,
                and managing of chargebacks or disputes.

                The PF will either have to build these tools them-
                selves or buy the needed tools from a software
                company that specializes in this like Infinicept.

Question: We have a lot of ISOs and agents reading this, is
                there an opportunity for them in this market?

TA:	There is a necessity for ISOs to evolve to the software model. ISOs have a limited period of time to adjust their business model in order to keep up with the fast moving software companies within the payments industry.
	The opportunity is to either sponsor PFs, become a PF, or both.
	There is an ongoing trend that software is eating payments. The reality is that software is taking over the most important parts of the payments ecosystem and ISOs have to decide how they want to play in this evolving world. Some of them can sponsor and help these software companies get to their rightful position in payments and in return benefit from this. Or they can build or buy software companies because in the future software providers will have the most important role.
	There are currently examples of ISOs taking both approaches. For instance, Global Payments and Clearent have been buying software companies while Worldpay and Nuvei are sponsoring software companies becoming payment facilitators.
Question:	Are ISOs becoming PayFacs and if so, why?
TA:	Yes they are because it allows them to operate in a much more efficient and effective way. They are leveraging these tools to allow them to grow faster and become a much better operation.
Question:	Other than Payment Facilitation, what products or technologies do you see being deployed or developed that might impact the industry in the coming years?
TA:	I am very excited about B2B hubs, virtual card payouts, and network level tokenization.

For B2B hubs this is where you have corporates and all of their suppliers and you link them together to do payment electronically. Everything B2B is a huge opportunity.

INTERVIEW ALLAN LACOSTE

(EVP OF PARTNERSHIPS & MARKETING, NUVEI)

Question: Please tell us how you got in the industry and what you are focused on today?

AL: *I got into the merchant services industry at the young age of 18. I graduated Malibu High and needed a way to pay for my education. I actually studied Computer Science. I had four jobs of which one was a database designer for a small Cardservice International in Calabasas, building systems that calculated residuals to pay our agents on time.*

I was then given an opportunity to work alongside my stepdad and mom, whom were in the business, at a start-up. All three of us opened a Cardservice International ISO. We moved up the ranks quickly and for many years in a row we out-sold and out-closed the majority of all registered CSI offices. I personal wrote 100+ deals a month (and got my first Porsche 911). Eventually, we sold that portfolio and cashed out when my stepdad had health concerns that later claimed his life. I credit him for teaching me the industry and sales. What a damn good salesman he was!

At that point, my wife and I opened our very own ISO of North American Bancard. I was "King Kong" at NAB back then! I closed up to 1,000 deals a month for many, many years. And I learned a lot from Marc Gardner and Gary Rutledge.

I went on to open Powerhouse Payments, a full risk, liability ISO with First Data and Wells Fargo. I processed for giants and grew to over 4,000 deals a month. Six years later, I sold that and opened another ISO with a group of friends. That's when I went on to work for Joe Kaplan as his ISO Director for Total Merchant Services. I guess you could call it my first "real" job!

I was looking for something different. I had known Joe for a long time. I remember Joe cruising around Calabasas in his black Porsche 911. Joe taught me a lot. He had an entirely different style than I was used to. I learned how to manage a big organization while at TMS.

When Joe and I parted ways, I moved on and landed my dream opportunity with Phil Fayer (CEO and founder of Pivotal Payments) as EVP of Partnerships and Marketing, right around the time of the rebrand to Nuvei. Phil was, and still is, one of my favorite players in the industry. His values, both in business and family, are remarkable. I wanted some of that to rub off on me. And it has!

Fast-forward, my focus today is on managing the overall growth of Nuvei's North American sales and *marketing teams. I determine the best ways to maximize revenues, exceed expectations and shorten our sales cycle, ultimately adding more value to our partner distribution channels.*

Question: In your opinion what have been the major changes in the payments space over the last 5-10 years?

AL: *Nothing has changed. And everything has changed. After all, there is nothing more important in the business world than someone with the ability to sell and close. It doesn't matter what you do or what technology gets released. Nothing happens until that sale is made.*

However, there are now more ways to sell through distribution channels. The integrated software vendor (ISV) market is booming. Integrating payments directly within a software or app adds more value for the software vendor while now making the sale seamless. Payment processing is a huge opportunity for ISVs.

The growth of payment facilitation is also important. These companies can benefit from adding the payment facilitator function to what they do. Not only does this create additional value for the customers, but it provides key advantages for the ISVs and SaaS providers as well in ease of operating within the client systems and added revenue for the providers.

Some ISVs continue to leave money on the table by failing to integrate payment processing into their software. By doing so, they're losing a large volume of potential revenue. Aligning with someone like Nuvei that simplifies and speeds up integration of payments creates a potentially powerful revenue stream that can't be overlooked.

Question:	Do you see any significant trends occurring that will have a major impact on the industry as a whole?

I believe the shift from brick and mortar to online has been accelerating at an incredible pace, even over the last 5 years. Omnichannel is no longer a buzzword, it's a necessity for retailers to survive.

Multichannel commerce is also more prevalent. Consumers are using more and more channels to make purchases, and merchants are increasingly needing to accept debit and credit payments wherever their client's shop: a physical store, website, via app, an online marketplace and more.

ISOs and merchant account resellers need to align with payment processors such as Nuvei who are deeply aware of these shifts and focused on technology. Having the capability to deliver payment processing to support merchants in providing a consistent level of service and user experience across all channels is critical.

Question:	Do you still feel that there is still an opportunity for ISOs and agents to build a book of business and earn a good living?

AL:	*Absolutely. There is no doubt that both ISOs and agents have a huge opportunity, not only to make a comfortable living but to live their dreams. I have personally helped many "small fries" become giant players while at Nuvei through our ISO Guru program.*

We realized that even experienced sales professionals can benefit by learning from someone who has been a merchant reseller or who has worked closely with them.

Question: There has been quite a bit of change and disrup-
              tion over the years, what do you think are the main
              challenges ISOs and agents are facing today?

AL: *Consolidation is something on the top of every-
              one's mind these days. There isn't a week that
              goes by where you don't hear about a huge player
              buying up another, or merging. Will service suffer?
              Will bonus or residual income decrease? ISOs and
              agent worry about these things constantly.*

              *Automation, real-time fraud management, a strong
              developer portal with robust APIs to support devel-
              opers. These are all important and what today's
              merchant is looking for. ISOs and agents must be
              able to answer these questions and deliver the right
              solution, custom-tailored for each opportunity and
              merchant type.*

              *The growth of eCommerce has also flipped the
              traditional ISO model on its head. With the retail
              industry becoming digitized, more merchants are
              looking to provide an omnichannel experience. An
              ISO or agent must be able to provide it. The Square
              model of direct-to-merchant sales is also compet-
              ing with traditional ISOs.*

Question: What products or technologies do you see feel will
              impact the industry the most in the coming years?

AL: *Real-time analytics. Fintech and bank fusion.
              Innovations in transaction security. They're all
              important. But I think the biggest impact will be
              the growth of online global commerce.*

              *Global acquiring and the support for a global pay-
              ment processing model has and will continue to
              impact the industry in a big way. Cross-border
              transactions can deliver big growth to online*

retailers of all sizes, however the cost involved in scaling and expertise needed can sometimes be daunting. Getting that expert advice is just as important as the technology behind it.

It's one reason Nuvei acquired SafeCharge for nearly $900 million in August 2019. Having direct connections to all major payment card schemes worldwide, supporting over 150 currencies and 180 payment types, along with being able to provide the expertise involved in growing successfully is paramount.

Question: Nuvei has made several acquisitions recently, what was the thinking behind acquiring those companies?

AL: *Nuvei is always looking for ways to increase the value it provides to merchants and distribution partners, all while increasing revenue. When it comes to acquisitions, we're always on the lookout for meaningful opportunities. Driving growth by acquiring tech giants such as SafeCharge is one way. Acquiring merchant portfolios is another.*

The SafeCharge acquisition specifically strengthens our technology platforms by leveraging the innovative, cutting edge technology they developed, and improves our go-to-market positioning. We've improved our ability to provide incredible payment solutions to our technology partners, merchants and resellers.

Question: Any additional comments or thoughts that you would like to share?

AL: *I've been in the industry since I was a teen, so believe me when I say that aligning with a payments partner who can deliver the tech, knowledge and training to be successful is vital to competing and growing long term in this industry.*

With fintech bleeding more into traditional sales, keeping on top of emerging trends is without a doubt the biggest challenge ISOs and agent face. At Nuvei, we promote a payment technology network where collaboration extends beyond typical boundaries, giving way to bigger and better opportunities.

INTERVIEW AMY ZIRKLE

(VP INDUSTRY AFFAIRS ETA)

Bio located at: *www.surviveandthrive.biz/resources*

Question: Where do you think we are as an industry today?

AZ: *The payments industry best exemplifies market*
                 growth built on technological innovation to enable
                 development and deployment of new products and
                 services bringing speed, security, and sophisticated
                 solutions to market. Technology further means that
                 the pace for the transformational change taking
                 place in the industry happens at a far more rapid
                 pace. Think about where we are with mobile pay-
                 ments, disruption at the point of sale, expansion of
                 software, growth of new players – the paradigm shift
                 in payments is fueled by technology and technology
                 will continue to shape the future of the industry.

Question: What do you feel is the biggest trend occurring within
                 the space and how could that affect ISOs and Agents?

AZ:	*ISOs and Agents need to recognize that they must be knowledgeable of industry trends and impact of new technologies to better serve customers. They must position themselves as payments consultants to meet the needs of current customers and work to engage new customers. Being strategic and understanding the shifts underway in the payments industry is vital to long-term growth as a knowledgeable and expert partner to clients.*
Question:	With all the competition and mergers in the space, do you feel like this is still a good opportunity for new entrants to the business?
AZ:	*There are significant opportunities for new entrants into the payments space. The ability and awareness to harness technology, design creative product solutions and serve growing market segments provides a rich point of entry for new players. Deepening work in the software space to bring value add has created energy and excitement about the potential to reach the SMB space to support the unique needs of this segment. Growth in ancillary services based on software solutions are significant as well. These services can bring enhancements to payments offerings in the way of loyalty programs, rewards, improvements to back-office functions and new ways to serve the B2B space.*
Question:	What advice would you give to a new salesperson entering the industry?
AZ:	*Understand the role that technology plays for this industry – it is critical and essential to gaining insight about where the market is and how it may evolve. Continue to be a student to gain fluency in growth of new solutions. Recognize too, the basics that underly the industry – the foundations of payments*

– that remains core. Rules and requirements of the card networks exist to establish baseline parameters and "rules of the road," however recognize too that the innovation in the market exists as well. Function as a parallel processor, bringing knowledge of the industry to your customers but also serve them as they serve their customers with the innovative product solutions.

Question: What do you think are the major challenges our industry is facing?

AZ: *Staying ahead of changes spurred by technology and innovation, new entrants that may not be fully versed or knowledgeable of the foundations of the ecosystem. These new players could present challenges in terms of introducing risk (unintentionally) into the system. The pace of merger activities creates some additional challenges that the industry must wrestle with as these newly merged entities change the landscape. Regardless, these challenges present more to be excited about in terms of the vibrancy of the payment ecosystem.*

Question: What role can the ETA play to help with these challenges?

AZ: *As the nonprofit trade association for the payments industry we are the network, the community, and the resource to provide all the elements to ensure our members recognize the challenges well in advance of their emergence and support and guide them in leveraging challenges as new opportunities for growth.*

Question: Do you see any major government intervention or regulation on the horizon that might affect payment professionals?

AZ:	ETA continues to work across federal and state arenas to ensure that government regulations and policies create an environment conducive to fostering economic growth and innovation in the payments space and do not limit or harm operations. We are working closely with federal and state policymakers to address issues dealing with the growing focus on privacy matters as a matter of near-term interest.

Question:	What will be the major priorities during your tenure at the ETA?

AZ:	The payments technology industry is undergoing significant change spurred by rapid technological innovation and new partnerships which will define our future. ETA has expanded our work to capture the new players to the payment ecosystem. As the premier trade association of the payments industry, we have always embraced the acquiring channel as its core. But that channel is changing.

The industry is at an inflection point due to innovation, market consolidation, and the entry of new players. How we, as an association, respond to those changes, meet the needs of the industry, and define opportunities going forward will be key to our second wave of growth.

And for different companies or segments, the needs are different. But the common element members derive from the association are the benefits to their business and enhanced business opportunities.

INTERVIEW KATE GILLESPIE

(CEO, GREENSHEET)

Bio located at: *www.surviveandthrive.biz/resources*

Question: Tell us a little bit about the Green Sheet and its mission?

KG: *The Green Sheet has been on the beat since 1983 empowering merchant level sales professionals to achieve success. Our twice monthly magazine and web site are relied upon by tens of thousands of MLSs for the news, analysis, educational and networking resources that help keep them at the top of their games.*

Question: Do you still feel that there is still an opportunity for ISOs and agents to build a book of business and earn a good living?

KG: *Always. We've witnessed many changes in this industry over the years, and with these changes have come new opportunities. The key to success in this business is being able to evolve with the industry. MLSs can no longer just sell; they need to be business consultants. Those that make this shift will do well,*

Question: There has been quite a bit of change and disruption over the years, what do you think are the main challenges ISOs and agents are facing today?

KG: *The biggest challenges are those presented by emerging and evolving technologies. Keeping up with these changes requires that a MLS be able to navigate a steep learning curve and remain open minded and flexible.*

Question: Do you see any significant trends occurring that will have a major impact on the industry as a whole?

KG: *Ongoing mergers and acquisitions, particularly among acquiring partners. This is not a new trend, but rather cyclical. Still, it has an impact on everyone. The thing to remember is that the sky is not falling. We have seen similar cycles many times in the past and they are likely to continue. The role of the MLS – the feet on the street who are the first line of contact for merchants – transcends these consolidation maneuvers.*

Question: What do you think the future looks like?

KG: *The future continues to look bright for MLSs. Banks and processors do not have a reach to most small business, whether these are brick and mortar establishments or ecommerce businesses. MLSs are uniquely positioned to provide that connection.*

Question: In your opinion, how will ISOs and agents need to adapt or change to continue to enjoy success?

KG:	It is imperative that they not be locked into the "old" ways of doing business. They need to be consultants that help merchants grow their businesses. Anyone who just sells equipment and processing and focuses on pricing above service will not survive in this business long term. Every MLS needs to keep in mind that a merchant's business success is their success.
Question:	Do you have any thoughts or comments on future products or technologies that might have a major impact on the business?
KG:	I am still watching crypto currency. It will be interesting to see if it ever becomes mainstream. I believe the jury is still out on that one.
Question:	Any additional comments or thoughts that you would like to share?
KG:	I have been in this industry for 20 years. I have seen many changes and heard about the demise of the MLS and ISO over many of those years. However, the need to support the exchange of value for goods and services will always remain. It may look different, but our industry has proven to be very creative and resilient. The future remains bright for those MLSs who educate themselves and adapt to changes.

INTERVIEW WITH MARK DUNN

(FOUNDER, FIELD GUIDE ENTERPRISES)

Bio located at: *www.surviveandthrive.biz/resources*

Question: Why don't you start by telling us a little bit about
              your background and how you got in the business?

MD: *I got into electronic payments in 1989. I had a
              contact in the industry who was president of an
              early processor and this particular processor was
              a telecommunications company, primarily, who
              specialized in electronic payments connectivity. I
              was able to get a sales position focusing in on sev-
              eral markets. I was with that company for about a
              year and a half and had connections at the time,
              and knew several people working for Verifone, and
              ended up moving over to Verifone from the payment
              processing side. So, I was off to the races from there.
              I really started in on, not so much the merchant
              services side, but on the processor equipment side
              and migrated into merchant services. When I was*

at Verifone, *many of the people that I was training on Verifone equipment were sales agents or sales representatives and I saw what they were doing and became very interested in merchant services sales, and over a period of time migrated into that side of the business. I became national sales manager of an ISO and have now worked the last 15 years as an independent consultant based on the previous 15 years of experience.*

One of the great things about the last 15 years is that I've gotten to see behind the scenes, behind the curtain I guess you would say, what's going on at more than 150 small to medium sized ISOs in our industry.

Question: I know you're involved at the Midwest acquirers association (MWAA), so tell us a little bit about what you're doing at the MWAA and how you're serving ISOs as well.

MD: *Well, I am the last remaining co-founder on the board of MWAA and I was president through the first 4 years of MWAA's existence and since then I've been the treasurer of the organization.*

MWAA has as its mission the education of the agent, ISO and bankcard community. We try to provide a forum for discussion, for education, for contacts and developing business within the industry. We think we've done a pretty good job of that over the last 17 years.

We started off following the model created by the Northeast Acquirers Association (NEAA) and have adapted that model significantly. We think that we provide a great opportunity for vendors, processors, ISOs, agents and other players in the merchant services community to spend a couple of days together and find out what's going on and make new connections.

Question: We've known each other for many years. When I look at your background, I see a real interesting perspective on the industry. Not only do you work with people from the consulting side of the house, but you also have the MWAA show where you get to meet and see all these ISOs and agents and probably have a very unique perspective on what is going on. In your opinion where do you think the payments industry is today? Where do you think we're at with all the disruptors in the market, with everything going on, what's the state of the industry today?

MD: *Well one of the key elements of merchant services traditionally has been face-to-face sales contact between merchant services salespeople and merchants, and business owners. Many of the disruptor's models are not based on that; they're based on internet contact primarily and setting a service up remotely without the overhead of an in-person, in the field, dedicated sales force. So that has implications for the traditional ISO model.*

I haven't been able to determine whether the traditional ISO model is threatened and will be gone within 5 years or 10 years, but I do know this; that business people like to have solid resources and individuals they can depend on to deliver solutions and answers for them. They have to rely on that and to the extent that ISOs can continue to provide that and continue to afford to provide that I think business owners will always turn to a personal contact.

Of course, one of the realities is that there's a generational change in business and retail right now. As millennials and other young people become business owners, they operate differently. When they are shopping for services they look online. They are downloading apps on a smartphone or tablet, and that's how they buy. It remains to be seen whether that decision-making process will up-end the traditional ISO model.

Question:	So, the ISOs and businesses today want that personal (or crave or want or desire) a personal relationship. And if I was a new rep just looking at our business, and looking at other industries, and I've got some sales experience and I'm thinking about coming in to merchant services, is there any advice that you would give that new rep that might help them started or get off the ground running when they get into the biz?
MD:	*Yes, you have to take a long-term approach and I know that that's very difficult for young people to do, for new people in the industry.*
	I used to tell people it takes 2 years to learn the merchant services business. Most people today don't have that kind of patience. If they're on quota, if they have a highly leveraged compensation plan, they probably don't have that kind of time.
	So, I think it's critically important that the salesperson coming into the industry evaluate the training program that they're going into. They have to ask a lot of tough questions about how many resources are you going to make available to me to learn this job as quickly as I can? Because the time to productivity is critical, both for the organization whose program is being sold, and for the individual whose compensation is dependent on productivity.

Question:	That's great point. When a new person gets in the business, I guess one of the tools that you would recommend would be a good training program. Any other tools or things that you think are import-ant for those reps to be successful as well?
MD:	*You need to become a student of solutions. So, you must understand the basic operations of a simple credit card terminal. But you also need to understand the value-add that integration of different software provides. And you have to be able to compare and contrast one solution to another and be able to rec-ommend to the business owner why one would be a better fit for them than the other. If you're not prepared to talk to that level of detail, you're probably just going to be hustling price, and hustling price is not any-where near as effective as it was 5 to 7 years ago.*
	It's not selling value when your leading question is "What's your rate?" and your response to their answer is "Oh I can beat that."
	What keeps merchants on board is realizing that the value of the processing, the rate that they're getting, the data that they're able to get from the payment side of the business and the reporting and the ease with which it operates, is more valuable than the cost that they're paying; that's what keeps merchants on board.
Question:	A little bit earlier you talked about millennials, you talked a little bit about the internet, our potential challenges to ISOs or agents. When you look at the industry today, and you see some of these dis-ruptors, what are some of the other— or are there other— challenges that are really headwinds for ISOs and agents today?

MD: *I think it's a question of the resources that the agent or ISO is able to bring to the table. I recently saw an RSA report about card not present fraud. CNP fraud is skyrocketing and with the introduction of the EMV chip, plastic card fraud is way down.*

The fraudsters are going online. So, the question is: what resources does the ISO bring to allow the online merchants to stay a step ahead of the fraudsters, those who are submitting fraudulent orders using stolen credit card data?

Unfortunately you have to be able to address these important issues down to the granular level with the merchants because if you're not able to do that you're not going to touch a need or determine a need in a conversation that you have with him or her about their business.

Question: As far as technology goes (and I know every year when I come to the show there are always new products and new vendors and interesting things in the market place) are there any trends or anything that you're seeing from a technology perspective that you feel might be a game changer in the near future or down the road?

MD: *The sophistication of the applications that are being implemented today is just amazing.*

I think that technology on every level is changing or has the potential to change everything about the merchant services business. But I think that the integrated solution, where an ISV is providing software that addresses the entire enterprise, addresses the need for critical data of the business owner to manage their business, to report important developments daily to guide their business and then provides payments as a part of that integrated solution, is one of the most powerful developments that we have going on right now. I see it every day. And where payments are integrated as part of the enterprise approach, payments stay locked in. It's virtually impossible to separate payments processing out, send it to a new processor, when it's integrated in that way.

Some service providers will allow their customer to designate a certain processor but many of them take the approach that here's our solution, this is our payment processing— if you want to do business with us, this is how it's done.

Question: That's a trend I'm seeing as well. Okay I think that covers most of it. Now is there anything that you would like to add or comments or thoughts that you'd like to share?

MD: *I'm a strong believer in the importance of merchant services and payments processing as an industry. I think that, where money and technology and the merchants' paycheck— which is really what payment processing is— come together, you have a powerful incentive for change, for improvement, for better value, and I believe that the industry will continue to grow. And I don't think we'll ever get to a cashless society, but predominance of electronic payments will continue. And I believe it's a great career for the individual who will invest the time and surf the changes to stay on top of what's happening in our industry. I think if you're good at electronic payments, you won't ever be without a job— a good job.*

INTERVIEW MATT HOSKINS

(FOUNDER PAYPROTEC)

Question:	Tell us how you got into the payment business?
MH:	*Payments was a natural transition for me due to my background in insurance sales. Both are very similar in the concept of selling your product/service once and then reaping the benefits of that sale monthly so long as the client stays with you.*
Question:	What advice would you give to a new salesperson entering the industry?
MH:	*My first piece of advice is to understand that the opportunity today is greater than it ever has been in the past. Too many salespeople believe the fallacy of the "good ole days" being the only time you could succeed. As technology gets better, and it certainly has, new opportunities present themselves daily.*
Question:	In your opinion what are the critical characteristics

that salespeople in this industry need to possess to be successful?

MH: *Salespeople in any industry need tenacity. The payments space is no different. We need to be experts in our understanding of our product offerings and then believe in your ability to truly help business owners. Couple these traits with the persistence to keep showing up at businesses until they are ready for your products and you have a successful sales agent. Every time.*

Question: What do you think the future looks like for the industry?

MH: *The future of payments follows the path of cell phone software consolidations. For example: Today's smart phones are cameras, calculators, internet computers, video devices, televisions, books, notepads, and a hundred other things I could mention. Heck, you can even make a call on them too! We are already seeing the credit card machine morph into a similar tool for business owners. Payments, cash register, inventory, payroll, computer, internet, camera, CRM, accounting (accounts payable, accounts receivable, & tax calculations) just to name a few. All these features save business owners time and that is their most valuable asset.*

Question: What challenges do you feel our industry is facing?

MH: *The payments space has traditionally flown under the radar. Wall Street has taken notice of the handful of bigger players, but with the startups like Square, Braintree, Adyen, & Stripe hitting the scene over the last 5-7 years we now see the big money pouring into payments. While I don't necessarily see this as a threat, the challenge is getting to the business owners before they DIY patents for themselves. Basically, any business owner can get on the internet and find a payments system for their business before an outside sales rep even knows about the new business opening. Of course, like anything bought over the internet, the vast majority of those systems are not the best fit for the business. Our value is understanding each product and giving product demos in person or over the phone with the business owner. This custom fitting can never be replaced with online shopping.*

Question: What products or technologies do you see coming out that will impact the industry the most in the coming years?

MH: *I am really excited about same day settlement & instant funding for businesses. Most small business owners (1-5 employees) say their number one struggle is cash flow. If given the ability to have today's transactions in their bank account today, basically making plastic the same as cash, I believe business owners run toward these products with full abandon. I am also a huge fan of subscription-based membership. What would ordering pizza or grocery shopping look like if one monthly fee covered your purchases - unlimited each month? You heard it here first!*

Question: Are there any comments you'd like to make?

MH: *The payments space is small, intimate, and very rewarding. My advice for anyone wanting to make a career in payments is simple; make friends regardless of who they represent at the time of your introduction. Things change quickly and many small companies grow into big companies very quickly.*

	You will likely be teammates with folks who wear different brands when you first meet them. There is plenty of opportunity for everyone. Don't burn bridges over money.
Question:	How will ISOs and agents need to adapt or change to continue to enjoy success?
MH:	*I get the distinct pleasure of speaking to many current ISO owners & sales agents on a daily basis. I am always fascinated by their ability to adapt, create, and forge new ideas as things change. For me, just have an open mind & explore the endless possibilities of what the future holds. We all know technology will evolve and that will present new windows of growth potential for every one of us. It's the person who thinks they know everything already or is just certain that the payments world is going to end next year who finds themselves at a huge disadvantage.*
Question:	Any additional comments or thoughts that you would like to share?
MH:	*Payments has been very good to me and my family. I have met some of the best people in this industry and I have been all over the world. There is no better place to hang your hat. No better place to build a foundation for you & your family. Jump in. Get reinvigorated. Dream big! Always here to help.*

INTERVIEW WITH PAUL RIANDA

(LAW OFFICES OF PAUL A. RIANDA)

Bio located at: *www.surviveandthrive.biz/resources*

Question: How did you get started focusing on the bankcard
              industry?

PR: *I was working for a law firm in 1995 when I was ran-*
              domly assigned a client that was a sales agent in
              the bankcard industry. Over the next few years, that
              agent grew and eventually was large enough that
              I suggested they hire me in-house to take care of
              their legal work. The client, by then an ISO, thought
              it was a good idea and I went to work for the com-
              pany in 1999. I worked at the ISO for three years
              learning the business and eventually was made
              the Chief Operating Officer in charge of customer
              service, risk monitoring, credit underwriting, and
              all other operational functions. When the ISO was
              bought out in 2002 as part of the iPayment roll up
              before it went public, I went back to private law

practice and decided I should focus on the bank-card industry. I tried to write as many articles as I could, get speaking engagements, and generally get involved in the industry to try to increase my client base in the bankcard industry. Luckily, I was able to build up enough clients to establish my own private practice so that now I can to devote myself full time to the bankcard industry.

Question: What are the key items a sales agent should be concerned with prior to signing an agent agreement?

PR: *The first thing is to make sure that you are dealing with a reputable company that will be there to pay your residuals and support you in the long term. The most important thing in the agent agreement is making sure that the residual payments are protected. Some of my clients demand that the agent agreement state that the residuals can never be terminated, even if the agreement is terminated. At a minimum, I like to see the agent agreement reflect that the residuals can only be terminated for a material breach of the agreement that is not cured after 30 days written notice. In addition, it is important to look out for things like making sure the agreement cannot be amended without the agent's consent, that there is a right to sell your residuals (subject to a right of first refusal), ensuring that your pricing cannot be changed except by the exact amount interchange and the like change, the agreement is non-exclusive, there are no minimum production requirements and that all relevant provisions are mutual, such as indemnity and confidentiality.*

Question: What are the main items agents who are considering becoming a registered ISO should concern themselves with?

PR: *In my experience, people don't fully understand
                    what registering really is all about. They think that
                    the decision to register grants them certain spe-
                    cial rights to do things when it really does not. All
                    registering does is allows you to market in your
                    own company name and to have sales agents. The
                    more important question in my mind is whether
                    you should take the responsibility for underwriting
                    the merchants, monitoring risk, and accepting lia-
                    bility for merchant chargebacks, losses, and fees.
                    You must register to do all those things; but in my
                    mind, those are the critical decision points over and
                    above just registering. Usually, you have to decide
                    if you want to just focus on sales and marketing or
                    if you want to become a full-service ISO that takes
                    care of essentially all the merchants' needs.*

Question: Do you see any common mistakes that new
                    entrants to the business should avoid?

PR: *The most common mistake I see is that sales agents
                    get themselves stuck in an exclusive agent agree-
                    ment and/or with a less-than-reputable company
                    because they do not educate themselves about the
                    business. These agents invariably find out they are
                    making less than they could elsewhere. The prob-
                    lem is that, if they want to move to another ISO, they
                    risk losing all their residuals. So, they are stuck with
                    a low-paying partner with no way to get out. My
                    advice is that agents need to educate themselves
                    by reading bankcard publications and by talking to
                    people in the industry before they decide on which
                    ISO they should partner with. Also, never sign an
                    exclusive agent agreement.*

Question: What do you feel are the major legal issues facing
                    the industry currently?

PR:	The major legal issues right now are the continuing lawsuits filed against the card associations and the threatened litigation relating to interchange. These dual threats have the potential to take how interchange is determined out of the hands of the card associations and arbitrarily reduce interchange fees to a much lower figure. If that happens, my concern is that the sales agents and ISOs could be squeezed out of the profit picture and made obsolete. In addition, other laws that arc passcd rcgarding things like termination fees could have a lesser impact on our industry. Overall though, legislatures enacting new laws on a state or federal level are my main concern.
Question:	What do you think the industry will look like 5 to 10 years from now?
PR:	I hope it will look pretty much the same. Right now, we have reached the point that the climate is pretty stable between the agents and ISOs. The profit splits between agents and ISOs, along with the pricing points, have stayed constant for a number of years. That said, the overall profits that are there to split have been dropping because sales agents mainly compete on the basis of price to the merchants. This compression of available profits is leading more and more of the larger ISOs to originate merchants in-house rather than through independent contractor sale agents. I think that this process will continue, but that there will always be a place for the independent sales agent. Sales agents who are successful in the future will need to have a niche in order to survive because they will not be able to compete for the general merchant base given the pricing advantages that the larger ISOs can offer a merchant in a direct relationship.

Question: Do you see any noteworthy trends taking place
              that will affect ISOs, agents, or the industry as a
              whole?

PR: *The continued consolidation among the big pro-
              cessors is leading to less choices for sale agents
              and ISOs. I used to see a lot more variety in the
              companies that my clients were signing up with on
              the sales agent side. Now it is down to a handful of
              main players that are offering the most competitive
              sales agent programs and getting most of the sale
              agents. On the ISO side also, there seems to be
              lees choice. It remains to be seen if some of the
              larger processors might completely abandon their
              ISO programs with their small margins to instead
              focus on originating more merchants in house.*

SECTION 6

TOOLS & RESOURCES

In order to keep content fresh and accessible I have moved all resources online; you can grab these at:

www.surviveandthrive.biz/resouces

TOOLS AVAILABLE:

- Income Goal Sheet and Video Training
- Daily Call Tracker
- Developing a Telemarketing Script
- Sample Client Questionnaire
- Pain and Pleasure Exercise
- Preventing Objections Worksheet
- Advertising 101
- The Framework Production System

And much more.

SECTION 7

INDUSTRY GLOSSARY

The Industry Glossary is located at our resource website:
www.surviveandthrive.biz/resources

*"He who conquers others is strong;
he who conquers himself is mighty."*

—Lao-tzu

Made in the USA
Columbia, SC
04 February 2020